NAKED EMPERORS

NAKED EMPERORS

Criticisms of English Contemporary Art
from the *London Evening Standard*

Brian Sewell

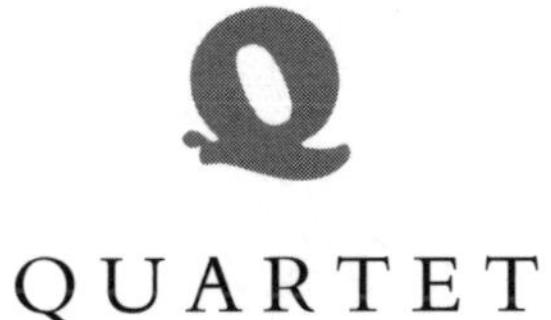

QUARTET

First published in 2012 by
Quartet Books Limited
A member of the Namara Group
27 Goodge Street, London W1T 2LD

A catalogue record for this book
is available from the British Library

ISBN 978 0 7043 7282 5

Typeset by Antony Gray
Printed and bound in Great Britain by
T J International Ltd, Padstow, Cornwall

To the many arts editors of the *Evening Standard*
who have let me have my head:

Roy Wright
1984–1987

Vicky Weir
1986–1987

John Walsh
1988

John Preston
1988–1990

Ian Irvine
1990–1991

Annalena Macafee
1991–1993

Alex Renton
1994–1995

Alison Roberts
1995–1999

Annabel Freyberg
1999–2001

Fiona Hughes
2001–2012 and beyond

The Publishers have inserted urls, where appropriate, underneath the review which will link the reader to gallery sites or individual artists' websites. All were correct at the time of publication.

Contents

NAKED EMPERORS

Introduction

It was in 1994 that my reviews for the *Evening Standard* were last gathered into a book, *The Reviews that Caused the Rumpus*. Then it was as a riposte to thirty-five of the self-proclaimed great and good of the art world who, early in the year, had complained of my countless bigotries, demanding that the editor replace me; now it is in response to the many more than thirty-five not in or of the art world, who share my scepticism and downright disrespect for the narrow and artificial orthodoxy of the very small but arrogant and condescending clique that, publicly subsidised, controls the visual arts in England. There has been no subsequent rumpus; the enemy's weapon now is the insidious 'he would say that, wouldn't he' response that relieves them of all responsibility to question what they do and defend their case. Besides, whatever it was that they feared in 1994, has not come to pass; successive governments in control of arts policy and purse-strings have been comatose in their contentment with the status quo, and the clique is more entrenched than ever, wholly in control of the institutions and the cash, the propaganda, the promotion and even of the attitude of broadcasters and the press.

No one in the visual arts has ever been more securely established, more in control, than Nicholas Serota; with his multiplying Tates and satrapies from Newcastle to Margate, his influence on the Arts and British Councils, his Trojan Horses at the gates of the National Gallery and Royal Academy, his Tendency is everywhere. It is embodied in cronies, critics and curators (the collective noun for all is creep or crawl), theorists and academics, and expressed in obscurities of jargon that from *de haut en bas* intellectually exclude the wider public, whether drawn to contemporary art in the spirit of enquiry and the hope of aesthetic reward or, as Hirst's flies to rotting flesh, drawn by the promise of exhibits freakish, grotesque, repugnant and bizarre, but aesthetically barren.

In my young day I too was intrigued by immediately contemporary art before time and common sense had separated wheat from chaff. In the Fifties and Sixties of the last century contemporary art could come and go as swiftly as contemporary pop music, but visual art now is an expensive tangible commodity with a perhaps even higher second-hand value, and empty husks cannot be discarded as though they are a disc or album by a fallen Pop Idol. To attack Hirst or Emin is to attempt the pricking of a bubble of Croesusian extravagance and were the pricking to succeed, the losses of face for critics and financial investment for collectors that must follow, are too frightening for them to contemplate. If, however, on such false foundations as assertion and loose cash Hirst and Emin are here to stay, this should not mean that those who practise the ancestral forms and traditions of art must be reviled, ignored and deprived of state patronage – as is the case – because their work is not fashionably cutting-edge. While a dozen or two Serota Darlings, famous and fortunate in his support, repeatedly scoop the cash and opportunities provided by the taxpayer, a thousand other artists, often technically, intellectually and aesthetically their superiors and not restricted to variations on one single notorious idea, but denied state support and opportunity, are all but invisible. It should surprise no one that this volume of reviews from the last twenty years or so rails against a system that is so slanted and so blind.

How It Began

In the early months of 2000 the Whitechapel Gallery mounted an exhibition that looked back to art in the years 1965–1975, when my enthusiasm for contemporary art was fading. The following review perfectly encapsulates my disillusion.

Live in your Head: English Art 1965–1975

WHITECHAPEL GALLERY, FEBRUARY–APRIL 2000

Evening Standard, 25 February 2000

It all seems so long ago and hardly worth remembering except that, at the time, in the haze of cannabis smoke it seemed so hopeful, innocent and flower-powerful, a time to reject the materialism of the past and escape into Kate Greenaway land. The first of those ten years was marked by 'I can't get no satisfaction' sung by the Rolling Stones, and by the first shaven-headed children of the Hare Krishna movement; the last saw in sombre gloom the execution of Malcolm X and the election of Margaret Thatcher as the preposterous leader of the Conservative Party. In the years between, the Notting Hill Festival came into being, freedom was crushed by Russian tanks in Czechoslovakia, a human egg was fertilised in a test tube, a heart transplanted in South Africa, Greenpeace founded, Britain joined the Common Market and Bloody Sunday brought to a head the murderous divisions that had troubled Ireland since the founding of Sinn Fein in 1905. The years in question are those from 1965, in the middle of the Swinging Sixties, to 1975, when Britain was struggling to recover from the devastating effects of the oil crisis and an inflation rate of 28 per cent; they have now been identified by the panjandrums of the Whitechapel Gallery as a significant era in the history of English art. In that few artists of the day knew in which direction art should develop, it was a decade of uncertainties, but of two things they were sure — that the ancestral conventions of painting and sculpture need no longer be observed (indeed, could cheerfully be abandoned), and that all an artist need do was to proclaim himself an artist, for what then followed was that anything he made or did, by whatever means or none, must necessarily be art – a simple logic widely accepted and merrily agreed by the empty-headed critics of the day. Art could be anything, anywhere, or nothing; an idea, quite invisible, or a happening that could not happen, with no material evidence of either, could be just as much a work of art as Michelangelo's Sistine Ceiling, provided that its perpetrator had made the essential declaration 'I AM AN ARTIST'. Enthusiastic enquirer that I then was, I well remember intruding on the business of a Bloomsbury solicitor to inspect lengths (uneven) of coarse and hairy parcel string suspended from drawing pins in the ceiling (the work of an artist in residence there), contemplating in an otherwise empty room of the Hayward Gallery an empty matchbox, open to reveal its emptiness, setting off for Germany to fight my way into, across and out of a vast room filled from wall to wall and floor to ceiling with shredded paper, and for New York to see an exhibition of canvases blankly white but for the stencilled inscriptions THIS IS A STILL LIFE, a portrait, a landscape and so on. I smoked my fair share of cannabis, ate it in salads and home-baked cakes, and spent unending evenings in the company of art students in the wilder shores of London drifting into the intellectually incapacitated daze induced by bhang, dagga, grass, ganja, rama, shit and all the other names by which it went and of which they pretended the kind of connoisseurship now expended on mediocre wines in Islington. Swallowing LSD on sugar cubes, I surrendered to fantasies that made the paintings of Salvador Dalí in his prime seem the poor, pale, pedestrian inventions of a plodding mind. In New York I joined the languid throng that lay at Warhol's feet.

This I confess only because it was, I am certain, a necessary concomitant without which the absurd and intellectually trivial art of this period could neither have come into existence nor been accepted by critics and curators who should have known better. To some extent artists were deliberately testing the critical response, seeing how far they could go before critical rebellion came into play, but rebellion there never was and artists were encouraged in self-belief and became aggressive; dissidents among them were regarded as traitors, shouted down and violently excluded from this company of angels. Everybody of importance in the contemporary art world of the day was an angel too – the ICA, the Arts Council, the art magazines, the organisers of great international exhibitions, and the new art swiftly became invincible; its apologists and propagandists founded what is now the universal jargon of criticism and theory, and their heirs have become the high priests of today's Arts and British Councils, today's Department of Culture, today's Tate Gallery and Royal Academy, today's art schools and universities, today's new galleries funded by the Lottery and the Millennium Fund.

In revisiting this pretentious and dull trivia, the Whitechapel Gallery reminds us how arid it all was to both eye and intellect, and how utterly familiar it is, partly because the work of those contributing artists who are still alive has changed so little in the passage of a generation, and partly because so much of what they did has been done again and again by student imitators imitating imitations. It is all very well to argue that art must be disassociated from the skills of art, but to disassociate so far that the skills become disreputable, their exercise clear proof that the practitioner is not an artist, results in visual mayhem – though that is perhaps too exciting a word for literary and conceptual things that are incomprehensible without written explanations and obstinately unrewarding in any sense even when explained. When the students of the immediately post-Hockney years at the Royal College declared that 'Every convention in art is now dispensible' and believed it, they were expressing with the glee of the adolescent iconoclast what Derek Jarman, their contemporary at the Slade, described with melancholy as 'the final solution' – a phrase as telling in this context of culture-control as in the history of the Jews, for it has indeed meant the death of art as once we knew it. This is the art at once of an Orwell world, preaching, hortative, domineering, and the art of the silly and frivolous, the art of those who, like communists, fascists and low church Christians have a message and insist on delivering it, and the art of those who haven't the foggiest notion of what their work may mean, but take the chance that to someone, somewhere, it may mean something.

The only famous work on view is the tumbler of water on a glass shelf that Michael Craig-Martin, now Gauleiter of Goldsmith's and in his second term as an influential Trustee of the Tate Gallery, tells us is an Oak Tree. In 1973 he repeatedly asserted that the glass and the water had become an oak tree because he said so, and that it was and would remain an oak tree until he reversed his spell. As he was, it seems, persuasive at the time and twenty-seven years later is so still, the sceptics among us should think ourselves confounded. If, indeed, it has become a tree, and if, indeed, I am persuaded that this is so and am content to genuflect to the miracle, one nagging question remains — why and how is it a work of art fit only for a gallery, and not some thaumaturgical object venerated in a church? Why is the glass of gin deliberately (and in homage) left in my garden twenty-seven years ago, not now a lofty juniper? Why when I burnt almost all my life's work as a painter, did I not think of bottling the ashes — as Susan Hiller did — and call that a work of art? Why is the pyramid of oranges just within the Gallery door a work of art, unless it is to tell us that every greengrocer is a Michelangelo? We are invited to help ourselves, making it the perfect interactive sculpture to repeat on the empty plinth in Trafalgar Square. How is a filing cabinet a work of art — unless, as is the case, Wittgenstein is filed under S? How is a vitrine filled with much the same memorabilia that all of us can muster, a work of art? Oh the serious mysteries of art . . . oh the wonders to behold.

If cleaners came in and cleared it all away this might be another rich stage in the being of this work, reduced to absolute minimalism and then reborn through conceptual reconstruction. Why not? If the years 1965 to 1975 gave us, the wretched public, anything in art, it gave us the right to conceptualise, to assert that in our minds the light switch and the fire extinguisher in every gallery have as much claim to be works of art as anything exhibited by artists. These years made artists of us all, or of none of us, made everything a work of art, or nothing. Look about you at this dreary exhibition and see it for what it is – to make art of it both cannabis and LSD are the essential open sesames.

THE INSTITUTIONS

THE ARTS COUNCIL

The English, though much given to glorifying adventurers who did and died and do-gooders single-minded enough to do the good themselves, are at heart a nation of committee members, cosy only in the comfort of corporate responsibility and the safety of numbers.

Of this the Arts Council is a prize example, burdened with committees on which some members sat – David Sylvester, Marina Vaizey and Richard Cork, for example – not for mere years but even for decades, and some sat on half a dozen, concurrently and in sequence, bending their patronage to their own purposes and those of buddy-boys. Once a broad church in the visual arts, mounting exhibitions devoted to old masters as well as modern, it now, with mightily increased funding, restricts its quite uncritical activities all but entirely to the support of immediately contemporary art, and is one of the engines that establishes and maintains the fame and fortune of the favoured few. This it contrives by excluding from its advisory groupies, and particularly from the rank of Councillors, all who have ever been critical of its activities. Margaret Thatcher when Prime Minister once expressed her wish to extinguish this nest of vipers, but neither she nor any minister since has seized the opportunity. Beyond reform, only by shutting it down and sending into exile all who have served on it or in its arrogant bureaucracy, starting again with a tabula rasa, shall we ever be able to devise a system for funding the arts that is not buddy-boy back-scratching and bureaucratic, but fair, simple, broadly based and swiftly effective.

I am not alone in my view that in the visual arts the Arts Council is now an irrelevance to the great majority of working painters and sculptors in this country, to whom it offers neither financial support nor exposure in exhibitions: nor, to those who, not artists, but whose taxes fund it, yet to whom it offers no direct benefit of any kind (and precious little that is indirect), is the Council of the slightest use or interest.

A Nest of Vipers

Evening Standard, 24 November 1999

For twenty years I have locked horns with successive chairmen, panjandrums, secretaries and Councillors of the Arts Council, probing their Byzantine methods of selection and appointment, their often outrageous exploitation of appointment for professional advantage, and their buddy-boy and back-scratching patronage and subsidy, and with every poke and prod the stink of corruption has oozed from this long-standing midden.

For twenty years its worthies, often drawn from the battalions of the great and good, have blustered, blethered, dissembled, written furious letters to submissive editors and, in the case of the then Sir William Rees-Mogg, have abruptly terminated correspondence on the grounds that my interest in the Council was malevolent. I treasure contradictory letters of 1982, one from an Arts Councillor telling me that I had been proposed for membership of an advisory panel, the other from the Secretary-General telling me that I most certainly had not. I treasure hand-written letters from Luke Rittner, a later Secretary-General, telling me that I was very near the truth and nudging me nearer still – hand-written in confidence, with no copies for the files. I treasure similar letters from junior press officers who could not bear the lying and deceit with which senior officers of the Council consistently obstructed my enquiries.

I have every reason to think that some current Councillors are as self-seeking and self-serving as any of their predecessors, and that the current Chief Executive, Peter Hewitt, is as valiant in defence of the indefensible as was Sir Roy Shaw, Secretary-General from 1975 to 1983. A letter of June this year asking, yet again, for the precise dates and figures of an Arts Council Lottery Award involving a six-, perhaps eventually even a seven-figure commission to Anish Kapoor, a Councillor, has been ignored; so too were my complaints of misinformation and, to other points, of responses that had been, shall we say, diversionary and evasive.

Two decades or so ago the Arts Council gave money to Helen Chadwick (she who pissed in deep snow and made bronze casts of the consequent cavities – the *Piss Flowers* of the Serpentine) to go on a Yorkshire pub crawl and to other artists for going down a coalmine, for running after scrap paper in the street hoping to find shopping lists, sweeping rubbish into artistic heaps in a high wind, walking about with a scaffold pole balanced on his head and for exhibiting horse droppings in the Serpentine – Chris Ofili was not the first there with a clod of dung. Little has changed since, and from its policy of promoting only what it perceived as breaking the boundaries of art (though it once had a duty to exhibit the odd Wagner or Beethoven of painting) grew the present power of the Serota Tendency with its dead horse hanging in the entrance of the Tate, its vast new premises at Bankside and the freak shows of the Turner Prize, and now even Cabinet Ministers seek to brand themselves as Britpop-smart by demanding elephant turds and pickled herrings for their offices. We, the common people, have meanwhile gazed in adoration on works of art in the mediums of human blood, semen, urine and the fluff discovered in an artist's navel, and one of next year's candidates for the Turner Prize is even now at work on a marvellous monument composed entirely of snot and toe-jam.

Unlike the walls of Jericho, no Joshua has ever cracked open the ghastly edifice of contemporary art with its twin towers of the Tate and the Arts Council – until now. Suddenly a little fissure has appeared and a Cabinet Minister, Chris Smith no less, Gauleiter of Culture, has turned, if not into a Trojan Horse, at least into a Trojan Dormouse. It is a funny little tale: David Lee, editor of *Art Review*, who has been gunning for the contemporary art establishment almost as long as I have, published an article on what he dubs 'the usual suspects' in the *Spectator*. It was powerful stuff naming and shaming the 17 officials, trustees, directors of galleries subsidised by the Arts Council, art dealers and one critic, 'the reliably uncritical Richard Cork' (my predecessor on the *Evening Standard*), who share among themselves and their friends the visual arts tranche of the £500 million or so that the Arts Council now dispenses every year. The article was read by the Arts Editor of the *Sunday Times*, who took Chris Smith to lunch and quizzed him, and the Minister, surely an old hand with journalists and leaks, let slip a certain misgiving about the extremes of contemporary art and, wondering what has happened to painting and drawing, suggested that the narrow nominations for the Turner Prize, perhaps chosen only for controversy's sake, are 'unrepresentative of British art'.

In the consequent *brouhaha* Antony Gormley, Arts Councillor and in one way and another a recipient of Arts Council funds beyond the dreams of avarice, rounded on the very Minister who in 1998 had appointed him a Councillor for his 'expert under-standing and committed leadership'. Well yes – never a truer word, perhaps, for few have been more expert and committed to leading the Arts Council whither it can most favour themselves and their friends. 'It sounds to me,' he jeered, 'as if Chris Smith wants a dinosaur park' – a revealing riposte, for it suggests profound contempt not only for the materials and techniques of painting and drawing, but for all who ever practised them, contempt for Michel-angelo and Raphael, Picasso and Deanna Petherbridge – and if readers know nothing of Petherbridge, then we must blame the Arts Council and the Tate, for she is perhaps the most accomplished draughtsman of this quarter-century.

The Department of Culture has, of course, been plastering the crack. 'No, no, the Minister was chewing on a jellied eel and, not entirely audible, was misheard and misinterpreted . . . he loves the shark, the sheep and the medicine chest . . . for Gilbert and George when fainting in coils his admiration is quite unalloyed . . . it's just that painting in oils has been chucked into the Waters of Oblivion by the Arts Council and the Serota Tendency.' If Chris Smith wants to revive it, the remedy is obvious – throw Gormley and Kapoor off the Arts Council and replace them with others for whom the arts of the past are as present as the present. The officials of the Arts Council are heart and soul engaged in visiting the wilder shores of contemporary art, a few dealers, Nick Serota and Charles Saatchi their fellow-travellers, and it is time that we had Councillors capable of navigating other courses. I can think of half a dozen informed journalists who would serve the people and the Minister well, but above them all let me nominate David Lee for the Arts Council, the honest sceptic whose article revealed a significant doubt in Chris Smith's mind. From that small misgiving should come great change.

How to Improve the World

THE ARTS COUNCIL COLLECTION

Evening Standard, 8 September 2006

The Hayward Gallery has a new director, Ralph Rugoff, an innocent from California, who cannot have known that his first exhibition here – of largely familiar works selected from the Arts Council's Collection – could only be greeted by a groan. Poor soul – in a foreword to an entirely unnecessary and expensive catalogue he writes of this random accumulation of whatever happened to be available within each of the past sixty financial years, and cheap, and second-rate, or subsidised by other purses, as a museum without walls, a collection of key works democratically selected by leading artists, writers, critics and 'a changing cast of curators from the Arts Council' who made shrewd choices with 'remarkable under-standing of the moment'. Poor soul – he may think himself the new and vigorous director of a gallery that for years the sane man has thought moribund, but he has immediately become the dummy on the knee of the Arts Council, whose Collection is none of the boastful things he claims for it.

Whenever previous directors of the Hayward could think of nothing better for its ill-lit prison glooms, they trotted out yet another survey of the Arts Council Collection – hence the groan. Now of some 7,500 paintings, sculptures, photographs, assemblages, installations and defiantly unclassifiable Lord-knows-what, much of the tiny tip of the iceberg that we thus are allowed to see is what we have been allowed to see before. The sceptic concludes that, far from being a vast collection of key works (and ground-breaking to boot), it is one of doubtful or even embarrassingly dismal quality of which even the prideful Council is ashamed. That another writer in the catalogue puts up the ninepin that the Collection is 'an oversize bag of sweets' from which favourite flavours can be picked, only to knock the notion down, is a powerful indication of misgiving within the Arts Council; the Collection is an entity, he asserts, its very identity discerned through its variety – but that argument surely proves it to be the very bag of sweets that he denies.

Buyers for the Collection are, like the judges of the Turner Prize, 'people we can work with' – as an Arts Council spokesman once put it to me – carefully chosen always to choose works that in their eyes are cutting-edge, boundary-breaking or any other cliché of the contemporary arts and their mountebanks and jokers, responding only 'to activity in the present'. Heaven forfend that the Collection should ever fill a gap with a decent picture from the past – no, no, it must go forward, press on, be the willing victim of every whimsical and transitory fad and fashion, responding only to art of the immediate moment, even the split second point in time. Come video, film, digital media and sculpture in sound, light, human waste or fifth dimension, the Arts Council must have it without a moment's hesitation – it is now that matters, not posterity.

The exhibition thus offers an opportunity to judge how well these various nows have worn. The curators, in quoting the title of another exhibition, rashly challenge us to do just that – 'Look at that picture . . . How does it appear to you now? Does it seem to be persisting?' I have long argued that this is precisely what the private collector must do, and if a picture (or any other work of art) does not 'persist' he should get rid of it; in purchasing he can, perhaps, afford to be a little casual, take a risk and give it time; in our museums, however, we have no culture of de-accessioning and these must take much greater care in acquisition. Is the Arts Council Collection, our museum without walls, private or public in this sense? I ask the question because I see no point in public ownership of 7,500 (and increasing) works of art that are bought only because they are cheap and of the moment, if the largely hopeless rubbish that is inevitable in a collection based on such a principle, cannot be shed when time has passed and serious connoisseurship been applied.

That there is such a collection is an accident of history, the idea inherited from CEMA, the Arts Council's wartime predecessor six decades ago. During the war all our galleries were closed and their treasures evacuated, and we were glad of cheap and cheerful shows of contemporary art that tomorrow might be blitzed. With the war at an end, the newly formed Arts Council found itself in possession of CEMA's pictures and continued to supplement them, doing what the Tate Gallery could not, for at that stage it had a government purchase grant of only £2,000 a year to cover all its responsibilities for historic British art and modern foreign painting and sculpture. The Tate's grant grew very slowly to £40,000 in 1960, but when it rose to a peak of over £2,000,000 in 1984–5, a period in which it bought heavily, judiciously considered paintings by contemporary British artists, the Arts Council should at least have considered whether there was any point in its continuing to duplicate the Tate's purposes with a collection of its own, providing – as it does – generous, even blatant, patronage for little friends whose work fits the current fancy. The number of artists given that patronage, who within a quinquennium or a decade have slid into total obscurity, is disconcerting.

Why should the Council continue to believe that the possession, expansion, conservation, storage, transport, staffing and administration of a collection of briefly contemporary works of art is still part of its business? In all other aspects of its work it is an enabling agency, a promoter of drama, opera and music, literature and poetry – only in the visual arts does it become the owner; if it enables the public to buy subsidised seats at the performance arts, why does it not support exhibitions at which the works of art are for sale? As a collector it faces appalling costs and problems, for contemporary art is no longer the comparatively manageable framed canvas or sculpture in bronze and stone, but is often an unmanageable monster – witness the Antony Gormley *Field* that it owns, its 40,000 constituent figures inherently fragile, their unpacked and unprotected weight a full 25 tons, their volume that of 25 Mercedes cars. In comparison the pram, washbasin and other life-size impedimenta of Cathy Wilkes' *She's pregnant again* is child's play, but like so much video art, this installation requires a selfishly large space to make its feeble point and is of the moment only in that interest in it is no more than momentary. Purchased only last year, this is its first outing in London – but is it a work that could only have been made in 2005 and of that moment? Is it not just one more of an innumerable kind that has been littering gallery floors for at least a generation?

Nothing in this exhibition lifts the spirit, and in one form or another we have seen it all before. Damien Hirst's *He tried to internalise Everything* of 1992 is one of a group of steel cage pieces that I immediately interpreted as evoking the beastliness of man to man; at the time I thought too that they marked his transition from empty-headed joker to serious thinker, but in the light of subsequent work I question that judgement and now believe that I imposed my perception on the piece and that Damien's meaning was incoherent and far shallower. Ian Davenport's *Poured Lines* of 1995, bought from the best of Cork Street dealers in that year, seems as ingeniously empty now as it did then, and a canvas of exactly that kind could have been bought direct from the artist himself while still a student for a tenth of the price. Has Anish Kapoor's stainless steel orifice – *Untitled*, 1995 – gained in meaning and significance since it was bought? Indeed, did it ever have more to say than a distorting mirror in a fairground? Could the Collection have bought two worse works by Patrick Caulfield or one less promising by Hockney? Of course the Hockney holds some interest in being early, deliberately bad and openly homosexual in subject – *We Two Boys Together Clinging*, of 1961, not only represents a homage to Walt Whitman whose poem goes on to describe them as clutching, sleeping and loving, but is a wry image of

Hockney himself clinging to Cliff Richard (now there's a thought, half a century on) – but is it good enough to be in a publicly owned collection, a key ground-breaking work? Surely Hockney's ground-breaking moment was when he began to draw well enough to make a boy look like a boy and not a preposterous rag doll.

The best of this drab Collection lies in its early works. The small Bacon, *Head VI*, of 1949, has lost none of its power with familiarity, the four small bronzes by Henry Moore from the period 1951–62 are utterly enviable, Bridget Riley's *Movement in Squares*, of 1961, is as freshly disciplined as her work can be, and another painting without colour, Victor Pasmore's *Snowstorm Spiral Motif*, of 1950–1, is simply beautiful, a painterly as well as a visionary abstraction from reality; a picture that I fancy Leonardo would have liked. Compared with these, the more recent paintings of Craig Martin, Kossoff, Auerbach, Doig, Bob Law and, particularly, Chris Ofili, seem empty and insignificant, the sculptures of Camilla Law, Angela Bulloch, Bill Woodrow and Roger Hiorns wilfully frivolous. Hiorns' *Nunhead*, of 2004, perfectly makes my point about the curatorial difficulties posed by contemporary artists; it consists of two BMW engines encrusted with copper sulphate crystals standing on a steel table, and to keep the crystals immaculate these heavy machines will have to be regularly re-dunked in copper sulphate solution; this is enthusiastically described by the curator as a fearless adventure in acquisition, but to me it is tomfoolery.

If this exhibition demonstrates anything, it is the pressing need for the Arts Minister, of this or any future administration, to undo the Arts Council altogether and devise some better instrument for giving public subsidies to the arts than a body that is patently undemocratic, answerable to nobody, judge, jury and propagandist for itself, stubbornly reliant on a very narrow-minded group of dominant advisers, and, within the visual arts, unrepresentative of anything other than the Serota Tendency but without the connoisseurship and shrewd judgement that is occasionally evident in the various and several Tates. In the visual arts the Arts Council's activity amounts to regimentation, absolute control, censorship and such favouritism in patronage that accusations of, if not downright corruption, moral turpitude seem justified. Now that we have the DCMS we do not need the Arts Council. Now that we have Tate Modern we do not need an Arts Council Collection.

How to Improve the World, The Arts Council Collection 2006

Damien Hirst, *He Tried to Internalise Everything* (1992)

Ian Davenport, *Poured Lines* (1995)

Anish Kapoor, *Untitled* (1997)

David Hockney, *We Two Boys Together Clinging* (1961)

Francis Bacon, *Head VI* (1949)

Henry Moore, *Working Model for Reclining Figure: Internal/ External Form* (1951)

Bridget Riley, *Movement in Squares* (1961)

Victor Pasmore, *The Snowstorm: Spiral Motif in Black and White* (1950–1)

Roger Hiorns, *Nunhead* (2004)
http://www.artscouncilcollection.org.uk/

As an example of Arts Council exhibition patronage I offer
the British Art Shows instituted in 1979.

In the Days of the Comet:
British Art Show 7

HAYWARD GALLERY

Evening Standard, 17 February 2011

In 1979 the British Art Show (BAS), in spite of a slightly shaky start, seemed a sound and sensible idea – every five years we were to stare into the goldfish bowl and distinguish between clear water and the mephitic fish-shit at its bottom. We knew then that we had had a number of artists worthy of international reputation since the end of the war in 1945 and that London had trounced the School of Paris into oblivion, but there were grave uncertainties about the generation from which the new Moore and Sutherland must rise. The old certainties then lay in the hands of Caro, Freud and Auerbach, but even of these we were not quite sure, for the promise of Hockney had already proved fugitive, the promise of Procktor was quite gone, and far too many proudly presented as The Future by Bryan Robertson and John Russell in *Private View*, their seminal tome of 1965, had, in the fourteen years since, fizzled and sputtered to a standstill. A scrupulous survey of who was in, who out and who coming up on the outside might have clarified our hopes and opinions, but the very first BAS, with over a hundred artists in it had the air of uncritical pluralism and inclusivity for its own sake, and proved to be just another rambling exhibition. As it was not shown in London, few saw it, fewer cared, and it had no influence.

In 1984 BAS2 had a fashionable Arts Council slant to it

but, again seen only in the provinces, was a great thing of no importance. Only in 1990 did the BAS come to London and the Hayward Gallery, by then reduced to forty-two artists, of whom three were soon to be nominated for the Turner Prize; in this, at least, it was Art Now, but in claiming that it was 'the most controversial exhibition of the decade' its curators were impertinent. Then it spread its wings again and in its absence for two whole decades its London audience has to all intents and purposes forgotten that there ever was a BAS. It was damned silly of the Hayward Gallery, to which the show 'belongs', to let loose its grip and allow London to be deprived of it. I know all the arguments for sharing shows of every kind with the far-flung provinces and am wholly in sympathy with them, but London provides by far the largest audience and should never have been eliminated from the circuit. It is in London, more than anywhere, that continuity matters for both the artist and the informed critical audience. Enthusiastically and unreservedly I welcome the return of the BAS and hope that five years hence I shall again see it in the Hayward.

There is, alas, not much for me in BAS7. In his foreword to the catalogue the Hayward's Director, Ralph Rugoff (who is unlikely to have seen any previous BAS), remarks that 'changes in curatorial approaches and attitudes have radically affected what art means'. They have indeed. The curator has become the artist. The artist needs only the junk yard, the junk shop and the local branch of Curry's to discover equipment, materials and objects that, at first glance unrelated to any aesthetic endeavour, can be converted into art by the interpretation of the curator – a few words of mumbo-jumbo in the catalogue and the Arts Council or the Tate will buy it. The two curators of BAS7, one from the Hayward, the other from the Henry Moore Institute, have rejected the basic but useful convention of the comprehensive survey and imposed a theme – *In the Days of the Comet* – potentially a Bed of Procrustes on which every exhibit must be made to fit, not by chopping off the legs or stretching them, but by ingenious curatorial elasticity. The intellectual compression and extensibility in apology and exegesis of the show's twin curators is almost Jesuitical, their calling on authoritative sources worthy of doctors of theology.

Their comet is derived from the title of a novel by H. G. Wells that sank without a trace of interest or influence, his vein of science fiction exhausted. That it was published in 1906 but set in 1910 immediately suggests that the curators too are looking a little into the future, beyond their bailiwick of British Art in the quin-quennium 2005–10, but there is nothing on view in the Hayward that is not dull-mindedly rooted in the recent past. Given the theme of the comet and the superstitions attached to it as a portent of change and its almost dependable regularity in orbiting, the chosen artists have largely ignored it – the curators thus shift their ground, and argue with Jesuitical casuistry that the comet was less a theme imposed than 'a set of coordinates and a method of navigation'.

They also argue that as a comet is not constrained by national boundaries, the Britishness of a British Art Show need not be British in any sense that the BNP might recognise – nor should it be, for what now passes for art is very much in international idioms devoid of national characteristics. But why continue to call this The British Art Show rather than Art in Britain Now?

When the curators go on to admit that 'art of the present requires no specialist knowledge; we are all experts in the present', they are in danger of explaining themselves away. If they are not experts, why are they in charge of this exhibition? Why should we believe anything they say of it or its exhibits?

Old fossil that they may think me, they have given me equality and I shall use it to declare that nothing in this exhibition is art as I understand it. The inept practitioners of video and film should be packed off to the fields of cinema and television to see if their pretentious amateur productions, when deprived of the label 'art', hack it as information or entertainment. Was there ever an 'art' of more selfish form in terms of time and space? All take whole rooms and one exhibit in this genre endures for 24 hours, others of the ilk requiring a mere 6 hours and 45 minutes between them; has the Hayward made provision for overnight visitors?

There is no painting here of any interest or quality – indeed, one might well argue that to attract the interest of the contemporary curator a painter must be technically maladroit and bungling and the daubing meaningless. Varda Caivano's muddied canvases make the point, yet here are praised as 'fields of vision communicated with the least possible means and the greatest possible effort'. Whoopee. Milena Dragicevic paints ugly heads so 'unknowable' even to her that she wonders how they reached the canvas. Terrific. Michael Fullerton claims to be in debt to Reynolds but his portraits could surely never scrape into the National Portrait Gallery's increasingly dire annual award for portraiture. Wicked. The best that the curators can say for Phoebe Unwin is that her paint, when applied to the canvas, 'often visibly becomes painting'. Shit and molasses. What is it when it doesn't become painting? And who decides?

As for sculpture, Sarah Lucas puts it neatly with her declaration that as well as standing up, 'a dick with two balls' can do and be everything else expected of the sculptor. 'Michelangelo?' I murmur, 'Bernini? Rodin?' With Roger Hiorns and Wolfgang Tillmans she was in BAS6 in 2005, and all three are now brought back into the light described as 'major artists . . . currently making the best work of their careers'. In Lucas's *NUDS* I see nothing but a repellent variation of an obsession first revealed by Charles Saatchi in 1997, foul flesh in visceral embrace. Hiorns, the dominant contributor to the show, is an ingenious fellow given to stuffing mind-controlling drugs into aircraft engines and growing copper sulphate crystals in council flats, and in Athens he smeared semen on the spotlights of the Acropolis. Speculation on the how of this last jape must render us incredulous – even with the help of a hundred fifth-formers in an all-boys public school . . . And this was sculpture? Well yes, quite clearly so to Sarah Lucas as well as to the curators who write movingly of his 'visible and invisible tools of manipulation'. In the Hayward his sculptures, all untitled 'transformations', are disappointingly untransformed, the Mercedes engine a Mercedes engine, the naked boy a boy, the epoxy resin girl a model from a Top Shop window.

As is always the way in the world of contemporary art, the curators present their chosen artists as thinker, seer, philosopher and shaman to whom we must bend the acquiescent knee. We should do nothing of the kind. There is no wisdom here. The curators' choice of hapless artists and their wretched art is utterly conventional, rooted in the narrow orthodoxy and even narrower patronage of the Arts Council and the Tate, absolutely safe for aspiring young professionals with their eyes on the ladder of preferment. Here there is nothing that in some sense we have not seen before, that in concept and execution veers from Saatchi–Serota precedents; the names change, but the ideas remain the same, the execution growing shoddier. Nothing in this modish show is beautiful, intense, deep or desirable, nothing is even decently well made. It tells a truth, however – that the contemporary art now institutional in Britain is a thing of infantile decadence – but not the whole truth; I fervently believe that curators of independent mind could find an altogether other truth, founded, not on fad and fashion, but on honest connoisseurship.

In the Days of the Comet: British Art Show 7,
Hayward Gallery 2011

Varda Caivano, *Untitled* (2011)

Milena Dragicevic, *Supplicant 202* (2009)
http://www.artscouncilcollection.org.uk/

THE ROYAL ACADEMY

Founded in 1768, the Royal Academy has ever since, with its Summer Exhibition, been an annual event attended by more than 100,000 visitors with scant interest in art – art's Boat Race, so to speak. Nevertheless, it used to stand for qualities in drawing, painting and sculpture that were ancestral, reaching back to the Italian academies of the late Renaissance and the industrious workshops of the earlier, back further still to ancient Greece and Rome. Not good at housekeeping, it fell on hard times in the early 1960s and had to sell its greatest treasure, the Leonardo Cartoon now in the National Gallery, but for a paltry sum; and when times were hard again it began to change the character of the Summer Exhibition, invited the collaboration of the Hirsts and Emins, and bestowed the enviable title Royal Academician on celebrities of the Serota Tendency who can neither draw nor paint. With the ludicrous appointments to the Royal Academy Schools of Tracey Emin, Fiona Rae and Richard Wilson as, respectively, Professors of Drawing, Painting and Sculpture, this abandonment of integrity now gravely infects its teaching in every skill-based hereditary sense; Perspective has fallen so far into redundancy that no fit Professor for this discipline can be found for the appointment.

I do not invariably review the annual show – that would be tediously repetitious – but five years ago was provoked to write what follows.

The Summer Exhibition

ROYAL ACADEMY

Evening Standard, 11 June 2007

Dear Jake and Dinos Chapman – A decade has passed since the Royal Academy revealed Charles Saatchi's collection of contemporary art. That I left the building utterly sickened by what I had seen was as much your fault as that of any other artist, you the first among equals with your mutant children, their faces, genitals and anuses confused, though the crude obscenities of Sarah Lucas were hard on the heels of your immaculate conceptions. Never before had I experienced such nausea, such revulsion, at the sight of fully realised ideas masquerading as works of art. I walked away, walked home indeed, and passing Jagger's *Royal Artillery Memorial* at Hyde Park – one of the greatest, truest and most heartfelt sculptures of the twentieth century and a match for Picasso's *Guernica* – paused to mourn, not the deaths of soldiers, but the deliberate death of art at the hands of those who should sustain it.

Since then I have grown to respect you, your *Tragic Anatomies* seeming now to have been an aberration perhaps engendered by working as assistants to Gilbert and George. To any man a boy during World War II, your *Hell*, perfectly encapsulated the horrors of oppression, a powerful evocation of the darkness of man's mind. Your pseudo-ethnic sculptures carried kindred implications, but without the simple promptings of a war their meanings were more complex. Your embellishments of Goya's prints (an expensive but worthless late edition deserving, in itself, no veneration or respect) significantly heightened the old man's emotion. Your own recent etchings must touch every nerve of those who care for handmade prints, technically brave and beautiful, exciting the lust for possession. But when the Royal Academicians invited you to join their number, you accepted and then poked them in the eye with the nastiest squalid little offering you could devise.

Now you insult the Academy again, with dinosaurs in the forecourt. They are big – as dinosaurs must be – and they are heavy, but they are the whimsical concept of the child with paper and scissors realised by shipyard workers without a ship to build. They may be both joke and jibe – Academicians have long been likened to dinosaurs and you yourselves point to the emptiness of Richard Serra's rusting abstract constructions in iron plate – but the joke is too thin and the jibe too blunt, for your Jurassic monsters have far less aesthetic merit than anything produced by Serra. Reproduced in pink plastic they have a future among the swings and roundabouts of the children's playground, but the Academy's forecourt is a place for gravitas. I know that the Academy likes to make a fool of itself at the Summer Exhibition, to surrender to the amateur, to be coy and winsome as well as self-important, to let in the this and that for which the fairground barker can shout 'Roll up, roll up!', and to attract the idiots of the media with things outlandish and bizarre, but you are serious and capable artists who should not join in the jape.

That you should be perceived to have insulted the Academy may well be your intention, but as the Academy regularly insults the rest of us with the dross it offers at the Summer Exhibition, you risk seeming to be part of that offence. Stop it. You are too good for such nonsense. Indeed, you are too good for the Academy.

Yours in friendship, BS

Dear David Hockney – We have been on nodding terms for more than forty years, and there was a time, in the Seventies, when I thought you one of the finest draughtsmen of the twentieth century. To that view I remain absolutely firm, but for the last twenty-five years or so you have done nothing that is worth a second glance. Your portraiture has been unworthy even of the street painters of Montmartre; you insult your beloved dogs with daubs; and your watercolours would hang unnoticed among those of amateurs in any provincial festival of arts. Your publishers trumpet your foolish views on lenses and the *camera obscura* as though you are a second Leonardo – but you are not and you are wrong, and had you been some unheard-of Dick or Harry, no publisher would have given you the time of day. Only the preparatory studies for your *Grand Canyon* paintings at the Summer Exhibition of 1999 have had any merit in your protracted dotage and decline.

And now you fill the west wall of the largest gallery in the Academy with the largest picture you have ever painted and the largest anyone has ever painted in the open air – just the sort of 'Roll up!' features publicity demands. 'Oooh!', we are expected to respond – but it is only the gross inflation of the landscapes that you exhibited with your dealer last year. 'Very beautiful,' you said of those yourself, though 'embarrassingly incompetent' would have been the modest truth. With the compilation of canvases increased from six to fifty, the overall size has risen from some two metres by four to some five by thirteen, and with a computer to plot it and a painter to assist, you completed it in 'one breathless three week sprint' – as one of your doting admirers put it.

I am compelled to say that it looks like three weeks' work. I have seen better backdrops in provincial pantomimes and I dare say that the Theatre Royal in Scunthorpe could make use of it for *Babes in the Wood* next winter. But this boastful failure is perhaps the true Hockney, the man who as a boy was the 'Number one character' at the Royal College, in every ploy determined to be noticed, the man who as a man has always pushed himself into the public eye, ignoring adverse criticism. And you are secure from it, for you surround yourself with sycophants who, like the courtiers of Darius, daily greet you with 'Oh King, live for ever.' Through fawning curators you control your propaganda and to your other toadies, doddypolls and dunderheads, you can do no wrong – but, dear David, you can do and you do – and you do it here.

It is a measure of your vanity that you usurped, as though by right, the best wall in the whole Academy, assuming that not one of your peers there would say nay – and not one did. You took a space that could have accommodated the work of a dozen other painters and I understand that it is your intention next year to do so again. How's that for selfishness and arrogance. Your fellows will, no doubt, let you have it without demur, even in perpetuity, for they know the value of the publicity you generate for yourself and are grateful when scraps of it, by association, fall on them, but the Academy's Summer Exhibition, ghastly though it is, should never be your personal instrument.

Your once ardent admirer, BS

Dear Michael Craig-Martin – It should surprise no one that the Academicians asked you to become one of their number, for they long since sold their souls to Mammon, but that you, the Eminence Grise of contemporary art in Britain, the calculating Trotsky of it, should have accepted their invitation, is astonishing. It is not only a significant change of heart on your part, but the point at which the onlooker must recognise that the ancestral traditions of painting have for so long been abandoned by the very institution that for so long has been trusted to maintain them. No wooden horse was needed for your Trojan victory. You speak of older Academicians as reactionary, as wanting to steer art into retrograde and provincial dead ends (how then can you bear to go to bed with Hockney?), 'but that's not going to happen', you assert. Such conviction suggests that a coup has quietly taken place.

Let me compare you with Rembrandt, a man who drew models in his studio, drew landscapes to and fro, drew such curiosities as elephants when they occurred, drew on impulse and in careful preparation for a painting or a print; he could paint thick or thin, light or dark, swiftly or with care; he could change his mind midway, submerging what would become a pentimento; he could even turn his brush about and scribble with the point of its handle in wet paint. You work with a bank of simple outline images stored in a computer's memory, and can, at the press of a button, generate consequential designs on a scale impossible by hand; you play with scale, the grand piano smaller than the shoe, a latchkey larger than a ladder, you like your line to be thick, even and bleakly insensitive, with no duty other than mere outline – nothing to do with drawing as Rembrandt understood it. You like your colour to be flat, opaque, unmodulated and nauseating in its bright deliberate dissonance, with no evidence of texture in the paint itself any in the thing it represents.

All this is evident in your revision of Seurat's *Bathers* in the National Gallery, your major offering at the Academy. Anything Howard Hodgkin does, you can do better, I suppose, but the Seurat is again the victim; 'rarely,' I said of the Hodgkin, 'has one painter misunderstood so grossly the subtleties and purposes of another,' but at least it was in oil on timber and the brushwork evident, but yours, in acrylic on a sheet of aluminium, is so vilely alien to the original, so vulgar, so featureless, so dead, that it could be mass-manufactured by machines and not even Richard Cork, your gospeller, could tell the difference.

Contemplating your *Reconstructing Seurat (Orange)* (will variants in purple, apple green and chrome yellow be on view at the Academy next year?), I could think of no aesthetic reason for inviting you to become one of the Olympians of Piccadilly, and none for your acceptance other than subversion; with you in Burlington House it will soon be Tate Modern's west end branch.

Yours in profound misgiving, BS

DEAR ROYAL ACADEMICIANS – That each year you mount a Summer Exhibition that is worse than any predecessor, is a remarkable achievement. That in doing so you collaborate with the enemy and in embracing the darlings of the Serota Tendency, join it, narrowing the band of Academic patronage to those who already have support in abundance from both Tates and the Arts and British Councils, is deplorable. I have no doubt that you quell your consciences with cash, for the commissions on £65,000 for a Craig-Martin and £70,000 for a Gary Hume are far far above those to be earned by selling the works of longer established Academicians (with the exception of the execrable Tom Phillips and the deluded Bellany), or the worthy but unfashionable painters for whom the Academy is the only opportunity for exhibiting in London; this year there is an overwhelming sense of loyalty and principle abandoned.

In your many galleries you hang, crowded and confused, an exhibition that in part is no better than the railings of Green Park, that in part resembles the final year show of any art school in the land, that overlaps the Triennial surveys mounted by Tate Britain and the shows to which we are accustomed at the Saatchi Gallery and the various outstations of the Arts Council and the Tate. You have made ignoble a once illustrious institution and reduced the Summer Exhibition to a ghastly hotch-potch at which only Sunday Painters and the millionaire artists of the new establishment wish to show their wares. At the Royal Academy, it must be said, merit does not matter any more.

Your obedient servant, BS

The Summer Exhibition, Royal Academy 2007

Jake & Dinos Chapman, *The Meek Shall Inherit the Earth But Not the Mineral Rights* (2007)
http://www.royalacademy.org.uk/exhibitions/summerexhibition2007/
chapman-brothers-sculpture-in-the-annenberg-courtyard,397,AR.html

Royal Artillery Memorial at Hyde Park
http://www.guardian.co.uk/artanddesign/jonathanjonesblog/2011/nov/
07/royal-artillery-memorial-english-heritage

David Hockney, *Double Study for 'A Closer Grand Canyon'*
(1998)
http://www.racollection.org.uk/asset_arena/photo/large/28/
PL000528.jpg

Michael Craig-Martin, *Reconstructing Seurat (Orange)*
http://www.telegraph.co.uk/culture/cultural-olympiad/8594148/
British-artists-to-make-Olympics-posters.html

Apocalypse

ROYAL ACADEMY

Evening Standard, 22 September 2000

Shock Treatment. The Art of Outrage. Welcome to the Freak Show. These are three of the circus-barking headlines in the broadsheets that for the past few weeks have been leaking news and opinions of *Apocalypse*, the Royal Academy's autumn exhibition. Ostensibly intended to explore beauty and horror in international contemporary art, the exhibition's propaganda has cynically whipped up rage in Tunbridge Wells, where the expectation of nausea and repugnance, pornography and filth, has set moustaches twitching, while in the purlieus of the polytechnic university, hordes of the ignorant young are marshalled to the show's defence. This is *Time Out* readers' stuff, informed by *Time Out* gush.

A freak show? Shock and Horror? Outrage deliberately provoked? No, not at all. Distaste, but not disgust, numbness rather than response, weariness with the familiarity of it all and disappointment with its feebleness. Anger would be a far more enjoyable response, adrenalin flowing, pupils widening, words effortlessly tripping from the tongue, but with boredom there is nothing of this, and one wanders disconsolately from room to room in the hope that something seen a second time, a third indeed, will engender an aesthetic frisson, no matter how slight and transitory. Nothing does, however, and it is abundantly evident that contemporary art has lost its cutting edge. Only the exhibition's junior curator, Max Wigram, who should perhaps have worn jackboots and a Nazi uniform for the press view, roused, not anger, but exasperation with his bullying – 'I know what you're going to say about this exhibition. I could write your reviews for you.'

Norman Rosenthal, the exhibition's senior showman, contributes a wayward essay to its sky blue and mendaciously illustrated catalogue, anxiously giving his chosen artists historical authority, for most of them are unfamiliar to an English audience. This exhibition should be, he demands, 'a jolt to the assumed pattern of art', and then accuses us of only ever wanting 'pleasurable experience' from the visual arts, as if the high point in our aesthetic lives is the prettiness of little pictures by the old Royal Academicians whom he so despises. Artists are seers, he tells us, who have always been obsessed with expressing the illusion of suspended time, and at this point Bosch and Bruegel are brought into play, Titian and Caravaggio, Goya and Cézanne, Wagner, Stravinsky and Shakespeare – the artists he shows us now, we are to assume, must be of equal company.

Artists of that calibre were indeed seers of a kind, visionaries certainly, able to inform us by involving us as immediate spectators who, breaking through the veil of the picture plane, are there at the event, be it the Crucifixion or the wayside murder, the cannibal's feast or the roasting of St Lawrence on his grid. For them, horror and beauty were the two most powerful instruments of empathy, pathos and catharsis, their vile and violent subjects metaphors and synecdochisms for all kinds of inhumanity, but in lifting them above the literal and scrupulously descriptive even if only in the application and exploitation of paint, and in lending them beauty, even if only the physical beauty that stirs loins, these painters took their imagery far beyond the mere portrayal of lessons to be learned, of warnings and precepts to be observed, of martyred saints to be invoked for superstition's sake, and gave us art that is unarguably art – and with it, insight and understanding; so too composers with their orchestras and poets with their words.

With these artists summoned to his elbow, Velázquez too, and Chardin, Beuys, Murillo, Poussin and Brancusi, with Charlotte Salomon adduced as proof of burgeoning public interest in the details of the Holocaust, one senses 'spin' worthy of 10 Downing

Street in this marshalling of antecedents, and one recognises the deceit of it when all but a pair of exhibitors express not the slightest interest in, or respect for, the past of his once learned profession. Can Tim Noble and Sue Webster, joint pilers of black plastic rubbish bags, even spell Arcimboldo, whom Rosenthal designates their forerunner?

'How are young artists today reflecting the inevitable contemporary abyss?' asks Rosenthal, to which the answer, with the exception of the notorious Chapman Brothers, is that they are not. Remove the brothers' work and this becomes an exhibition of stale ideas that once, in other men's hands a generation and more since, touched in some degree the aesthetics of astonishment, the gasp of incredulity, but to which now, at second and third hand, we can only say that we have seen it all before and its aesthetic interest has not grown with repetition and the grand scale of the Academy. This is an exhibition of exhausted art, of art forms that, though visual, belong in the cinema rather than an art gallery (and even less in an academy of painting and sculpture) and are crude fairground entertainment.

'There is nothing inherently wrong with entertainment as such except that, in itself, it contributes nothing to the process of self-knowledge that makes the viewing of art such an enriching experience,' prates Rosenthal. If that is so, then the visitor to this exhibition should ask how much he gains in self-knowledge when, crouching low as a dog, he squeezes through the kennel entrance. This sets the tone of the Rosenthal Rocky but hardly Horror Show – an immediate indignity inflicted on the old and lame, the overweight and the claustrophobe, as he struggles into a simulated cellar, musty and damp; in terms of squalid misery this is of the ilk of the Tracey Emin bed – a relic, a token, the petrified remains, the keepsake of a pathological condition requiring analysis and not, in itself, a work of art.

The paintings of Luc Tuymans are etiolated nothings; blanched and almost colourless, this stuff of the fumbling first-year student here must pass for the masterpiece, Max Wigram erupting in angry pleasure over them. Maurizio Cattelan – he of the Tate's hanging horse (a full-page illustration in the catalogue to remind us of that pointless exercise) – strikes down the Pope, a life-sized waxwork, with a meteorite; the art historian could, no doubt, tie this lampoon to a thousand anti-clerical caricatures and it will be much enjoyed by the patriots of Ulster, but when all is said and done it is peepshow Tussaud stuff. What used to be the great Gallery III contains an absurd pavilion by the pretentious and silly Japanese girl, Mariko Mori, of whom no one would have heard were merit the reason for her fame (her father is an influential magnate); in the idiom of television staging, shining bright, it would look well enough as the host's set on a TV home video show. Is my self-knowledge enhanced by any of these?

Mike Kelley gives us a video of amateur actors desperately performing the stilted script of a domestic squabble – the Tooting Thespian Society, perhaps? – together with the furnished set. If Chris Cunningham has indeed installed a pornographic video, then with its flashing lights, balletic ballyhoo and deafening noise, all but the compulsively prurient will be driven away before they witness conjugation. By Wolfgang Tillmans we have photographs, the soft pornography of a boy playing Christ for doubting Thomas and the grotesquely enlarged perineum or rima area of pink denim shorts, the most remarkable among them. Is anyone enlightened by such trivia? And who cares who carefully constructed the piles of black bagged and loose rubbish topped by Disney shadows, or who in-stalled the new bus stations for Auschwitz? How is my self-knowledge deepened by these things? I bow to no one in my respect for the ghosts of German concentration camps, scarred as my memory is by the discovery of Belsen, scarred by the photographs given me by Robert Spanski, the first Allied Forces photographer to enter Dachau. New bus shelters trivialise the beastliness and Rosenthal, a Jew, should know it.

The work of these and other inadequates of the blunt edge of contemporary art will take the visitor ten minutes – no more – the intellectual effort no greater than flipping the pages of *Hello*. And then we come to the Chapman Brothers. Though disturbed, engrossed, fascinated and compelled by their nine extended tableaux in glass cases, I am not wholly convinced that these are works of art, but they are outstanding in the wretched company forced on them by Rosenthal and Wigram. Exploiting every idiom of the Cult of the Terrible they make reference to every variation of the Martyrdom of the Ten Thousand Soldiers on Mount Ararat, crucified, beheaded, thrown into pits, hanged and spiked on broken branches; here are apocalyptic horsemen, the Knight, Death and the Devil, the waxwork dead of crypts in southern Italy, the medieval Dance of Death and the horrors of the Thirty Years War in central Europe as recorded in contemporary accounts; here is the film vocabulary of *A Bridge Too Far*, *Bridge Over the River Kwai* and *The Bridge at Remagen*; the height of the huge glass cases and the angle at which the spectator sees *into* the grisly spectacles, recalls the filming from helicopters that made *Apocalypse Now* so immediate and telling. Mutant figures are still part of the Chapman language, but the sexual shock has gone and with its elimination one may brood on every genocide, Armenian, Ugandan, Rwandan, Bosnian, Kurdish, Greek of Turk and Turk of Greek, as well as on the Holocaust of Jews. This is an evocation of history, not Hell.

These tableaux are perhaps dangerously near the expensive toy and the tactical exercise table of the army in my day – indeed, were they paintings or conventional sculpture they would at once be damned by the all–powerful 'Turds are art' brigade as too specific, too precise, too skill-based to be art, and their destiny may be as Tate Modern's occasional Christmas treat for boys on the cusp of puberty. In this company, however, only the Chapman Brothers have any claim to be taken seriously as artists, touching the visionary, jolting the assumed pattern, suspending time, and even, if not contributing to self-knowledge, reviving it. Apart from their contributions, this exhibition, offering no challenge, not even pessimism, only banality, is not the promised sequel to *Sensation*, and like the artists of his choice, Rosenthal too has lost his cutting edge. Perhaps he should now spend more time with his family.

Apocalypse, Royal Academy 2000

Tim Noble & Sue Webster
http://www.timnobleandsuewebster.com/tnsw_biblio/
apocalypse_168-9.jpg

Maurizio Cattelan, *The Ninth Hour* (1999)
http://www.christies.com/lotfinder/LargeImage.aspx?image=/
lotfinderimages/d20516/d2051684x.jpg

CHARLES SAATCHI AND HIS GALLERIES

Long before Nicholas Serota became Director of the Tate Gallery in 1988, Charles Saatchi slipped discreetly into the art world as a serious collector of work by well-established contemporary artists, American, German and English. A free spirit, untrammelled by trustees and the constraints of a public Gallery's bureaucracy, rich as Croesus and able to buy at whim, he was doing what the Tate should have done but was too impoverished. Having opened his own gallery in 1985, showing the wonders of Warhol, Schnabel, Judd, Koons, Guston, Nauman, Kiefer and many others of whom we could hardly have known had they been left to the Tate, Saatchi then began to venture into the riskier field of the unestablished artist and was quickly on the way to forming the collection of work by Young British Artists (the YBAs) for which he is notorious; this the Tate could never have done.

There is no doubt that just as Hirst made a dead shark into a work of art and Emin her squalid bed, so Saatchi, with his taste for art that is crudely literal, bizarre, grotesque, sexual and calculatedly offensive, made them into artists. His admirers see him as a Medici, his detractors as Svengali. He is neither; since 1980 or so he has matured from enthusiastic (almost manic) private acquisition, to the very public role of demonstrating what has been happening in art, both national and international, to a far greater extent than Serota and his multiplying Tates – if we know anything of the undertows of art it is from his many exhibitions, not Serota's. As the reviews that follow clearly demonstrate, my response to his work has radically changed, and I am now convinced that for our constantly nourished awareness of immediately contemporary art over the past three decades, its decline and degradation, we are deeply in Saatchi's debt – though that does not mean that we must admire it.

Sensation

THE ROYAL ACADEMY

Evening Standard, 18 September 1997

The proper response of a critic to the Royal Academy's exhibition of Charles Saatchi's notorious collection is to ignore it, for deprived of praise and exegesis, with controversy left unroused, the breathless broadcasters of radio and television silent, all microphones muffled, all typewriters stilled, it would slip quietly into oblivion, the state that it deserves. This course, however and alas, cannot be pursued for whatever the exhibition may not be in aesthetic and intellectual terms, there can be no doubt that as news of a peculiarly distasteful sort, it is grist to the newspaper's mill; the unwilling critic must therefore put aside his natural and wholly commendable antipathy, and write.

Why is he antipathetic, when it is constantly claimed by the compliant critics of the Serota Tendency (by far the majority) that Mr Saatchi leads the world in taste and connoisseurship, and that his chosen artists are the cutting edge, the breakers of bounds and the leapers of boundaries, while the toadies of the Culture Minister promote the notion that their international success at home brings down the price of bread? He is antipathetic because he sees them as nothing of the kind, but as exploiters of a stale tradition of outrage almost as old as the century and now so familiar that it has lost its force, desperately seeking variations on themes first established by Duchamp, Malevich and other innovators and explorers eighty years ago, and renewed and expanded since the war by Arte Povera, Beuys and Fluxus. They are at best remarkable for their pointless ingenuity, and at worst for a puerility, particularly striking among the women, with which no boy beyond the age of fourteen is comfortable.

The title of the exhibition is Sensation – intended, no doubt, as a self-fulfilling prophecy. If we take this to have the meaning common in newspapers, then it is reasonably accurate, for this is an accumulation of freakish, monstrous and anomalous images and objects calculated to affront, disturb and generally excite an emotional or highly charged response, and to divide utterly those determined to support it from those revolted and repelled. Shock, horror, bewilderment and boredom are the legitimate responses in the Royal Academy this autumn, the first three deliberately intended and provoked by Mr Saatchi and the deferential lackeys who dogsbody for him in a flatulent, acquiescent and superficial catalogue, the fourth the subversive response of all who have over the past decade been reasonably attentive to the activities of the Serota Tendency.

Mr Saatchi's is, to put no fine point on it, a collection of the most familiar work by the most self-important and self-seeking contributors to exhibitions of contemporary art since 1985, and no one who has done regular rounds of the Tate, Serpentine, Whitechapel and South London Galleries, the ICA, the Camden Art Centre and Mr Saatchi's own premises in nether St John's Wood, will be in the least shocked or horrified. To some extent the experienced may remain bewildered, though less by the content and meaning of the exhibited material than by Mr Saatchi's need to possess it (the province of the Freudian analyst rather than the art critic), but the powerful and abiding response is boredom, for everything we see is too familiar, and so too is the misery of seeing it again.

We have seen it all before, again, and again, and again – and if not precisely these things, then things so familiar in idiom, material and scale that there is nothing to distinguish them; and here's the rub – Mr Saatchi is an advertising man, of whom none is more skilled in the slick business of the message in a moment – which is precisely what he respects in contemporary art, and therefore buys it. He is not interested in layers of meaning, in contemplation, empathy, catharsis or the elevation of the spirit; the abstract values of art, proportion, balance, colour, tone, and the management and exploitation of pictorial space, are of no value to him, whether in a non-figurative sense or as supports for figures in an implied narrative. He seeks only the flash of recognition that is the transitory response of the commuting traveller to the glimpsed hoarding, or the idle reader turning the pages of a trashy magazine, and his collection can be seen as quickly. We must go further: we must accuse Mr Saatchi of having not the foggiest idea of what has for more than two millennia in western Europe been man's intelligent response to art, its purpose, the complexity of it, the emotional and intellectual intensity of its demands of us, our passionate need for the romance and reason of it, the nobility and gravitas of it, the mysticism of it, and even the sense of the exiled soul redeemed by it. Mr Saatchi's collection is a package of inflated playthings for the shallow mind.

They are, of course, the inflated playthings of the Arts and British Councils too, the playthings of the pretentious panjandrums who run the Venice Biennale, the Kassel Documenta, the Turner Prize, and every international exhibition that depends on causing a sensation among the Pavlov dogs of television and the press. Through the Tate Gallery and the Arts and British Councils the public pours enormous quantities of tax into the pockets and purses of these artists, and the more they do so, the more Mr Saatchi purrs as his investment swells. Now the Academy has joined them in this boosting of his profit (for there is much evidence that he is a dealer and entrepreneur at least as much as a collector), his Trojan Horse there Norman Rosenthal, the Exhibition Secretary.

The Royal Academy has fallen on hard times – complacency, indolence, an embezzler and huge debts have seen to that – and Mr Saatchi's collection was, as it were, easily at hand to fill the gap when this winter's exhibition had to be cancelled at short notice, the cost of showing it minimal, the potential profit enough to widen the eyes of the most cupiditous if public interest could be whipped into a froth. It was. In high summer the Academy revealed that it was to exhibit Marcus Harvey's portrait of Myra Hindley, each patch of paint the size and shape of a child's handprint. This was the first specific information about the exhibition – nothing of the same kind was offered about other artists and their contributions – and the challenge to public sensibilities was quite deliberate. The consequent ballyhoo was sufficient for the RA to issue another press release late in July, protesting that it shared the public's revulsion and abhorrence, but that any suggestion that it 'was motivated to mount this exhibition by exploitative financial concerns is wholly wrong' – an act calculated to continue the controversy. The picture, a meretricious work of painting-by-numbers ingenuity, has not been withdrawn from the exhibition and now hangs in so prominent a position that the Academicians' breast-beating is revealed as intentional hypocrisy.

The Academy has uttered other platitudes, protesting that it has a duty to exhibit works by young British artists who, at our expense, have been furnished with international reputations, and on its behalf, Norman Rosenthal's essay in the catalogue likens Mr Saatchi's artists to the Pre-Raphaelites and the painters grouped round Sickert, to Manet, Goya and Bosch – the deceitful alignment of a fraudulent present with a triumphant past, the arguments and implications spurious. The Academy has no such duty; on the contrary, if duty it has, it is to preach another gospel altogether – that there is life yet in the old dogs of painting and sculpture, and in the ancestral traditions and techniques. If there is anything more deplorable about this exhibition than the exhibition itself, it is the Academy's betrayal of academic teaching in the RA Schools, the Academicians' alliance with the enemies of art, and their reckless scramble onto the Serota–Saatchi bandwagon.

This is an exhibition of vast and vulgar photographs, the pre-pubescent female dummies of the window-dress trans-sexually perverted and engaged, the distorting mirror, pseudo-Victorian dresses, black ethnicity enlivened with the turds of elephants, and waxwork figures. An atmosphere of crude sexual fantasy hangs heavy in the galleries. We are reminded of Mona Hatoum's gullet as a sexual instrument with the video of her *Deep Throat*, the business of her eating confused with oral sex; Sarah Lucas too is obsessed with sexual imagery, the erect cucumber conventionally phallic, the overturned bucket and half-consumed kebab preposterous metaphors for the vagina; and we have Tracey Emin's tent emblazoned with the names of all with whom she has slept but who have not necessarily penetrated her body. Jenny Saville, by contrast, avoids the childish pornographic trap, and sustains her promise as a serious painter of female flesh. With its washbasin in a padded velvet case, the portrait head in refrigerated blood, and explicit mutilations, the exhibition provides bizarre accompaniment for what, in terms of quantity, is something of a retrospective for Rachel Whiteread and Damien Hirst, vain winners of the Turner Prize. Whiteread remains depressingly devoid of ideas, her exploitation of unlikely spaces never bettered than in the cast taken by filling her hot water bottle with plaster of Paris, but growing ever larger and increasingly banal. Hirst remains a wayward, undisciplined intelligence who might, one day, if gross flattery and easy wealth do not undo him, produce a work of art; for the moment he seems pleased to vary the contents of his formaldehyde aquaria, and little more; his *Thousand Years* of 1990, a confection of maggots, bluebottles, and the flayed head, rotting, of a cow, fills the gallery with a foul stink.

Sensation has a meaning other than that of the newspaper man and the advertising guru – the awareness of touch or taste, pain or pleasure, for example. In this sense, the exhibition elicits one reaction above all other; forget shock and horror, both of which can be accompanied by a strange inverted thrill; forget the bewilderment and boredom that blind the eye and anaesthetise the spirit; here in the Royal Academy the overwhelming sensation, abiding, unremitting, absolute, is nausea. Mr Saatchi's assemblage of freaks, frauds and feeble failures makes the sane man sick. It has, however and unwittingly, one valuable purpose – it reminds us that this is the stuff applauded by the Serota Tendency, and that to house more of it, much more, we spend our Lottery millions on the new Tate Gallery on Bankside.

Sensation, The Royal Academy 1997

Mona Hatoum, *Deep Throat* (1996)
http://www.christies.com/lotfinder/LargeImage.aspx?image=/
lotfinderimages/d46582/d4658294x.jpg

Tracy Emin, *Everyone I Have Ever Slept With 1963–95* (1995)
http://upload.wikimedia.org/wikipedia/en/a/a5/Emin-Tent-Interior.jpg

Damien Hirst, *A Thousand Years* (1990)
http://www.artchive.com/viewer/z.htm

Ant Noises

THE SAATCHI GALLERY

Evening Standard, 5 May 2000

If Charles Saatchi has a deserved claim to the respect of the art world, it lies in his seeing – or in his being taught to see – the possibilities of an industrial building on the extreme northern fringe of St John's Wood, as an art gallery. From a disused paint factory on a site ideal for a property speculator to erect half a dozen mock-Georgian villas in a security-conscious close, he made instead the largest private gallery in Britain, spare and functional, a place of struts, plain walls and roof in which lights, changing floor levels and wide stairs shape the spaces, make some seem vast and others almost intimate, and subtly control the wandering visitor's steps. Paradoxically, though inviting vast canvases and superhuman sculptures, small works are not overwhelmed by all this space and light, for the visitor establishes his own comfortable relationship with everything that is to be seen, stepping forward, stepping back, as he and the exhibit define the space they need. The space is thus infinitely flexible, subtle, anonymous, undemanding and, not deliberately given new character to obliterate the old, its origin is still evident. Consciously or unconsciously, Saatchi's conversion of this building must have sown a seed in the minds of those who now, in Tate Modern down on Bankside, have created what its promoters claim to be 'the world's greatest gallery devoted to modern art'.

Saatchi as a collector is a different matter – phenomenally influential, but not for the good. He has the eye, not of a connoisseur, not of a man who prizes aesthetic response as the essential currency of the artist and his patron, but of a showman, a circus ring-master, a fairground barker, a Barnum or Bailey with a caravan of freaks to attract the curious and gull the gullible. A lurking presence in the market place, he has for many years been an influence on dealers, curators and young artists, his symbiotic relationships occasionally smothering them and not invariably beneficial. Long a mysterious influence rather than a public figure, his wholesale emergence into open view at the Royal Academy, *Sensation* the well-chosen and prophetically punning title for his collection of all that is bizarre, obscene, grotesque and calculatedly offensive in contemporary art, made him public property, and he has since courted similar publicity in America as another unofficial ambassador of British culture, more manipulatively skilful than the Spice Girls and, because so much money is invested in the current market value of his possessions, disturbingly effective. Without the constant promotion of his collection, each addition swiftly and shrewdly made notorious, Nick Serota's Tate Modern would not have been a dream come true; without it the British Council would not be parading his chosen artists in every major and minor arena round the world, the Arts Council would not seem an adjunct of his business, and our Minister of Culture would have to stand in awe of someone else.

Saatchi's mind and eye are neatly encapsulated in his current exhibition, *Ant Noises*, an anagram of *Sensation*. The great work here is Damien Hirst's *Hymn* – a hymn of praise to Him or him, a work only weeks old and already as worldwide famous as Michelangelo's *David*. If only it were as beautiful as that hobbledehoy of a youth, speaking as openly of the sculptor's physical desire as of the subject's inner spirit and the weight of history and heroism upon him – but it is not, and indeed is not beautiful at all. Its apologists see it in terms of the Greek and Roman sculptures of the ancient gods, a new Olympian Jupiter, a gigantic kouros, and are not the least discomfited to be told that it is the gross replica of a plastic toy intended to teach children the rudiments of human anatomy. They prattle of the superhuman bronzes, brightly painted, that were once housed in the stadia and temples of the antique south, they prate of Leonardo da Vinci, George Stubbs, the anatomist Vesalius and the flayed figures from which art students and budding surgeons once learned the function and the whereabouts of sinews, muscles, arteries. They excuse the flagrant plagiarism by telling us that Rodin hardly ever touched his sculpture but left it all to his now forgotten workmen; and they justify it by telling us that this is what Duchamp would have done, had he been alive to do it.

Twenty feet tall, in glossy colours that recall the current range employed on sports cars by Mercedes-Benz, weighing six tons, bought for £1,000,000 — the apologists reel off the statistics as if these alone were justification enough for making *Hymn* — it was bound to become headline news, and bound to be headline news again when the designer of the original plastic toy did what Hirst himself did when British Airways used large round spots of colour in their advertisements — 'Hey,' said Hirst, 'those spots are mine and I've 500 spot paintings to prove it.' But when Norman Emms said 'Hey — that's my design and it can be had for fifteen quid in every toyshop in the land,' Saatchi's lackey critics told him that he should be overwhelmed with gratitude to have been the inspiration for so great a man as Damien Hirst — 'Be off with you,' they said, 'Hirst has converted your poxy plastic gew-gaw into one of the greatest sculptures of the twentieth century and a divinity for the twenty-first, a monumentally powerful meditation on the frailty of the human condition.'

It is nothing of the kind — dull and featureless at back and sides, it is not even an effective sculpture in the round. It is nothing but another novelty, another freak, another caprice to captivate an audience mindless enough to mistake an elaborate prank for art. Epstein's *Adam* did not deserve its years in peepshows in New York and Blackpool — but this is all that Hirst's *Hymn* is fit for, except that it hasn't the balls to shock an audience.

As for the other exhibits, these too are wretched. We have seen them all before, or very like, and seeing them again does nothing to enrich acquaintance. Jenny Saville's once immodest promise as a bold painter of fat women is dissipated on canvases of even greater scale, with a consequent welter of flaccid slapping brushstrokes in which is evident no grasp of form or structure, the dead dull paint hopelessly disciplined with the tedious precision of mannered ticks and strokes that echo old Coldstream's formula for diverting attention from the drabness of his nudes. Ron Mueck, no Michelangelo, is no more than a modeller of Tussaud waxworks that depend for impact on shifting the scale to well above or below life size while clinging to uncanny realism; he shares the least appealing characteristics of Jeff Koons, even the religiosity of images that could serve well in Spanish and Bavarian churches; and in the final analysis his work is, if not exactly sentimental, twee enough to be sold through Sunday supplements in limited editions for the mantelshelf.

Sarah Lucas — she of *Sensation*'s erect cucumber and stained mattress (the springboard for the Emin bed) — offers us a cigarette between the lips of a vagina and a pair of old flea-market bronzes joined energetically in sexual frottage. Chris Ofili's paintings, fussy in detail, composition not even attempted, are feeble studio sweepings that give the lie to whispers of genius. Rachel Whiteread's hundred casts of the space under an upright chair, in jelly-baby colours and translucence, would look well as an advertisement for a confectioner.

In spite of the utterly undeserved success thrust upon them by all the state agencies as well as Saatchi, these artists, well into maturity, now seem irredeemably lightweight, frivolous and silly, mischief their only asset. Hirst, though wayward, once seemed capable of high seriousness, and Saville once drew a little and could control a brush, but both have abandoned what small integrity they had. Lucas is contemptible, Whiteread a pretentious bore, and Mueck — alone here in technical skill — perhaps has macabre imagination enough to make a Chamber of Horrors for Tussaud. Ant Noises they may be, but there is no Sensation here.

Ant Noises, Saatchi Gallery

Damien Hirst, *Hymn* (1996)
http://www.artnet.com/galleries/artwork_detail.asp?G=&gid
=414&which=&ViewArtistBy=&aid=8315&wid=32316&source=
artist&sortby=i mgorder&rta=http://www.artnet.com

New Labour

THE SAATCHI GALLERY

Evening Standard, 18 May 2001

Thirteen years have passed since Peter Langan, friend, restaurateur and serial lecher, died. I am reminded of him often, and in small things he has a kind of immortality, in bubble and squeak, ripe figs and mature women with black hair, but none of these triggers of recollection has ever been so immediate and powerful as a so-called work of art in the latest exhibition mounted by Charles Saatchi, that Satrap of the Serota Tendency. In this, a video by Liane Lang, a recent graduate of Goldsmith's College, the too much admired hot-house of the cutting-edge in art, the ugly spatula fingers of a plasticine hand pleasure the plasticine clitoris that peeps from a loose-lipped plasticine vagina; to give this enigmatic art object a realistic setting, Miss Lang appears to have plucked her own black pubic hair and re-rooted it in pale inner thighs of yet more plasticine. One wonders at her state of mind as she set to work with the tweezers – or did she simply retrieve loose hairs from her knickers or the plug-hole of her bath?

Langan was fascinated by the techniques of female masturbation and so too, it seems, were artists as far apart as Titian and Augustus John if we enquire quite why the fingers of the hand fall in just that particular position in a painting of a female nude. It is a gesture of modesty, proclaim the professors of iconography – but is it? If modesty, then why not an outspread hand rather than one of which the fingers have slipped into the cleft? It can perhaps be argued that in touching on this subject Miss Lang works within the ancestral traditions of European art, but the tempering concept of modesty can surely not be one of which, she, a native of Munich, is aware. I doubt if she knows it even as *Bescheidenheit* or *Sittsamkeit*, for her exposure of an essentially private pursuit is a no holds barred, no secrets kept, demonstration of the activity, even if it is presented as some sort of Wallace and Gromit episode, and the video is called, not the fashionable evasion *Untitled No. 31*; but plain straightforward *Masturbating* (speakers of Turkish will recall that 31 in that language is slang for this activity, notorious in the harem of Topkapi).

In Mr Saatchi's catalogue, one Patricia Ellis relishes, drools over indeed the 'close-up beaver shot', describes what she sees as 'sticky, pink and clammy to the touch', and concludes that though Miss Lang's subject may be taboo, unmentionable and subversive, it is also so endearing and arousing that 'Spectators may cheer for girl-power while cringing in their seats'. Girl-power? – Miss Ellis is thirty years behind the times. Endearing and arousing? How can Miss Lang's realisation be either of these when in colour, texture and well-worn looks the hand and parts are less to be imagined as belonging to a Page 3 girl than to one of Macbeth's witches, so withered and so wild, things rather of the cauldron's brew than of the gates of paradise?

This video is the first thing and the last of which one is aware in the exhibition, its hail and farewell to us, for it is the nature of the television screen to vanquish all competitors for attention – in this case, just inside the entrance, a carelessly propped bicycle that few will realise is 135 per cent larger than it should be, and an armchair that apes Le Corbusier's 1926 design known as *Siège Grand Confort* but entirely constructed of the bright polystyrene foam sponges with which most of us wash dishes. These are, perhaps, forms that can be justified as art by categorising them as Surrealist or Duchampian though late, luke-warm and stale, but try as he might, the sane man cannot lift Miss Lang's 60 minutes of female masturbation above the level of schoolboy smut. Would Patricia Ellis have written as drooling a defence had the subject been an hour of male masturbation and would Mr Saatchi's lust to possess have been aroused by it? Did he buy Miss Lang's video because he thought it art or because he knew that showing it would cause debate and, with a stroke of luck, bring about another visit from censorious peelers?

To me it matters not a hoot what people see if they want to see it, and it may well be that pornography, even when reduced to adolescent bawdy, is an educational force of sorts and, wisely used, a dispeller of myths and mysteries, but that this video is in any sense a work of art seems utterly preposterous. If ever the idea that museums and galleries should lend their possessions to local pubs comes into force, as well it may if we have another four years of New Labour, then Miss Lang's *Masturbation* is an obvious candidate down at the Old Bull and Bush.

Perhaps even more objectionable as art are the gaudy pots of Grayson Perry, vulgar enough in form and glaze to be in sales of table lamps at Harrods twice a year, except that in the detail scribble of the decoration one is likely to discover episodes of sexual bondage, hermaphroditism, fellatio, a monkish figure brandishing a brace of dildos and more masturbation. These vases are now the commonplace of mixed exhibitions in such galleries such as Whitechapel, as though art must acknowledge craft as equal, but one of them stands more or less for all, and owning enough of them to make what Antony Gormley might call a 'Field' reduces Saatchi's connoisseurship to the level of philately, phillumeny and mania.

Smut is the core of the sculpture of Rebecca Warren too. She is another girl from Goldsmith's on whom wide-parted legs seem to have a fetish hold, male as well as female. She models in clay, as old sculptors often did, sometimes letting it dry penny plain, sometimes tuppence colouring it, crudely, in what appears to be unsubtle household gloss. Her references are to Rodin, who, genuinely lecherous, often touched a universal note far above the lust that stirred his loins; to Medardo Rosso's strange inventions in wax over plaster (1890s); to Umberto Boccioni, the lower limbs of whose *Unique Forms of Continuity in Space* (1913) obviously inspired her own pair of disconnected legs and to Lucio Fontana, to whose polychrome ceramic sculptures, much exhibited in recent years, she owes a formidable debt, and whose 1947 drawings for a crucified figure appear to be preparatory studies for her own, though she goes a good deal further with the idea of the erect penis and lascivious tongue. Why collect work that is so obviously begged, borrowed, stolen and so much worse than the originals that inspired it?

In sheer scale the exhibition is dominated by the vast decorative trifles of D. J. Simpson who gouges marine plywood with an electric router to construct abstract graffiti with vague landscape tendencies – the perfect trivia with which to embellish the tedious architectural conceits of Lord Rogers and Lord Foster. On a small scale and in paint on canvas they might have seemed to explore the shallows of Parisian art half a century ago, but inflated to the half acre they are merely empty wastes. The remaining contributors are Enrico David, a serious young Italian who embroiders large canvases with wool in much the same way as Scottie Wilson, an obsessive lunatic much loved by George Melly, constructed his small watercolours, and Martin Maloney, of whom and whose inept and contemptible pre-school primitivism the less said the better.

Oddly lacking in energy, this disappointing show, to which Mr Saatchi has given the title *New Labour*, is indeed laboured and laborious. It suggests that he has lost his eye. As a rule, in his challenges, he rouses a vigorous reaction and it hardly matters whether this is for him or against, for the debate is all and even those who have found his antics crude, ostentatious and occasionally deeply distasteful, have been able to discern something of quality amid the dross. Only a cynic might suggest that this is less his deliberate choice than the happy accident that arises from his buying as much as he does. In this exhibition, however, nothing redeems his offerings from utter, absolute and tedious banality.

Acquisition on Saatchi's scale must reflect a psychological condition governed by a need, above all, for frequent repetition of a fetishistic experience; it is not uncommon among collectors and can be an aspect of aggression, dominance, power and even a form of sexual activity − *to spend* was for centuries the euphemism for ejaculation − or masochism. It is not unknown for collectors to begin with the first, progress to the last, and then stop. Withdrawal symptoms are neither prolonged nor painful and the compensation for them is, in every case, an exhilarating sense of relief. The indications of this lacklustre exhibition are that Goldsmith's College is losing its status as the *ne plus ultra* of pretentious absurdity and Saatchi his ability to challenge. I have always argued that the Royal Academy's Summer Exhibition is the justification for the Saatchi group of favourites, but when these become as dull as those, there is no justification for either.

New Labour, Saatchi Gallery 2001

Liane Lang, *Masturbation* (1998)
http://www.saatchi-gallery.co.uk/artists/artpages/
liane_lang_masturbation1.htm

Grayson Perry, *Golden Ghosts* (2000)
http://www.saatchi-gallery.co.uk/artists/artpages/
grayson_perry_golden_ghosts.htm

In October 2008 Charles Saatchi opened his third gallery. His first, on the northern boundary of St John's Wood, he had outgrown; his second, in the old palatial premises of the Greater London Council before its extinction, had proved in many ways disagreeable; but in the handsome disused Duke of York's Barracks in Chelsea – a building to which I am sentimentally attached for it was my base while in the Army Reserve after National Service – his third incarnation has achieved perfection. It is large, but not overwhelming, beautifully lit, and in every aesthetic and functional sense a more comfortable gallery than Tate Modern. His first exhibition there was devoted to contemporary Chinese Art, an irrelevance in the context of this book but my review covered other points and, for the first time, expressed my grudging esteem for him; my comments on the exhibition are thus excluded.

Charles Saatchi, *Phase III*

Evening Standard, 10 October 2008

In Charles Saatchi's virtual absence for the past two years or so, the London Art World seemed diminished, as though two cylinders of a straight six engine had been cut from the firing order (it can be done). He has for so long been a major presence, his activities at times provocative and incomprehensible, at times an important prop to the hapless inactivity, narrowness and complacency of Tate Modern, that his absence was as evident as his presence has been since his first public incarnation, his St John's Wood Gallery, in March 1985. There, in that magic space where even the tiniest work of art could dictate the dimensions of its territory among the giants, he did what the Tate should have been doing – he showed us the great figures of art worlds established in Europe and America and gave us a wider intellectual context against which to set his own art world establishment, drawn from the very young and obstinately infantile Young British Artists.

In broad terms it must be argued that in everything Saatchi did, the panjandrums of the Tate were forced to follow, sheep deriving initiative and energy from his shepherding, yet it was Serota, stumbling along behind, who got the knighthood for doing what he was paid to do. Where would we have been, I wonder, if Saatchi had not shown him what was happening in British art? It was not Serota who mounted the notorious *Sensation* exhibition at the Royal Academy in 1997 – an exhibition that told a terrible truth and from which I departed feeling so physically and intellectually sick that I walked home through the wholesome ambience of Hyde Park and Kensington Gardens to cleanse my soul – but it was Serota who gained the greater advantage from it, for it opened the floodgates of the future for him, while Saatchi took the flak. Saatchi was so vilified for *Sensation* that for its three months duration he was the most hated man in Britain; the wounds of the abuse hurled then scar his reputation still.

With hindsight, however, it is clear that Saatchi, a cheerfully rootless innocent, the history of art a discipline unknown to him, his connoisseurship entirely uncluttered with the baggage of the past, sensing no debt even to the art of the earlier decades of the twentieth century, could establish his interests wholly in the later, in the art not of his lifetime (he is now in his sixties), but precisely of the moment. He was thus the perfect champion for artists wilfully ignorant of the past, wanting only to be new and different, wanting to be the new Duchamp and the new Beuys, the new breakers of boundaries and the new discarders of old definitions. As a consequence he has been the patron of an awful lot of rubbish, and the world of art, silly as it is, Serota its prime Pooh Bah, has unquestioningly adopted it.

But Saatchi has in recent years performed a more serious task and in its performance has again led the way for Tate Modern: he it is, not the Tate – which is much more given to gazing at the navels of Frida Kahlo, Louise Bourgeois and their ilk – who has given us heavyweight surveys with a broad sweep of contemporary art in America and Germany. I am far from convinced that these have been encyclopedic and suspect that Saatchi's often perverse and whimsical taste has governed them, rather than scrupulous diligence, but he brought them about and, in doing so, showed us a great deal of contemporary art of which we would have remained dimly ignorant had we had to depend on Serota for such revelations. It is with another of these semi-didactic exhibitions that the new Saatchi gallery in King's Road, Chelsea, opens – *New Art from China*.

I am grateful to Charles Saatchi for demonstrating so compellingly the bathetic dreadfulness of contemporary Chinese art, some of which has already been promoted into and above the tens of thousands of pounds, dollars and euros that are the price of trivia in the international art market. He has performed a useful service. I hope that he will perform another and another, proving the dreadfulness of art now in Australia and Nicaragua, Belarus and Bessarabia. His new gallery, light, bright, proportionate and functional, a very handsome classical skin given new life, is a friendly tool in which to perform such curatorial exposures, infinitely more comfortable than Tate Modern, its giant portico a thousand times more welcoming than the doom-laden nightmare entrance there.

He has taken a quarter of a century to do it but in this third incarnation of his gallery, both Saatchi and it have at last arrived and with it, for the first time, have an air of permanence. That air raises a very serious question. With Saatchi's death — and even he cannot go on for ever — what then? Saatchi has, against a great deal of scornful and angry opposition (including my own), performed a great good, ironically, even in his *Sensation* exhibition. We may have cared for very little of the work he has shown us over the years, but he enabled us to see it as it happened and, looking back, my impression is that he made no particular claims for any of it, that as a curator he was dispassionate, unlike those who work for state-owned galleries and invariably claim — as the Tate does with its Turner Prize and annual subsidised commissions — that their chosen contemporary artists are the old masters of the next generation. Saatchi, more than any man alive, has been responsible for letting us see art here immediately and in its infancy, and if, in *New Art from China*, we perceive the influence of British art a year or two ago, then that too is his direct responsibility.

We should honour him for it. It is my firm belief that the DCMS and its hapless ministers should long ago have entered into negotiation with him so that there is some lasting relic of all that he has done for art in Britain. His endeavours have been very different from those of Tate Modern and they deserve to be continued.

Third Saatchi Gallery

http://www.saatchi-gallery.co.uk/gallery/intro.htm

The Revolution Continues: New Art from China

http://www.saatchi-gallery.co.uk/current/nafc_installation_views.htm

NICHOLAS SEROTA
AND HIS TATES

Born 27 April 1946, Knighted in 1999, Director of the Tate Gallery since 1988 and thereafter of all that it has spawned, Nicholas Serota had not a silver spoon at birth, but – far more useful to a man of Macchiavellian character – immediate acquaintance with the corridors of power. To have been the son of an esteemed Labour politician, Beatrice Serota, created Baroness in 1967, rising from Hampstead councillor before his birth to Deputy Speaker of the House of Lords before his appointment to the Tate, her rare name everywhere respectfully recognised (particularly by the ignorant Conservative politicians who gave him the post), cannot have impeded his astonishing rise to power in the arts. Under his wing TATE has become as much a badge-engineered brand as British Leyland was, the original gallery re-named Tate Britain as its Austin, the disused power station on Bankside crudely converted into Tate Modern, its Triumph (and as unreliable), the rather more sympathetic conversion of a dockyard building into Tate Liverpool (realised by his predecessor) its Morris, and St Ives, that artificial, pretentious and whimsical joke of an art colony, has been endowed with a suitably futile dinky Tate of its own, the Motor Corporation's Riley Elf. All their contemporary offerings are much the same. All are run as satrapies, with surprisingly frequent resignations, while Serota remains the single Emperor. I am inclined to see him as a Lord Cherwell of the Arts: Cherwell it was who, to achieve their submission, advised the saturation bombing of German civilians in World War II and, expensively wrong in all his forecasts, failed; Serota too, in similarly saturating this country with the silliness of contemporary art, will ultimately fail.

Nevertheless, Serota, if not the best man for the Tate when he took over from Alan Bowness in 1988, was a better choice than his rivals on the final list, among them Norman Rosenthal of the Royal Academy, much disliked for his aggression, and Julian Spalding, then of Manchester City Art Galleries, much mistrusted as an unwise, even foolish, populariser. For the liveliness of his twelve years in charge of the Whitechapel Gallery, 1976–88, Londoners respected Serota, had even grown fond of him, and his appointment was largely applauded in the expectation that at the Tate we would have more of the same, but bigger and better. No one anticipated the extent to which the familiar old Tate was to become unfamiliar, the sense of historical development abandoned, the number of exhibits greatly reduced (often to only five hundred or so), the hanging pretentiously sparse and the displays so constantly disrupted for the benefit of sponsors (BP) that the gallery had, and still has, a disconcerting air of impermanence and unpredictability.

No one, while piously applauding the expansion into Tate Modern, expected Serota to remain in permanent command of both, diminishing Tate Britain to little more than an adjunct of Tate Modern, devoted to contemporary British artists, as though these are not wholeheartedly part of an international phenomenon. No one expected the Tates to become major instruments through which contemporary artists in early maturity would be able to charge millions for a single work of art, and thus frustrate and impoverish the permanent collections by making it virtually impossible for the Tates to buy either their works or important masterpieces of the past. Tate Modern will never close the huge gaps in its earlier twentieth-century collections and will always be third-rate; without a serious change in attitude by those who run it, Tate Britain will never again retain an historic masterpiece.

Nicholas Serota
Modern Painters, Summer 1992

The Tate Gallery is a victim of history, of the time-warps that bedevil museums in this country, of changing status, and of conflicting demands that it has never satisfied; it has always been, and is still, an anachronism. Opened in 1897, it was intended to serve only one purpose – to be the national collection of modern British art. In 1890, Sir Henry Tate had offered the National Gallery his modest collection of three bronzes and sixty-seven paintings by the ilk of Lady Butler and Briton Rivière (lifted a little by Millais' *Ophelia* and three marvellous Orchardsons), and been refused, but his subsequent offer to build a separate gallery was, after some demur, accepted by the Government, and in 1897 the Prince of Wales cut the pink ribbon and opened the door.

It was not, however, the independent gallery for which Tate had hoped, but was instead an adjunct of the National Gallery devoted to modern British art, and thus became a bastion of the exhausted and etiolated traditions fostered by the Royal Academy, its primary collection, Tate's, larded with the works of Dendy Sadler and the execrable Benjamin Williams Leader, the titles ranging from *Little Dormouse* and *Hush!* to *Cupid's Spell* and *A Country Cricket Match, Sussex.* Not until 1915 was it recommended that the purposes of the Tate Gallery should be revised, and, shortly after, it became the national collection of British art of all periods, and the national collection of modern foreign paintings; in 1937 it became the national collection of modern foreign sculpture.

These changes came far too late to let Tate's building serve its new purpose as a National Gallery of historic British Art. The National Gallery itself had its fair measure of British paintings, important and unimportant (a comparison between the catalogues of 1946 and 1986 demonstrates the extraordinary reduction of the holding), for in the 1820s, when Sir George Beaumont and his friends recognised the urgent need to found a National Gallery, British art of the past was deemed to be part of the mainstream of European art. As British art of the then present was not in general thought to be part of the National Gallery's purpose (the Turner Bequest of 1856 was something of an embarrassment), it was inevitable that with the foundation of the Victoria and Albert Museum (progressively from 1852 to 1857) John Sheepshanks should, in 1857, offer it his substantial collection of then modern and contemporary British paintings, with the intention of establishing a National Gallery of British Art to develop in parallel with the National Gallery in Trafalgar Square – his 531 paintings and drawings almost, at a stroke, equalled the holdings of the National Gallery, then only 560 paintings. Sheepshanks succeeded in providing a focus for other gifts of paintings (including the residue of Constable's workshop in 1888) that, though they make the V&A's holding of British art an unbroken thread over virtually the whole of the eighteenth and nineteenth centuries, alas divided the purpose of the Museum – a contrary pull that was not resolved with the founding of the Tate Gallery, and is still not resolved. The National Portrait Gallery, established in 1856, provided yet another home for major and minor British paintings. The British Museum, of course, ever since its foundation in 1753, has collected British prints and drawings in its Print Room.

It must be argued that the Tate Gallery was, at the revision of its purposes in 1915, either superfluous, in that historic British art was already adequately collected by four other London institutions, or a failure, in that it did not draw from these same institutions (excepting, for particular reasons, the National Portrait Gallery) works of art that were irrelevant to their larger purpose (it is still the case that the Print Rooms of the V&A and the British Museum compete with and overlap not only each other, but the Tate

Gallery, with the wasteful extravagance of unnecessary duplication at public expense). In the field of European art the Tate Gallery was certainly a failure, and without the energy and gift of Samuel Courtauld, hardly a single major Impressionist or Post-Impressionist painting would ever have graced its walls, though in these fields it was bedevilled by the curious arrangement with the National Gallery that whenever a painting reached the age of fifty it became an Old Master eligible for removal to Trafalgar Square. Without a purchase grant, acquisitions between the wars were made by gift, through the Contemporary Art Society, or by means of the Clark Fund of less than £600 per annum; no doubt it suited the Gallery in Fry-ridden, xenophobic, isolationist Britain, to become all but synonymous with resistance to the continental avant-garde, even in its feeblest forms, but its collections now suffer gravely from past failure to recognise, if not the importance of, at least the interest inherent in Cubism, Futurism, Expressionism, Constructivism, Dada and Surrealism – no work by Salvador Dalí entered the collection until 1968.

In international terms the Tate Gallery's holding of major works of art from Impressionism to Surrealism ranks lower than many a minor museum in provincial Germany – it lacks, for example, worthy paintings by such popular and prolific artists as Degas, Renoir and Van Gogh. Sir John Rothenstein roused the Gallery from torpor when he became Director in 1938, but was never given sufficient money to close the gaps in the collection – the Government first gave him an annual purchase grant in 1946, of £2,000 (a derisory sum even then). At the end of his administration, torpor returned, and under Norman Reid and Alan Bowness the Gallery was remarkable only for frightful Sixties-style interventions in the building, and such random sentimental acquisitions as the outrageously expensive cabinet pictures by Picasso and De Chirico that had belonged to Herbert Read, and, of course, Carl Andre's bricks, the subject of much indignant and scurrilous comment by a popular press wholly ignorant of the

Gallery's duty to build and maintain a national collection of modern foreign sculpture.

Two decades have passed since the bricks, *Equivalent VIII*, a work of 1966, were bought in 1972; sixteen years before the Age of Serota was established, they not only became an engaging episode in the Gallery's mythology, but marked a radical change in the public perception of the Gallery's purpose, adding to its functions the new duty to be the nation's gallery of contemporary art. More than any other work, the bricks established for the British that art may be made of any material, may introduce any technical medium or trickery, and may so cross, extend and confuse the conventional distinctions of and between painting, sculpture, photography, theatre, cinema and the *objet trouvé* . . . that the historically accepted meanings and purposes of art may be altogether abandoned.

This change of mood and interpretation has long been reinforced by the exhibitions of the Arts Council and the British Council, by such influential dealers as Nicholas Logsdail, Leslie Waddington and Anthony d'Offay, by the Kassel Documenta and the Venice Biennale, and by exhibitions at the Whitechapel Gallery and even the Royal Academy. No exhibition (other than, perhaps, *Picasso and Matisse* at the V&A in 1945) has caused more outrage and protest than *A New Spirit in Painting* at the Royal Academy in 1981; that eleven years on it now seems remarkably tame and un-controversial, is a measure both of the then British ignorance of the international avant-garde (for want of a better term) and its current awareness — an awareness for which one of its two British organisers, Nicholas Serota, is primarily responsible through his programme of exhibitions as Director of the Whitechapel Gallery. It can be argued that for at least two decades, in addition to internal curatorial pressures, the Tate Gallery has been under constant external pressure to establish and maintain a position as the National Gallery of Contemporary Art, partly from long and self-serving cliques within the Arts and British Councils, partly from self-serving dealers, partly from the unwarrantedly famous artists whom those dealers support, partly from Friends and Patrons, and partly from its own Trustees: all these small groups are financially, politically and professionally powerful, and most are cross-pollinated in symbiosis.

When Nicholas Serota became Director of the Tate Gallery in 1988 we knew that it would be subject to rapid and radical change. Though a post-graduate student at the Courtauld Institute, his appointment had nothing to do with the elite Courtauld Mafia in which so many believe, but was in most sane minds the logical consequence of his twelve years' work as Director of the White-chapel Gallery. It is not, however, without significance that his first professional post was as a Regional Art Officer and Exhibition Organiser with the Arts Council (1970–3), that since 1976 he has been a member of the Fine Arts Advisory Committee of the British Council, and that for the years 1983–7 he was a Trustee of the Public Art Development Trust – all remarkable opportunities for patronage at the time, and for continuing influence since; the years 1973–6 were spent as Director of the Museum of Modern Art in Oxford.

At Whitechapel, as well as paying necessary lip service to local needs with the transitory dross of amateur, ethnic and popular events (I have in mind particularly the *Whitechapel Open*) forced on any curator who has as paymaster a local authority (of any political complexion), Serota mounted a series of exhibitions of contemporary British, European and American artists that some might describe as inspired – Richter, Lüpertz, Baselitz, Marden, Kiefer, Kounellis, Guston, McLean, Morley, Hodgkin, Kirkeby, Schnabel and Twombly (all painters chosen for *A New Spirit*), and Long, Andre, Webb, Fulton, Cragg, Gormley, Gilbert and George (local amateurs, perhaps), Flanagan, Clemente, Smith, Nauman and Deacon – a series that not only declared Serota's interests and established his national position in the politics of art, but brought the Gallery itself a new level of international esteem, just as the Royal Academy had willy-nilly profited as Norman Rosenthal's instrument of personal aggrandisement (Rosenthal was Serota's rival for appointment to the Tate).

Since 1988 Serota's most obvious physical changes to the Tate Gallery have been his stripping it of wretched architectural interventions, thereby (among other things) restoring the bogus grandeur of barrel vault and domed rotunda that form the long axis through the heart of the building. His most obvious intellectual changes have been the annual re-hangings. The first of these was greeted with pleasure and delight, but the second, much less careful, startling change no longer blinded enthusiasts to the sad inadequacy of its claim to be 'a simple chronological path through the Collection', and the intellectual leaps required of the visitor as he moved from the historic British Collection to contemporary art induced unease; the fashionable wide-spaced hanging demanded a response not short of genuflexion and reduced the number of works on view to six hundred or fewer, and identification labels were so far and confusingly removed as to leave most visitors in ignorance; those who complained that masterpieces long resident in the galleries had been displaced by wretched rubbish and the second rate for the sake of bringing forward 'in turn, different aspects of the chronological sequence' were put down as domiciled in Tunbridge Wells. With the third annual hang, the novelty worn very thin, critical response was largely hostile, at last recognising the sense of insecurity that constant change had brought to the Gallery, the re-hanging now a disruption throughout the year, with rooms closed and the chronological paths diverted as elements in each new display proved to have a duration of not even half the promised year, and the number of works on view occasionally dropped to some four hundred and fifty.

In *Who's Who* Serota lists his recreation as 'hanging pictures'; in the Tate Gallery his private hobby has become his public political manoeuvre to demonstrate that it has vast resources but nowhere to put them on view – an argument undone by the wastefully sparse distribution of pictures on the walls (a small Magritte is separated from a small Dalí by fifteen feet of blank wall), the dismal quality of much that has been briefly resurrected (particularly of late nineteenth-century British pictures of the ilk of Farquharson and North), the pious extravagance of Minimalism, and the prodigal use of a whole gallery for the installation of a single work, of which Rebecca Horn's *Ballet of the Woodpeckers* (an absurdity within the immediate intellectual grasp of any who can comprehend a cuckoo clock) is an example. From such a manoeuvre we all suffer, for in turning the Tate into a constantly changing exhibition hall, though he may the more amuse those who live in London, Serota neglects a duty to the nation as a whole and to the international visitor, for these have reason to expect the Gallery's masterpieces to be permanently on view. Those from abroad who visit the Gallery now must not only have the most erratic impression of the history of British art (a whole room given to Gainsborough, but Reynolds reduced to one portrait, and that keeping rum company with Clarkson Stanfield, a range of Hogarths but no Stubbs), but believe that the National Gallery of Modern Foreign Painting is virtually devoid of representative Impressionists, Expressionists and most of this century's serious intellectual and aesthetic developments. His imposed pattern of fast change makes casualties of his best hanging; the Mondrians have never looked lovelier than in the second hang, seen in the little octagon with the Anrep mosaics, enchanting through an enfilade of rooms; these were replaced by the current witty hanging of William Roberts, but this comes down in May, destroying the telling balance with Fernand Léger in the pendant octagon. Add to the constantly changing stock from the permanent collection the disruption of temporary exhibitions in the Duveen Galleries of sculptors whose work, as in the case of Richard Long, is almost too well known and too frequently exhibited, and the management of the Gallery seems as giddy as a merry-go-round. Serota, in continuing the exhibition habits acquired as an Arts Council minion and long nurtured in Whitechapel, succeeds only in suggesting that the Tate's holdings are so weak and uneven as to put in doubt its standing as an international gallery, yet the sponsors of the annual re-hanging, British Petroleum, have announced that their support is to be extended for two more years (a decision made in advance of any critical response to this year's hang).

Perhaps in part this constant retrieval of forgotten works is a substitute for acquisition, for it is certain sure that the current annual purchase grant does not permit Serota to have a coherent acquisitions policy – he can do no more than fill an occasional small gap in the collections of the past, or point, as with Horn's *Wood-peckers*, to the immediate present. He is, in a sense, the victim of those with generous instincts, and must take what they give him (the recent Saatchi gift, for example), compromising on quality and interest if by so doing meagre funds can be applied elsewhere. In the open market he must buy what he can afford, when he can afford it, and not what he deems best – his penury defeats his duty as a curator and ensures that artists are represented by work that is neither their best nor of true museum quality. In this area Serota's work is thankless, for one worthy eighteenth-century British master-piece or great Bacon triptych may easily absorb all (and more) of an annual grant that would scarcely buy a straw hat by Renoir or a single sunflower from a bunch by Van Gogh, and no major painting could be imported from abroad; he is, moreover, frustrated by a 'Heritage' attitude that foreign works of art are only of interest if they have long been in this country – which means that the Tate is unlikely ever to acquire a major Matisse or Beckmann, indeed it will never have a significant holding of pre-war German art, for it will never be rich enough to go marketing abroad where it cannot call for the help of the NACF, the CAS, or the Heritage Fund.

Corporate sponsors, even at £25,000 a year, can hardly add real purchasing power to the paltry £1,800,000 annual purchase grant; nor can restaurants and bookstalls – generating income, these are now, it seems, fundamental to the well-being of all galleries, and if the sale of souvenirs and postcards takes the hanging space of pictures, so be it, for this is now the way of things and we should not complain. One thing, however, we should not tolerate in these small halls of Mammon – the sale of undistinguished coloured reproductions as limited edition prints, each bearing 'a certificate from the Tate Gallery', six for the 'special Connoisseurs' price of £395'. The Gallery is disgraced by such deceptive language, and no profit, however handsome, justifies lending its name to such a scurvy enterprise.

Serota's is an impossible task – but it was impossible even in Rothenstein's day and is worse now only in degree and in the Gallery's having to serve an extra purpose. The solution is, and has long been, obvious: the Tate Gallery should be divided into its constituent parts (though the divisions could never be precise), leaving the Turners and British art in Millbank, sending the ilk of Van Gogh, Degas, Matisse, Corinth, Munch and Kirchner to Trafalgar Square (where Neil MacGregor, in accepting the Berggruen loan, appears to have changed his mind about using *c.*1900 as the *terminus ante quem* of the collection) and opening an entirely new gallery (the Smithfield Market building would be perfect) for art of the kind that Serota clearly understands better than the rest of us, and for which, in half a century, our children may perhaps be grateful.

Tate Britain's Print Room
http://images.tate.org.uk/sites/default/files/styles/grid-normal-8-cols/
public/images/image/printmaking-student-group-prints-and-drawings-
rooms-tate-britain.jpg

Carl Andre, *Equivalent VIII* (1966)
http://beta.tate.org.uk/art/artworks/andre-equivalent-viii-t01534

Rebecca Horn, *Ballet of the Woodpeckers* (1986)
http://beta.tate.org.uk/art/artworks/horn-ballet-of-the-woodpeckers-
t06551

Nicholas Serota

Evening Standard, 10 August 1995

Nicholas Serota has been quietly reappointed Director of the Tate Gallery for another seven years. That this should be so should surprise none of us, for his first seven years ended with the planned conversion of the Bankside power station into the Tate Gallery of Modern Art far advanced in the project stage. This is an enterprise so vast, so grandiose and so magnificent that it is likely to gentrify the whole of Southwark, Bermondsey and Lambeth, educate the working classes, divert the taste of teenagers from hamburgers and coke to oysters and Piesporter, increase the gross national product and bring down the price of bread. With such a golden prospect, what could a poor witless Prime Minister do but reappoint the prophet making prophecies?

The Trustees of the Tate decided to commend Serota to the Prime Minister without, it seems, even contemplating the possibility that other candidates should be considered, and the post was not advertised. The Trustees are, of course, or have become, Serota's friends and fervent supporters, not the dispassionate and questioning watchdogs for the public interest that some of us might prefer; moreover, some were appointed to their posts at Serota's suggestion, if not urging, so that to the outsider the whole business seems a trifle back-scratching and perhaps even incestuous. Many of us realised that Serota's first stint was coming to an end when strong rumours from New York suggested that he might soon be lost to London; these ended when it became clear that a post for him at MOMA was implacably opposed by one particularly influential art historian, and that mass resignations there by long-standing curators might be a consequence. Had he been given a post in New York, who could have succeeded him in London? That there are no obvious candidates for the post of Director of the Tate is a severe indictment of the way we run museums and galleries in this country, for very few are national institutions with staff of international reputation, and the rest are municipal concerns bundled together with libraries, sport and entertainment, and more likely to be run by an employee of the local council whose previous experience has been planting the floral clock outside the mayoral parlour than by an art historian capable of mounting exhibitions and cataloguing the collections. Far too many of our provincial galleries are intent on providing low-grade entertainment for loutish schoolchildren — the last time I went to Leicester the main gallery was occupied by a length of railway track and a life-size cardboard replica of Stephenson's Rocket, yet this is the museum that houses the nation's best collection of twentieth-century German art and thus should provide a rung on the ladder of preferment that reaches to the heights of Millbank.

This rot runs deep in the profession. We should not forget that when Michael Levey retired from the post of Director of the National Gallery, for which a dozen British candidates should have been in strong contention, the Trustees could find no replacement in this country and proposed the appointment of a rich and very stupid American; public outcry rightly prevented this, and the present Director, the quietly studious but quite unknown Neil MacGregor, was then exhumed from the editor's office of *The Burlington Magazine* and brought to prominence. Surveying the provincial museums of this country now, none of the directors and curators is an obvious candidate for Serota's post, nor is one to be found among his staff at the Tate, for he has cultivated no Crown Prince to threaten his position, and we must suppose that, had he found a post in New York, the Tate's Trustees and the Prime Minister would to a man have been on bended knee imploring him to stay at Millbank.

His career from its very beginning with the Arts Council in 1970 has been that of a determined member of the Establishment, and he has become a man of considerable power and patronage beyond the normal workings of the Tate. Since 1976 – that is for an outrageous twenty years – he has been a member of the Visual Arts Committee of the British Council, and its Chairman since 1992, deciding which contemporary artists shall receive expensive state patronage abroad; he has the ear of those whose businesses generously sponsor the contemporary arts, using them, as is to be expected, to further his own plans and notions; he is invariably Chairman of those who have in their gift the Turner Prize.

Yet in international terms the Tate is a poor thing, with little to contribute to international exhibitions and thus often excluded from the circuit. It has no serious body of work by the Impressionists or Post-Impressionists, nor are the Fauves, the Cubists and Surrealists scrupulously represented; no one would turn to it to study Italian Futurism, and its holdings of German art of any kind are negligible. Serota has made no serious effort to fill these gaps; his acquisition policy has instead been devoted to Beuys, Rebecca Horn, Bill Viola and others who confuse the conventional distinctions between painting and sculpture of the past and the photography, video, *objet trouvé* and contraptions of the present – a change of mood and interpretation long reinforced by exhibitions of the Arts and British Councils, and by such influential dealers as Nicholas Logsdail and Anthony d'Offay. The Gallery is now the victim of these self-serving cliques, the Patrons of New Art, and even its own Trustees, all playing their part in reinforcing Serota's power base.

Since 1988 Serota's most obvious activity in the Gallery has been his once annual but now constant re-hanging, of which the novelty has worn very thin. In *Who's Who* Serota lists his recreation as 'hanging pictures', but his private hobby has become a public political manoeuvre, based on a profound misunderstanding of his public duty – which is not to entertain the Londoner with a frivolous merry-go-round of often dismal quality, but to serve the whole nation and the international visitor with the Gallery's masterpieces, of which far too many are the casualties of whim.

Nicholas Serota and his Tates

Over the next seven years, at vast and utterly unpredictable expense, we shall see Serota develop the Bankside power station into a new Tate for new art. We should not grudge him this, for part of a curator's duty is to represent the taste of the times (the failure of all previous directors of the Tate), and there is no doubt that current critics, dealers and the breathless gushers of the BBC delight in chocolate fountains and the urine splash, Heath Robinson contraptions and the life cycles of butterfly and bluebottle, faeces, semen and the deepest throat – the Tate's current exhibition, devoted to art for the end of the century, is a demonstration of the genre. But what has any of this to do with its founder's intentions for the Tate Gallery, and the subsequent revisions of 1915 and 1937, none of which could foresee that video and body fluids would replace canvas and oil paint? Why must Bankside be any part of the Tate? Can it not be an entirely separate enterprise called the Serota Gallery, given to him to get on with if the nation indeed wishes to have a monument to the degraded perversions that masquerade as art for the next millennium? Give him Bankside, by all means, for no official in this country is better qualified to guide us to the wilder shores of contemporary art, but he must be made to relinquish the existing Tate and all its contents. We cannot allow one man and one greedy body of Trustees to have absolute power over both.

Ideally the Tate Gallery should be split, not into two but three parts – British Art, European and American Art *c.*1870–*c.*1970, and the Wilder Shores or Serota Tendency. Only the first should be at Millbank, retaining the Tate name. The second should unite the holdings of the Tate and National Galleries in a new building, and be the subject of a determined acquisition programme in the Impressionist, Post-Impressionist, Expressionist and Surrealist fields. The third is already under way. Three directors are required, and three sets of trustees. This is the proper use of Lottery, Heritage and Millennium funding, the proper safeguard for a part of the nation's cultural heritage far too large to be in the hands of one empire-building bureaucrat and his biddable trustees.

Tate Exhibitions

As this volume is restricted to British art in very recent years and to living artists, the old grandees are largely absent, and only reviews of general exhibitions that have been mounted in Tate Britain, rather than Tate Modern, have been included.

Abracadabra

TATE BRITAIN

Evening Standard, 23 July 1999

The Tate Gallery has a dead racehorse hanging in its dinky little entrance dome. It is an exhibit in an exhibition for which the admission charge is more than a fiver, but this horse the visitor may see for nothing, for it is the equivalent of the supermarket's admonition 'Buy one, get one free' and the circus barker's bearded woman tempting the gullible to inspect, for payment, the more ghastly freaks within his tent. It must be admitted by the sceptic who has seen it all before, many times over and hither and yon, that the Tate has exploited the wretched nag with consummate skill in terms of free advertising and publicity, for even the Mona Lisa riding bareback all four apocalyptic horses of the Divine St John could not have roused such a rumpus on radio, television, the tabloids and the broadsheets – even the inhabitants of Lundy and St Kilda know of it. It has aroused grief, anger and outrage; small girls in tears and jodhpurs have gathered at the gallery's gates, their whips at half-mast, grown men have threatened to dump tons of stable sweepings on the steps, owners of racehorses talk of menacing the gallery's trustees with legal suits, and those of us who quietly love our cats, dogs and canaries are filled with misgiving at the thought that one day these too may end, not in a quiet garden grave, but as a work of art.

Ah, there's the rub, and there's the *Abracadabra*, of this show — for that is the title of the exhibition — for it is a demonstration of the hocus-pocus and mumbo-jumbo by which the false intellectuals of the art world are able to hey presto anything into art, be it the dung of elephants, the video record of a medical camera's examination of an artist's uterus, anus and digestive tract, an erect cucumber projecting from a stained mattress or a dead horse suspended in a dome. A dome? No. Any old dome won't do, for the magic here lies not merely in the declaration that a dead donkey is the stuff of aesthetic genius, but in displaying it in an art gallery. In a veterinary hospital the horse remains a horse and the cabbalistic incantations of an art curator are futile; hang it in the vestibule of 10 Downing Street and it remains a horse, for not even Tony Blair can play the warlock in this field; hang it in the stairwell of your own home, Dear Reader, and your children and your general practitioner will have you sectioned and taken to the loony-bin; but hang it in the Tate and — Abracadabra — it is at once a work of art and you, its stuffer, are a man of genius.

The ludicrously titled Curator of Interpretation, a puppet so well schooled in the jargon and the jabberwocky of propaganda for the Serota Tendency that he is incapable of talking sense, is the Tate's fall-guy on these occasions; a man from whose brain sweet reason fled on his appointment — his last logical act the decision that if he were to hold fast to his fatuous post he must abandon all forms of intellectual and aesthetic judgement and be prepared to coo with glee if, within the walls of the Tate Gallery, a man calling himself an artist pressed the morning's still warm turds into his hand — has been much in evidence these past few days. For him, *Abracadabra* has been a Command Performance, the great occasion for the

Tate's tame parrot to influence the ignoramuses who now pass for art critics, to give them for regurgitation the wholly uncritical cant and gibberish that is the voodoo language of his kind. For him the hanging horse expresses 'a powerful sense of pathos' and the exhibition as a whole reveals a new spirit in art of 'fantasy, humour, invention and provocation' – and the critics, like the jurors in *Alice in Wonderland*, all dutifully wrote 'stupid things' in their notebooks for repetition in their papers.

The horse is pathetic because its corpse has been abused, not because pathos has in any way been enhanced by the artist – formerly a mortuary technician. The horses blown limbless by the IRA in Hyde Park, screaming (I witnessed it), were a thousand times more telling; so too is an unconscious horse lying on an operating table; so too is a starving fallen horse beaten bleeding by its Pakistani master; so too is a wild Dartmoor pony sold to a Belgian butcher. These are matters of humanity and politics on which Goya and Géricault could have commented with effect and on which we should all have an active view, but that view is neither informed nor encouraged when a pretentious nincompoop in Italy – a country not much celebrated for its respect for animals – hangs a horse as art. If Maurizio Cattelan sought to make a general statement about the plight of animals in human hands, then he should turn the attention of his countrymen to the battery conditions in which they breed pigs and cattle for Parma ham and saltimbocca, and the appalling journeys by which English sheep are exported to their ghastly abattoirs. If Cattelan's intention was to engage our empathy in matters of animal welfare – which I doubt – then there are better ways of doing this than suspending his stuffed racehorse in the Tate.

The Tate's intention, of course, had nothing to do with man's ill treatment of the horse, though with half an ounce of wit and a brain not wholly petrified by working in that gallery – which for most employees there is akin to employment by Stalin in the Lubianka or the propaganda machine of Pravda – the Curator of Interpretation could have disarmed almost all opposition by asserting that it has everything to do with loving Dobbin. It is instead the visual equivalent of the 'Roll up, roll up!' cry for an exhibition that is less entertaining than the village fete and far less shocking than the circus or the fairground. Though the Tate apparently resents it, comparison with *Sensation*, the Saatchi circus at the Royal Academy two years ago, is inevitable, for it is imbued with the same overwhelming sense of the tacky, the tawdry and the pointless, the urge to shock for no reason, the whim to tickle fancy with the childish and the frivolous. The intellectual levels, however, are those of the amateur.

No smut, of course, no penises for noses and anuses for mouths, no cucumber jokes and no fried eggs for breasts – though one clever Dick has managed to slip in a woman emptying her bladder (but Picasso is a precedent for that). Apart from the dead horse the only nasty thing is the dead squirrel in the pose of a kitchen suicide – a macabre but not altogether surprising suggestion for updating *The Tales of Beatrix Potter* as soon as they run out of copyright. The clogs, clay models and cardboard Kalashnikov are all the stuff of village skills and holiday *trouvailles*, the videos could well be of any loutish stag night, the cartoon serial the offering that secured for Damien Hirst an E for art in his GCSE, the table football a discard from the Chelsea Arts Club, and the rest of it from a nearby Infants' School after a course in flame-throwing at bargain basement plastic buckets.

The Tate's wholly undistinguished accumulation of tat, junk and short-lived joke is in no way elevated by the waxworks of a pre-pubertal schoolboy whose hands are nailed by pencils to his desk (I forgot to look at his feet and side – oh what layers of meaning are to be discerned in such an image) and the Japanese businessman crawling abject on all fours. These merely confirm the impression that this is a sad little freak show from which the tattooed grandmother and the sword-swallower have resigned for want of proper company. No doubt apologists will claim that all these bits and pieces are justified by Duchamp, a deliberately mischievous innovator more than eighty years ago ('I threw the urinal in their faces and now they admire it for its aesthetic beauty'), and if not by him, then by Arte Povera and Fluxus, post-war movements for which discarded and random materials were essential and traditional professionalism anathema; but after almost a century of seeing 'found' materials and bathetic ready-mades impertinently presented as art over and over again, under the wing of the Arts Council and in every art school in the land, one wearies of such playthings for the shallow adult mind.

The curators of this international exhibition know nothing of empathy, catharsis or the elevation of the spirit, nothing of intellectual nourishment, nothing of awe and wonder, nothing of what is to be derived from, for example, the great Titians in the National Gallery. One of them asserts with jubilation that their choice of works is presented not 'as the last word but as the tip of an iceberg'; can there really be ten times more to come when a thousand times more has preceded it? Well yes, there can, for this is the rubbish so much applauded by the Serota Tendency and Serota, all-powerful, needs more, much more of it to fill the new Tate Gallery at Bankside.

Amid the unquestioning adulation of most other art critics, Serota cronies almost to a man, John McEwen shares my scepticism, describes the Curator of Interpretation as the thought police, writes of the exhibition that 'It really is the pits' and pointedly asks, 'Who needs a director with a programme so directionless . . . the Tate was intended to be a museum of art, not a fun palace . . . ' Is Serota, though an habitué of New Labour's corridors of power, fit to be the Tate's director?

Abracadabra, Tate Britain 1999

**Maurizio Cattelan, *The Ballad of Trotsky* (1996),
at Galerie Perrotin, Paris**
http://www.perrotin.com/Maurizio_Cattelan-works-oeuvres-5481-2.html

Intelligence

TATE BRITAIN

Evening Standard, 14 July 2000

Intelligence, an exhibition of only forty-two works pretending to survey the visual arts in Britain now, its boastful title utterly risible, is without doubt the silliest ever mounted by the Tate Gallery, a thing of vast pomposities, intellectually null and aesthetically void. Were it in Birmingham or Liverpool or Little Piddlehinton one could attribute it entirely to the Lottery-funded ignorance and vocal vanity that have, for the several years approaching the Millennium, prevailed throughout the provinces, as yet another case of the blind led by the blind, but as it is in London, at one of the nation's very few great galleries, and is entirely funded by the public, it cannot be ignored – commercial sponsorship, it seems, could not be found for artists 'of most of whom most people have never even heard', as a Tate spokesman neatly put it.

Those who care for painting need not go to this exhibition. Nor need those whose interest lies with sculpture. Drawing is represented by bands of shading diligently and laboriously and mindlessly applied by pencil directly to the plaster on the walls, the technique of the silly business ill-related to the demands of scale. The rest of the exhibition is neon, video and sound, lists of names and words and slogans, burnt cars covered in cork-tipped cigarettes, fibreglass figures and pathetic visual scraps of urban peasant culture that the politically correct insist are of as much significance and aesthetic profundity as any portrait of himself by Rembrandt.

The exhibition has no element of shock or horror, no hanging horse or suicidal squirrel, no upside-down piano, no seemingly bottomless sump of glistening black oil, nor even a halved

91

hippopotamus in aspic, and is of not the slightest interest to those in search of fairground freaks and thrills. Subscribers to *The Erotic Review* too will be disappointed, for here there are no body wastes and fluids and not a fanny or a phallus can be seen – unless, with grim determination, they stay the full five tedious minutes of a video in which the Nigerian artist who made it is seen naked in his bath (and perhaps not even then – I saw the episode but was numbed by boredom into inattention), his excuse for such self-revelation being that it fulfils the expectations of the lustful, fearful, envious white Caucasian.

The exhibition is not quite without painting of a sort – of the Michael Craig-Martin sort. This Trustee of the Tate Gallery contributes yet again the familiar unrelenting black outlines that he borrows from the comic strip, here applied to a frieze of banal objects common to the household, the workplace and the office, the stepladder jostled by the fire extinguisher, the lavatory pan by the filing cabinet, the wineglass by the paint brush and the overall. Few mural decorations – for that is what his paintings are – could, in spite of their patches of vulgar colour, so swiftly become unnoticeable and then invisible, so empty of content are they, so unrewarding to the sensual eye. One glance and one responsive wince at having to examine an image so commonplace, so deliberately tedious, so coolly drained of everything that might give the wanderer aesthetic gratification, so utterly pointless and unjustifiable, so contrary to everything that has emerged as pleasurable and intellectual in 2,000 years of European painting – and that is all. The sceptic stands before it unrewarded, asking only how it is that a Trustee of the Tate Gallery, a commercial artist in the sense that he is supported and promoted by one of Cork Street's most powerful and well-connected dealers, can remain a Trustee if in that capacity he is able to commission himself to paint a picture for exhibition in the Gallery? This *Study for Store Rooms* is painted directly on the wall and will be whitewashed into oblivion when the exhibition ends. This suggests some extraordinary contempt for the creative business of the painter, insulting to his assistants, but it seems that to Craig-Martin only the idea is important and of that he retains control. The Tate paid for the materials, and when the painting is destroyed at the end of September, Craig-Martin and his assistants can recreate it anywhere for anyone who, having seen it in the Tate, is crazed enough to want to have it as an embellishment for his factory or office premises. If we accept the general rule that a picture exhibited by a major institution is worth more than one that is not, then we have, again, the case of an artist holding an official and influential position risking the accusation that he uses it for his personal benefit and advertisement. We are compelled to wonder if Craig-Martin, had he not been for so long a Trustee, would have been chosen by the Tate to contribute to this exhibition, for he is hardly at Nick Serota's beloved cutting edge, but a man of almost pensionable age merely hacking out an empty mannerism fully developed a quarter of a century ago.

By the same token, a Trustee of the National Gallery, Christopher Le Brun, is an immodest contributor of execrable pictures to the execrable *Encounters* exhibition there; and Yinka Shonibare, an advisor to the Arts Council, has until late August a Council-supported one-man exhibition at the Camden Art Centre, as well as a waggish costume piece in *Intelligence*. Should we, in this context, again consider the flow of Arts Council funds into the work of Antony Gormley and Anish Kapoor, both of them fully-fledged Arts Councillors? Artists, it seems, are allowed licence forbidden in scrupulous professions.

Two more questions must be asked. Why is this vapid, lacklustre, lifeless cliché-ridden show presented in Tate Britain rather than Tate Modern? And why were these particular artists chosen for it? I am aware of the specious argument for continuity in British art, for the supposedly seamless transition from ancestral methods of painting to technically wretched video and witless installation, but to me the seam is all too evident in Tate Britain's reckless attempt to stitch together the traditional past and the transitory present —

they simply do not match or meld. The feeble attempts of artists in this exhibition to build on the conceptual and minimal explorations of the later twentieth century (then valid in their way, but dead ends nevertheless), are so stale, so threadbare, so hackneyed in invention, so banal and trite, that the wanderer through these rooms, detained by nothing beautiful, wonders what they have to do with the year 2000, and how the Tate can describe them as New, or even British, when so many of them are in idioms wholly international and at least as Transatlantic and European in origin and exploitation as they are British. Tate Modern is the place for such cosmopolitan recrement.

The curators of this nugatory show claim that it is a dialogue between art and audience, but it is far less so than between Donatello's sculptured saints and the urban poor of Florence in the fifteenth century or between Henry Moore's recumbent women and the chianti-drinking classes of his generation; if anything, lacking any element of revulsion or disquiet to challenge or amuse, dully hygienic to the core, it marks with absolute clarity the divorce of the Serota Tendency from the rest of the human race. The scruffy populace may make its way to Bankside as to a circus and its bearded-lady side-shows, but if, upstream, it expects much the same of *Intelligence*, then it should stay away, for here there are no frissons, thrills or laughter. *Intelligence* rewards the visitor with the torments of boredom and the required mood is one of suspended reason, abject reverence.

Intelligence, Tate Britain 2000

Michael Craig-Martin, *Study for Store Room* (2000)
http://db-artmag.com/en/51/feature/michael-craig-martin-the-pleasure-principle/#

TATE BRITAIN

Evening Standard, 7 March 2003

If the panjandrums of Tate Britain wish, every three years, to mount an exhibition that is a plain statement of the condition of contemporary British art, then I wholeheartedly support the project, no matter how depressing the material may be – but I wish the exhibitions could be called Triennial I, Triennial II and so on, instead of *Intelligence* and, now, *Days like these*. *Intelligence*, three years ago, was a silly title, asking for the crushing quip, and *Days like these* has the air of half a line misquoted from one of the more dim-witted ditties of Tennyson or Swinburne. Thirty such exhibitions, scrupulously assembled, scrupulously catalogued, should provide the perfect record of this century's art, but I doubt if, on the present slanted showing, the series will last much beyond Triennial III in 2006.

Intelligence was a directionless show, indulging the whims of its curators, and *Days like these* is self-indulgent too, gathered together by a pair of butterfly curators incapable of intellectual or aesthetic rigour. Physically it rambles, it sprawls, it invades vast areas of Tate Britain that would be better employed doing its duty as the great gallery of historic British art. It is so incoherent in layout that the visitor must be given a map so misleading that it directs him to cross the streams of Millbank traffic and leap into the Thames, and for Margaret Barron's paintings it points him, as it might a urinating dog, to the lamp posts and railings of Atterbury Street and right round the gallery's rear wings. Even so, the visitor is unlikely to see or hear (yes, hear – for this is an exhibition of sound as well as sight) everything in a single visit, for one exhibit, a CD player with loudspeakers is, it seems, played only at noon outside the Millbank entrance, another at irregular intervals in only half the rooms, and a third, a video projection of the subterranean world of men's public lavatories in London, is not on a continuous loop and the unlucky will, in this benighted company, take the screen empty of toilet bowls, to be as much a work of art as when replete with them. This useful information seems only to be available in small print on the verso of the map, and thus not to be seen when the map is in use.

The information in the catalogue is misleading too. At £19.99 this thin volume is an extravagance and a deceit. It begins with three short essays larded with the pomposities that in David Lee's *Jackdaw* are labelled Artbollocks, enlisting the support of authorities of whom only the insider cliques of contemporary art have ever heard. These attempt to set the scene, establish the context and justify the junk, but then run out of steam and slip into tedious descriptions of the work, in the course of which the writers discover secondary meanings – we learn, for example, that the Lockerbie Trial, at a deeper level, 'enacted a confrontation between Christian America and Islamic Libya'. One paragraph, and only part of that, makes any sense – 'Many of the most interesting artists working today don't believe in art. There is an aesthetic atheism . . . Ideas of art as . . . occupying a higher place in human culture, are rapidly losing ground . . . it is becoming clear that art and artists are not necessarily special.'

Following the essays we come to condensed sections devoted to the artists' lives and the discussion of works that it is reasonable to assume are in the exhibition. Some are, some are not. Some we find easily, for others we hunt in vain, for nowhere on the page is there the sensible helpful note 'Not included in the exhibition'. One attendant, trying to be helpful, directed me to a commercial gallery in Soho where he thought the missing works by Cornelia Parker were on view – and, considering what a hunt-the-slipper experience the exhibition had been, it seemed more than probable that her chunks of chalk from Beachy Head and earth from under the Leaning Tower of Pisa could be there, or even in Timbuktoo; they are illustrated in the catalogue, but are not in the exhibition. The one work by Miss Parker that is on view – the already notorious looping of a mile of string round Rodin's sculpture of *The Kiss* – is, to add to the confusion, nowhere illustrated, nowhere mentioned in the text.

Miss Parker's exploitation of the Rodin involved its removal from Tate Modern and return to Tate Britain, its former home – a wholly unnecessary risk to a fragile work regarded by many as a national treasure. The block of sugary white marble was, according to the contract, chosen by Rodin himself; the initial work on the figures was by an assistant but, according to a reliable contemporary witness, Rodin finished them and we should regard *The Kiss* as an authentic work of inestimable value.

As the Tate, in both its incarnations under Nicholas Serota, has behaved as though it holds the sculpture in contempt, never displaying it with even common sense and certainly not with sensibility, we should perhaps not be surprised that Miss Parker, an infinitely insignificant artist, but one once short-listed for the Turner Prize, has been allowed to have it moved so that she could have her whimsical way with it. Those of us who are serious about the nation's possessions must nevertheless ask why she was given such licence, and, with such a precedent, how many other contemporary artists will be allowed to do precisely what with treasures, not only in the Tate, but in the National Gallery, the V&A and the British Museum – shall we have Canova's naked Graces waving dildos and the Elgin Marbles drenched in treacle with public participation in the licking off? What were the trustees of the Tate thinking when they connived in Miss Parker's abuse of the Rodin? Should they not, with their tails between their legs, resign? Should not Serota be rebuked by the Minister? If ever there were a case for Government interference in a national gallery's affairs, this is it.

Does the exhibition fairly and accurately represent British art now? I do not think so – it would have been very different had the curators not been prostrate lackeys of the Arts Council and the Serota Tendency. The show is almost swamped by video projections, the by-products of cinema and television that have nothing to do with painting but are shown in art galleries because no Odeon audience would tolerate their tedium and unrelenting self-importance. Why do we believe those who say that they are art when they are perfect examples of the aesthetic atheism to which Jonathan Watkins, one of the two curators, refers in his essay, perfect proof of his assertion that artists are no longer, in any sense, special? And if they are not special, why include them in the exhibition? Why, indeed, mount the exhibition?

Much of the material is as old hat as it could be. Forty years must have passed since I first saw a plastic bucket masquerading as a work of art in Eindhoven, and more still since I first saw a canvas entirely covered in black paint. Surely screens of back-lit plexiglass in all its vulgar colours have long been the commonplace of art schools, even if not erected as bravely as the totem pole of them at the end of the long gallery. The useless ceramic object of hideous glaze and sculptural scale is the stock of every major garden centre, Hyacinth Bucket's one-upmanship response to the larger garden gnome or the *Venus de Milo* in white resin. Have we not seen a thousand times painting as the mimic of photography and photography as the mimic of painting? And hasn't Rachel Whiteread by now cast so many hidden and not hidden spaces that the repetition of the idiom on the life-size scale of her five-room flat and the staircase leading to it, has converted idiom to cliché and denied her one idea the energy and surprise that, in the eyes of some, it once had? I forecast years ago, when she made a plaster cast of the interior space of her hot water bottle (the result alarming in its resemblance to the torsos of plump women) that she would not stop until she had achieved her apotheosis with an interior cast of St Paul's — she has, alas, a long way to go yet. Like so many other sculptors — Gormley among them — she has been encouraged by critics and curators to believe that one solitary idea is quite enough. It is not. And the idea is diminished when the sculptor resorts to colossal scale; I observe in passing, that Kapoor's Ear Trumpet, Vagina, Enema or Gramophone Horn *Marsyas* in Tate Modern is undone by its size – visitors simply cease to see it before they have walked its length because the long protracted experience is so numbingly dull, its quality so thin.

There is, in this exhibition, not one single work of interest or merit. These are paintings that say with drip, splash and sweep of the brush, 'Look, look, I am a painting' – but drip, splash and sweep of the brush are merely marks that reflect the physical action of the painter and, meaningless without intelligent purpose, are not enough to make a painting. There is no sculpture other than the Rodin, and that – such gross impertinence – used only as an armature for string. There is a floor striped in dazzling sticky tape that might please the ghastly interior decorators of the BBC, or worse, set the pattern for Heathrow Airport's arrival corridors; hideous beyond a moment's tolerance, the damnable confection looks wild in photographs. There is Richard Hamilton's 1965–66 *Large Glass* replica of Duchamp's 1915–23 (smashed) invention – but what in the name of Methuselah has it to do with contemporary art? The only innovation is Margaret Barron's lunatic notion that she should paint tiny townscapes on strips of adhesive vinyl tape, and then stick them on nearby street furniture so that the paintings (if they can be found) and the views can be seen simultaneously. The paintings are, of course, vulnerable to wind, water, vandalism and theft – and where's the sense in that?

This exhibition has the scale to induce awe and in room after room, space after space, we are intimidated by its extent and the sheer size of many exhibits. But this is Fascist bombast, shallow, loud, vulgar, domineering and tyrannical. This is indeed art by artists who don't believe in art; this is indeed aesthetic atheism. Let me go further than the curator whose admission this is and who coined these phrases for his catalogue – to argue that any of this capricious anti–art is art in any sense, is perfect sophistry.

Days Like These, Tate Britain 2003

**Cornelia Parker, *The Distance (A Kiss with String Attached)*
(2003)**
http://www.frithstreetgallery.com/works/view/
the_distance_a_kiss_with_string_attached
auguste_rodins_the_kiss_1904_a_mile

Anish Kapoor, *Marsyas* (2002)
http://www.tate.org.uk/whats-on/tate-modern/exhibition/unilever-
series-anish-kapoor

Tate Triennial III

TATE BRITAIN

Evening Standard, 10 March 2006

Pure, unalloyed, unadulterated and incomprehensible post-modernism is all that can be said of Tate Britain's *Triennial*, its third reflection 'on the concerns and conditions of current art production . . . in Britain' – so current indeed that artists were still working on their installations up to the very moment of the press view and beyond. Should I, I wondered, turning up very late in the afternoon of that day, take an apparently discarded bundle of newspapers to be a work of art, a stepladder and tools to be another, and heap of miscellaneous detritus to be a third? Since the mid-1970s the visitor to contemporary art exhibitions has had to be wary of the fire-hydrant, the light-switch, the radiator and the dozing attendant in case they are what they are and not the works of art they seem.

There are, however, no dozing attendants in this *Triennial*, for not a chair is to be seen and the weary visitor of a certain age will find nothing on which to rest his bones while seeking enlightenment from the catalogue. Enlightenment? Alas, there's not much of that, for this is one of those catalogues – so fashionable now – not only of almost entirely different contents from the exhibition, but so extreme and unreadable in the modernity of its design that it is itself an exhibit of sorts. 'Look at me', this catalogue screams, but do not expect to read it, for its typefaces are ugly, its layout misleading, its essential information cramped in odd corners and columns, or printed in white on black so that the reader can make no notes; its essays are in black on yellow, and in illustrating things that are not on view and not illustrating things that are, it compounds confusion. This catalogue is a perfect example of post-modernist subversion in that it renders useless that which should be lastingly useful, it obscures what it should clarify, and on page after page its various contributors weave webs of anti-meaning on a weft of jabberwocky and a warp of gobbledygook.

The curator of this *Triennial* is Beatrix Ruf, of the Kunsthalle in Zürich. Why? Do not accuse me of xenophobia when I ask this question for I ask it in genuine surprise that Tate Britain could find no British curator, critic or historian of contemporary art capable of reflecting on British art now, on our art of this very minute. What can she know of it that we do not? Are her European perceptions of what is happening here much more acute than ours? Are we incapable of seeing British contemporary art in a larger international context? I doubt it, very deeply. No doubt the five curatorial collaborators provided by the Tate urged her to look at this artist and that, but the choices were, I am assured, entirely hers – and very odd they seem.

The collaborators prompt another question. I am certain that a major exhibition in this field put together by six men would have been greeted with screams and squawks reviling such gross political incorrectitude, but this *Triennial* is the creature of six women, yet not a murmur of protest has been heard. This is not a frivolous point – I have observed the curatorial attitudes of women often enough to know that, whether they work in fields that are now art historical or immediately current, their connoisseurship is too often flawed by feminism, corrupted indeed, politically deliberate at one extreme and whimsically indulgent at the other. No major art exhibition should ever be assembled by the monstrous regiment alone.

The ratio of two to one in favour of male artists suggests that there has been no gender bias in the choice, but in this accumulation of lifeless exhibits the critic must differentiate between the corpses and their faecal waste – and the women artists seem largely responsible for the latter. But it has long been so and we should worry far more over the curators' extremely narrow view of what now is art, for it is very much the blinkered view of the Tate and its outstations, very much the view of the Arts Council and the provincial galleries that it supports, and very much the view of the British Council when it exhibits British art abroad, purblind, prejudiced, authoritarian and ungenerous (and not noticeably Swiss).

I do not recognise this bleak exhibition as representing any specifically British trend in art or as in any sense art necessarily of the period 2004-6. It is essentially the same old tripe and trivia that curators have been peddling for three whole decades, as utterly familiar in Holland, Germany and Switzerland as it is here. No matter whether the artists are the old boys and girls of the Turner Prize, the even older boys of the pre-Serota Establishment, or are still in school, they contribute to the definition of post-modernism as a phenomenon of plagiarism – or as Miss Ruf has it, of appropriation and repetition, of 'democratic borrowing', and of the 'radical fictionalisation' of reality (by which I think she must mean the subversion of the work from which the artist steals – vandalism as well as theft).

One of her critical supporters describes this appropriation as a most basic procedure of contemporary art education as well as production, and the production of art as no more than the constant reshuffling of a basic set of cultural terms. These assertions are largely true, perhaps wholly so where the state's art schools are concerned, for here we are, almost a century since Duchamp first slapped his public's face, still reshuffling his ideas, reshuffling those of Beuys too. In art schools in which students might reasonably expect to be taught the low technical businesses of putting paint on canvas, modelling, carving and casting sculpture, and trying their hands at an infinite variety of print methods, these they are compelled by teachers (and the idiotic gaining of degrees) to abandon in favour of the concept, the thesis and the dissertation, for which they have neither the mature idea nor the command of language (unless they crib it from the internet as an example of reshuffling);

this surely is the subversion of all that they once believed to be canonical in art schools.

That teachers reject and cannot teach these ancestral skills because they themselves command none of them, is now accepted in every art school in the land — they command only the babble and hogwash of the Serota world. Imagine teaching French, not as a language, but as the concept of being French; imagine teaching music as a concept, discarding every instrument on which music can be made; imagine teaching surgery as a concept without a scalpel and a corpse. After a century wasted copying copies – let me suggest that we glance back to the fifteenth century in Florence, the century in which the Renaissance developed and consolidated step by step, that we measure the distance between Masaccio's Brancacci Chapel and Michelangelo's Sistine, and then that we compare this distance with that that inches from Duchamp to the feeble Duchampian insults of today.

Nothing in this exhibition is of any quality. Peter Doig, who once seemed to show the promise of a provincial Canadian painter, has contributed what may well be his worst painting, but that does not prevent a Tate curator from writing of his sophisticated visual language and conjuring associations with Gauguin, Matisse and Munch. Another Tate curator extols the work of Jonathan Monk who, having found some amateur drawings of women's heads dating from the 1920s, has embellished each with a drawing pin, thus converting them into his own work. This is less 'democratic borrowing' than downright theft, yet another Tate curator questioning our notions of authenticity, justifies it as a respectful reference to Duchamp and Rauschenberg. How can these curators write such drivel? I know of no other field in which such intellectual dishonesty could be acceptable.

There has long been need for a debate on the border territory between art and pornography, the only serious question raised by any exhibit – in this case by images of the kind given to sperm donors in fertility clinics. These date from the 1970s and are of

Christine Newby, whose professional name as a sex model was Cosey Fanni Tutti. Using the same name she is now an artist 're-framing her experience' in this form of 'performance art'. By the simple expedient of declaring herself an artist now, Miss Newby has elevated to the level of art, the plain, straightforward, gross photographic records of her sexual parts and what she and others did with them all those years ago, and there they are in Tate Britain, the temple of contemporary art, framed and hanging on the wall.

There is no point in expressing outrage at the exhibition of Miss Newby's parts – they and their ilk are familiar to every adolescent in the land – but there is some point in outrage at the feebleness of the argument for promoting them as art. Miss Newby and her apologists are naïve and silly women, not profound philosophers; these Tate curators would never exhibit pages torn from the trade organs of plumbers, boilermen and grocers 're-framing' their workaday experiences, nor elevate the life of a London rent-boy as performance art. What they give us here is a tiresome feminist argument, without merit and dishonest.

As there is a great deal of video in this exhibition the diligent visitor must set aside at least half a day for it (even if there is nowhere to sit) – half a day of such numbing boredom that advertisements on television seem, by comparison, engaging, witty, wise, beautiful and exquisitely constructed. The photography, every miserable scrap of it, we have seen a thousand times before – but that's post-modernist reshuffling. So too the installations. As for painting, drawing and sculpture – nothing here is worth a first glance, let alone a second. Had Beatrix Ruf gathered all this rubbish together in order to condemn it for its lack of aesthetic and intellectual weight, and demonstrate its arid conformity to the Serota Rules (though even he cannot be blamed for all the dismal banalities to which his mindless acolytes have sunk), this exhibition might have had some contrary merit, but she praises it, claims to understand it, seeks to interpret it, and with arguments of guileful sophistry, gulls the bewildered public yet again.

Tate Triennial III, Tate Britain 2006

Peter Doig, _Echo Lake_ (2000)
http://beta.tate.org.uk/art/artworks/doig-echo-lake-p78390

Cosey Fanni Tutti
http://throbbing-gristle.com/COSEYFANNITUTTI/content/content/
photo_2006_Tate_files/blocks_image_3_1.png

THE TURNER PRIZE

Instituted in 1984, four years before Serota's Rule was established, the Turner Prize was essentially the creature of the Patrons of New Art, a body formed to assist the Tate Gallery in its acquisition of works of contemporary art. From the very beginning it was much mocked (not only by the popular press), and the vicissitudes were so many that Serota began to take charge of it even in 1987 when he was still Director-designate. In 1990, with the bankruptcy of its sponsor, the Prize was suspended, its rules and purposes reconsidered. Relaunched in 1991 with the sponsorship of Channel 4 – partly Faustian Bargain, partly a symbiotic relationship that gives the television channel an inexpensive fixed feast every year and a great deal of popular exposure – it has been on a more or less even keel ever since. Many, however, aware of how manipulated the Prize has been within its very narrow orthodoxy, now feel that, having achieved its aim to popularise contemporary art (in which it has been far from alone), it has no purpose and, now habitual and dully consuetudinary, should be terminated.

I have never been able to take it seriously, so fumblingly inept were its beginnings and so obvious has been Serota's management of judges and artists, the former almost invariably his intellectual allies, the latter his favourites. In 2001 I wrote of the Prize exhibition that it was 'more vain and futile than any of its predecessors [it was the year of Martin Creed's electric light switched on and off] and we are compelled to wonder if the Prize has run its course and should now be abandoned . . . ' Nothing has changed.

The Turner Prize 2003

TATE BRITAIN

Evening Standard, 31 October 2003

The Turner Prize, the annual gladiatorial combat in Tate Britain, with the roar of applauding supporters and the thumbs down of a larger public longing for the gush of blood, is with us yet again, paradoxically celebrating its twentieth year with its nineteenth exhibition. This is to be explained by its having fallen into desuetude in 1990 after six successive years of rewarding artists rich and famous on the principle of Buggins' Turn and boring the public into indifference. In 1991, however, with the new security of sponsorship from Channel 4 – a cynical institution that saw in the association the chance of very cheap television programmes and a great deal of free congratulatory advertisement – the dead Prize was resurrected with rules that eliminate every eminent old Buggins and offer fame and fortune only to the comparatively young with a perceived disposition to stimulate disgust, scandal, outrage and incomprehension.

It hardly matters who is chosen for the short list (though sceptics believe this to be decided long before the year is out), or to whom the £20,000 is given by the judges, for the real and far larger arena is not within Tate Britain, but in the press, the media, the fashionable watering holes of Islington and at the mahogany dining tables of Tunbridge Wells. In all these quarters the Prize is seen as a Bruegelian bout between drunken Carnival and sober Lent, blind Folly and dumb Wisdom, so weighted in favour of the Serota Tendency that Carnival and Folly always win.

None of us need be serious about the Turner Prize. It makes not a jot of long-term difference to the winner or the rest of us, for most winners in its second incarnation – Gormley, Kapoor, Whiteread, Hirst and Ofili among them – had by then, with the aid of the British Council, been touched by the hand of international fame and the rest were already destined for oblivion. We must treat the Prize only as an entertainment; on our television sets we shall again watch poor gabblingly inarticulate Matthew Collings struggle wearily to appear to take it seriously, and in the general debate we shall, yet again, suffer the opinions of sub-celebrities who have no status in the matter – Janet Street-Porter and her ilk certainly among them – working themselves into a froth or treating the Prize as an event as theologically significant as the second coming of Christ. The sane, however, will see it as they see a pantomime – as a not too onerous obligation to adolescent children who will not be shocked by the obscenities. Let us rejoice in its clowning and leave support and indignation to poor souls without a sense of humour.

It is the custom of those who run the Prize to invite foreign critics and curators to be among the judges – readers will readily recall the participation of Bernhard Bürgi, Milada Slizinska, Bice Curiger and Kasper Koenig. This year I thought I might follow suit and called on Waltraut von Clausthal-Zellerfeld to add a little continental zest to my report on the four finalists. She is the Director of the Museum für Kunst und Gewerbe in Umpferstedt and, as an expert on contemporary pottery and porcelain, is particularly well qualified to be a judge, for London bookmakers are offering high odds on Grayson Perry, who is well known to the *cognoscenti* as Charles Saatchi's favourite potter. 'Und vot a potter,' said Miss Clausthal-Zellerfeld (CZ to her friends).

'Vot,' indeed. Perry's pots at first glance are the sort of thing for which the unthinking rich, attracted by the gilt and glister, pay too much in Harrods and turn into table lamps without realising that their decorative embellishments are not descended from elegant Japonaiseries, but are images of sex, violence and the lavatory. 'He is so subversive,' said Waltraut. 'Zese are powerful commentaries on ze cultural values of mittel England. Grayson is stifled by your consumerism and to ze only class zat buys vorks of art here, he sticks ze finger up. Zis is sexual socio-pathology; Grayson is a man dressed as a woman, but unter ze frilly skirt is an erect penis. He is just like his pots – you zink zey are vun zing, but zey are anozzer, and zey both say fuck you.'

Waltraut has a reputation for outspokenness, but I'd not expected vernacular English in a matter of such high seriousness. I drew her towards work less controversial, to the apple tree of Anya Gallaccio and the video of a running man by Willy Doherty. 'Ach, video,' was her response, the timbre of her voice disparaging. 'Ze new Rock und Roll of art. Vot rubbish. Zis has no business in an art gallery – in a cinema, perhaps, but not here. Und who is he? Vot is he running to and from? Und vy should I care? Is zis a seminal event?' I ventured that it is an allegory of politics in Ulster, to which she almost spat 'Und so? Zat is a justification for calling it art?'

Gallaccio's apple tree did nothing to mollify her. 'Vomanish,' she hissed, 'more feminine than Perry's pots. Und I have seen it all before, zis silly business of rotting daisies and rotting apples. Now zey are pretty, aber soon zey von't be. Und again, so vot? Rotting apples, rotting cabbage, rotting orchids – und so weiter und so vot? Show me sumsing new.'

'Zen tell me vot you sink of zis,' I heard myself reply as we turned to the work of the Chapman Brothers, for Waltraut's Dennis-the-Dachshund accent is alarmingly infectious. 'Ach! Ze famous naughty boys,' she said with the anticipatory grin of Germaine Greer about to lick honey from the upturned gluteus maximus of a hairless youth. 'Zese are ze New Futurists. Ze Old Futurists said zat venerating art is as pointless as ejaculating semen into a funerary urn – ve must regenerate it, no matter vot ze risk. Zat is vot zese boys do for Goya!' As it happens, I share her respect for the brothers' adjustments to Goya's etchings – sympathetic to the spirit of the original, politically pointed and technically delicate – but their sculpture of impaled corpses rotting is dully deliberate, over-calculated, and over-crowded, over-worked, drab in colour, tone and texture, and rather less intellectually entertaining than a fly-blown Damien Hirst or the Elfin Oak in Kensington Gardens. It is certainly no match for the gravity of Goya's original idea.

My reverie on maggots and bare bones was interrupted by a yelp from Waltraut. 'Look, look,' she said, 'sex' – pointing to what appeared to be a pair of inflatable sex dolls engaged in fellatio. 'No, no,' I said, 'according to the labels that is Death and the skeletons are Sex.' 'Zey have muddled zem,' she insisted, 'I know sex ven I see it und zat is sex. Look vot she is doing mit her mouse. Look at his erection. Sex is art und art is sex.' Hoping to restore order to her cerebral processes I asked if that might be her manifesto for 2003. 'Ja, ja – sex is art und art is sex' she began to murmur as a mantra, and seeing a glint in her eye that I would rather confront in the eyes of a great white shark, I slipped away from the gallery, its marble halls filled with the answering echoes, 'Sex is art und art is sex,' faintly dying, dying, dying.

In brief, this is as usual the worst Turner Prize show yet, and if the best that Serota can muster is the futile anger of the pimply adolescent and the taste of housewives in Hampstead Garden Suburb, then he should put an end to it. The bookmakers were right: Perry the Potter was the winner.

Turner Prize 2003

Grayson Perry
http://arts.guardian.co.uk/pictures/image/0,8543,-10704679481,00.html

Anya Gallacio, *Because I could not Stop* (2002)
http://arts.guardian.co.uk/pictures/image/0,8543,-10504679481,00.html

Turner Prize 2004

TATE BRITAIN

Evening Standard, 20 October 2004

Last October I vowed that never again I would review the Turner Prize, so null and nugatory had it become. Little could be said for it in its first incarnation in the 1980s as Buggins' Turn to win honour and spondulicks just for having been a minor figure in the art world for half a century, and even less when, for its second incarnation of 1991, it was re-jigged as a reward for any young whipper-snapper whom the British Council had sent to Yokohama to crumple paper and switch off a light. It has proved utterly indifferent to criticism and insult; to not unreasonable accusations of all but fixing the result its unconcern has been imperturbable and mutterings of intellectual corruption it has consistently ignored. It is a bandwagon that has always gone its own way down a very narrow track with a company of concubines and catamites, and the critic has despaired of ever influencing its course.

In a very serious sense the Turner Prize has lent weighty justification to much post-Duchampian tomfoolery as well as to the Hirstian assertion that whatever is seen in an art gallery must, by virtue of that simple fact, be art. To totter about the London Tates with a urinal on his back would now immediately mark a man as an old master, and were he to put anything at all in a glass case, with or without formaldehyde, would distinguish him as a new, but for most aspiring artists the mere declaration that he is an artist is enough and absolves him from the chores of creation.

Thus has art become largely meaningless. Artists now strive either to be different or the same; in difference they overwhelm the market with the banalities of mindless diversion, and in sameness they diminish rather than consolidate what has gone before. The twentieth century, in which we still seem to be, was congested with -isms of art that multiplied with the haste of bacteria in forgotten sausages, but it was no match for the fifteenth century in Florence – contrast, I beg you, the years between Masaccio and Michelangelo with those between Duchamp and Kapoor, and ask which left not only the arts but the world in a better state and which a worse? Quattrocento artists were, of course, intellectually disciplined by being the servants of a faith in which they had profound belief and of the despots, great and petty, who paid them for their propaganda. Artists of the twentieth century and this are, by and large, not the servants of church or state, but instead enjoy with dealers and curators symbiotic relationships without which none of them could survive, so powerful that church and state are now in kow-towing servitude to them. The Turner Prize is an instrument of this symbiosis: it promotes immediately contemporary art in all the galleries of the tentacular Tate, elevates the curators, exalts the judges and canonises artists no matter how meretricious and contemptible they may be.

This year, however, there is a hint of disconcertment among the artists of the Turner Prize, as though in the thin air of high Olympus they have wearied of their heady isolation from ordinary mortals and events; all have ventured into forms of social realism or political comment. The immediately apparent problem is that, for all their command of the video techniques that all employ, none is articulate in the sense that we fully comprehend what each is trying to say; they illustrate rather than illuminate. And not even that very well, for their unwarrantedly long and discursive films lack narrative clarity and purpose, and we can discern no argument. Video is a very selfish and greedy form of art – if it is art at all – and we are expected in this exhibition to sit for hours (yes, hours) in gross discomfort while so-called artists of no particular insight expose their credulity and lack of depth.

Above all things this exhibition reveals the futility of our adulation for any man declaring himself to be an artist. The experienced television journalists who produce investigative programmes and the best of Newsnight are far more worth a Turner Prize than these pretentious jokers, their work often visually exciting and certainly informative, their exploitation of stale idiom technically more accomplished, their views, based on longer and wider experience, far more mature.

Only one work offers anything in the way of visual and aesthetic nourishment, but it is something of a cheat. Yinka Shonibare, as much Nigerian as English and remarkable so far for little more than amusing the shallow with European costumes reconstructed in the bright fabrics of batik (subversion is too weighty a word for it), presents a ballet based on the assassination of Gustavus III of Sweden in 1792. Shonibare is not a choreographer: who then plotted the steps and actions of the ballet and why is no credit given to this vital grey eminence? Whose idea was it to dance without music and let only the sounds of dancing become the telling accompaniment to the dance? Indeed, whose idea was the ballet? – and to that the answer seems to be Swedish Television on which it was first broadcast. But all the credit is given to Shonibare, who made the insignificant costumes of which, within seconds, I was no longer aware, so absorbed was I in the dance. It is a ballet that I would like to see again, in reality or on the television screen for which it was designed, but with credits given to Shonibare only for the costumes, for surely to credit him with more must be preposterous.

As for the moral to be drawn from it, is Shonibare commending political assassination? If so, then I must argue that Gustavus III was ' . . . one of the most enlightened sovereigns of the eighteenth century . . . a liberal and sympathetic protector of the people against a corrupt nobility . . . a man of the Enlightenment'. And his enemies shot him in the back, the coward's way.

This exhibition is tedious to an extreme and no one interested in painting and sculpture, no one hoping for shock or visceral disturbance should waste his time and money on it. It is a show entirely for video nerds.

Turner Prize 2004

Yinka Shonibare, *The Swing* (2004)
http://arts.guardian.co.uk/pictures/image/0,8543,-10804926745,00.html

Turner Prize 2005

Evening Standard, December 2005

'I dunno.' It was much like listening to the William Books of Richmal Crompton that are sometimes read on Radio 4, 'I dunno' the hero's response, no matter how red-handed, whenever interrogated by his father, an angry neighbour or the parish priest. Simon Starling, winner of the Turner Prize with *Shedboatshed*, was indeed on Radio 4 gently interrogated for the morning news and, in the sense that he had just been awarded £25,000 for what only a very few, even in the art world, would define as art, was indeed red-handed with the loot, 'I dunno' his answer to every probing question.

Should we expect better from any artist now? The defence is that the artist speaks through his work and has no need to be articulate or literate, but I doubt if that was true of Rembrandt and Michelangelo. Most artists of the Renaissance and all the centuries since have been men of education, have even been men who furthered education – Leonardo and Vasari, Stubbs and Reynolds, for example – not in the conventional sense of school and university, but in the unconventional self-teaching sense of urgent enquiry and scepticism. I have no doubt that Rubens could debate theology with any divine of any denomination in his day, and that Wright of Derby did not just paint subjects of the Enlightenment, but was aware how they came about and of their implications; I cannot, however, think that Emin, Hirst, Ofili, Whiteread, Kapoor or any other recently sensational artist has anything of the intellectual depth and range of the great artists of the past.

For some years the main problem arising from the visual arts has been, not that they are incomprehensible in the context of the larger past, not that to many they are ludicrous, but that they have nourished an industry of interpreters who attribute wisdom to the artists they interpret, ennobling their contrived eccentricities. To be an artist a man need not draw, paint, sculpt or perform any ancestral function of the visual arts – he has merely to declare himself an artist; if he says 'I am an artist' and turns on a tap, turns out a light or empties his bladder in the snow, then an artist he must be. Now we go much further and appoint the artist sage, guru, mentor to us all, pundit for the press and savant for radio and television, trustee of national galleries and great Arts Councillor. To turn a shed into a boat and that boat back into a shed is to turn oneself into Merlin, Solomon and the Three Kings, to rival Plato and Aristotle, Spinoza and Descartes, to give 'Dunno' the same significance as 'Cogito ergo sum'.

Turner Prize 2005

Simon Starling, *Shedboatshed* (2005)
http://www.guardian.co.uk/uk/2005/dec/06/arts.turnerprize2005

Turner Prize: A Retrospective

TATE BRITAIN

Evening Standard, 5 October 2007

I can recall no exhibition, ever, so immediately disappointing as Tate Britain's new retrospective of the Turner Prize. The annual ballyhoo and cacafuego of the Prize itself is this year to take place in Liverpool as the opening broadside of that benighted city's futile attempt to merit its appointment as European Capital of Culture for 2008, and Londoners must make do with a meagre survey of its history. It seems very much a hurried afterthought, ill-conceived and ill-prepared; the entry charge is outrageously high.

At its start in 1984 no one in charge of the Turner Prize seemed to know what it should be. Its chosen judges nodded an acknowledgement to what many onlookers regarded as the extremes of contemporary art — 'three dustbins and a load of string,' as one commentator put it — but then played safe and gave the cash to some widely acceptable old boy. By the time that Patrick Caulfield, Richard Hamilton, Lucian Freud, Gillian Ayres and Paula Rego had been short-listed, and Malcolm Morley, Howard Hodgkin and Gilbert and George had won it, it was perceived only as a matter of Buggins' Turn for pensioners and ran into the sand. Suspended for a year, it was re-born in 1991 as the extravagant, intelligence-insulting, cynical, exclusive, manipulated and fraudulent event that we at first loved to hate but to which sane men are now largely indifferent, if not contemptuous.

For some years I have refrained from commenting on the Turner Prize and its accompanying exhibition, damning its organisation as duplicitous. The works may be different — 'eclecticism and verve' their prime characteristics according to a spokesman for Tate

Britain – but in every case the driving determination of their makers to be cutting-edge and break the boundaries is much the same, and the very difference grows wearisome. Difference is noted in a fraction of a second, and if difference is all that an artist has to offer, then there is no point in spending longer in its contemplation. For his very different *Shedboatshed* – in which an uncommonly large shed was converted into a boat, sailed to Xanadu and then turned back into a shed (the only form in which it was exhibited) – Simon Starling won the Prize two years ago more for the eccentricity of the idea than for any connection with ancestral forms of art. On what conventional grounds could the sane man commend it? Starling was not responsible for the design of the shed, nor for the colour and texture of the timber, nor for the wear and tear that aged it, and its double metamorphosis was more a matter of carpentry than art. Nevertheless, it provided yet another opportunity for the curators and critics of contemporary art to write of the many layers of meaning that they could perceive not only in the concept but in the labour of its embodiment. This is now what curators do – apply meaning to the meaningless.

Since its second incarnation I have held the Turner Prize in contempt for its exclusive approach to art, for its blindness to the quality of anything not definable as cutting-edge, for the narrow interests of its judges and their back-scratching with dealers, for the secrecy that surrounds it and the evident management of the result. The Tate is perhaps no worse than the Royal Academy in this respect – 'The Academy must look after its own,' a past PRA, Roger de Grey, once said to me, excusing his manipulation of a prize in which I had been involved – but its deliberate and flamboyant exploitation by the Tate for the purposes of publicity adds a deplorable gloss. I do not for one moment believe that all their selections for the short-list are insincere, but many must have been chosen and the Prize occasionally awarded to provoke the predictable response of writers in the *Sun* and *Daily Mail*, papers whose froth of outrage is known to rouse the interest of millions of readers. The Tate could not possibly pay for the advertising value of the column inches that it generates simply by being perverse, and the immediate reward for perversity is a flock of visitors, to be counted in their thousands as proof of the Tate's success. But these numbers mean nothing: indoctrinated art students will come to the Turner Prize in fairly constant troops, but attendance by the populace at large depends entirely on how close the exhibits come to the freakish, to the bearded lady, the Elephant Man and the Hottentot Venus, for at the Turner Prizes it is not art that the public seeks or expects but the enjoyable frissons of dismay, incomprehension and distaste.

All this said, as a man who in his early life worked on major exhibitions, I was astonished by the Tate's wretched retrospective view of the Turner Prize. It is as though they have lost faith in it. How could the exhibition be so thin, so unambitious, so unsympathetic to its subject? How could it omit so many memorable things? How could it represent so many artists with works so few and second-rate? I had expected to be overwhelmed not only by 'eclecticism and verve', but by the sheer fecundity of contemporary British artists over the past quarter century and by the very things that had caused so much brouhaha; instead, in a characteristically austere Serota hang with everything widely dispersed for iconic contemplation rarely deserved, we have a ragged patchwork that recalls nothing of the thrill and challenge of the period, nothing of the spirit of the YBAs. I felt that, though consistently hostile to the Turner Prize, I could have served it better than the curators of this exhibition, that with the discipline of an art historian I could have assembled a far bolder, braver, truer and more exhilarating exhibition. When I reached the last room I could not believe that I had done so, but I had.

Where were the paintings of Lucian Freud – twice short-listed, never the winner? Where were those of Thérèse Oulton, once thought to be of brilliant promise, and where those of Patrick Caulfield? Where were Derek Jarman's exotic film *Caravaggio* and

Vong Phaophanit's *Neon Rice Field*? Where were the disturbing illusionist paintings of Glenn Brown, the confusion of detritus (rubbish) collected by Tomoko Takahashi and the Zobop zig-zag floors of Jim Lambie in gaudy sticky tape? Where, above all, were Emin's tumbled bed and the morbid horrors of the Chapman Brothers? None of these won the Prize, but their work was far more interesting than that of many who did, and all are essential to our understanding of the workings of the Prize and the incomprehensibly erratic judgements of those who awarded it.

Whole rooms are devoted to single works – and so they must be, for contemporary art is a selfish and greedy business as well as shallow. Martin Creed must have an empty room for his light switched on and off, a work that offers nothing in terms of visual and intellectual nourishment and gains nothing in being seen again. Antony Gormley must have another for his five identical figures stiffly bent on ceiling, walls and floor, for had they to share the space their 'psychological Cubism' would hardly be apparent, nor would their connections with outer space, the calamity of Hiroshima, the polymorphousness of the self and the fundamental nature of our engagement with the earth – all these the perceptions urged on us by the exhibition's curator (I looked in vain for the word silly). As with the tedious videos of Gillian Wearing and Steve McQueen (sillier still), Anish Kapoor has a whole room for three large hollow forms in fibreglass covered in the matt light-absorbent blue pigment that was so long his obsession; they make a simple statement about our visual confusions when our sense of form, volume and depth is disrupted by the near elimination of reflected light – but why make so grossly large a work to demonstrate so small and obvious a point; it is remarkably ugly for a so-called work of art.

Damien Hirst is represented by a spot painting and by *Mother and Child Divided*, a cow and a calf sliced through from nose to tail, each of the halves separately encased in a tank of formaldehyde. Both were conceived in 1993; fourteen years later Hirst's workshop is still hacking out the spot paintings, smaller, cheaper to make and more marketable; fourteen years later, the original *Mother and Child* not available for this exhibition (one tank leaks and the others are suspect), the Hirst production line has made a replica, to all intents and purposes identical. With the acceptance of such commodification of his work it should be possible for him, on his dying day, to produce again his earliest conceptions, perhaps for the umpteenth time and, if his affairs are properly managed, for production to be continued posthumously – as it is by the Musée Rodin with the old man's bronzes. And if Hirst can contrive this, then so can all other contemporary artists – now there's a gloomy thought.

A gloomier thought, perhaps, is how swiftly forgotten many of the short-listed artists have been, how even the Turner Prize has brought them no more than Warhol's promised fifteen minutes of fame. Who now remembers Terry Atkinson and John Walker, Boyd Webb, Giuseppe Penone or Grenville Davey? Who can recall distinctly the work of Alison Wilding or David Tremlett or Hannah Collins? Were Willy Doherty's videos in any way memorable, are Shirazeh Houshiary's sculptures easily recalled? Callum Innes, Douglas Gordon, Craigie Horsfield, Simon Patterson, Christine Borland, Angela Bulloch, Steven Pippin, Michael Raedecker, Isaac Julien, Mike Nelson, Fiona Banner, Catherine Yass, Willy Doherty, Darren Almond, Gillian Carnegie, Phil Collins, Mark Titchner and Rebecca Warren – have any of these become a household name? No – winner takes all but not inevitably and always. The real immediate winner of the Turner Prize is always the Tate Gallery but in the longer term it is the very few associated dealers too, for they make the huge cash profit from the accolade.

Turner Prize: A Retrospective 1984–2006, Tate Britain 2007
http://www.tate.org.uk/whats-on/exhibition/turner-prize-retrospective/
exhibition-guide/turner-prize-02-05

Damien Hirst, *Mother and Child Divided*
http://arts.guardian.co.uk/pictures/image/0,8543,-17404774275,00.html

THE WHITECHAPEL GALLERY

It was in 1881 that the Vicar of St Jude's, Whitechapel, mounted the first of a series of art exhibitions for the enlightenment of his parishioners and others in the neighbourhood – a worthy purpose close to that of the founders of the National Gallery in 1824 in the belief that art is a language that does not depend on literacy, but speaks directly to man's soul. In 1897–9 the vicar's efforts were followed by the construction of the Whitechapel Gallery. In my lifetime it has had two great Directors, Bryan Robertson, 1952–68, and Nicholas Serota, 1976–88, but in more recent years its direction has become weak to the point of foolish and, in spite of recent expansion at vast expense, it is now a centre of fashionable but empty entertainment. No exhibition since that refurbishment has been worth a first glance, and certainly not a second. One review, of an exhibition that demonstrated the steep intellectual descent of the gallery after Serota's departure, is included only because it raises more matters than proof that the rot was well set in before the twentieth century ended.

The Whitechapel Gallery
http://www.whitechapelgallery.org/about-us

Examining Pictures

WHITECHAPEL GALLERY

Evening Standard, 20 May 1999

Examining Pictures is a rotten title for a shoddy little show that is a disgrace to the Whitechapel Gallery. Though the press release announced it as the great beginning of a new programme of exhibitions, the catalogue tells another tale – that far from being part of a coherent programme this exhibition is no more than an ill considered impulse stemming from chance cocktail party chatter. To this the sane man's only possible response is that the curators should have known that sound exhibitions depend on much more than whim and the heady whiff of alcohol, take many months to prepare, and are founded on a proper thesis rather than cod-aesthetics that expose them to accusations of intellectual incapability.

Their sixty odd pictures by sixty odd artists – and odd is certainly the word for most of both – give the impression of an entirely random choice, a morning's shopping for the dregs of Cork Street, the discards of collectors who have learned something of connoisseurship since acquiring them, or the leftovers from a sale at Sotheby's; the last thing in the world we could assume from them is that they represent the survival and resurgence of the art of painting – and yet this is the claim made by these curators.

Insofar as it is possible to fathom their intellectual confusion, evasion and casuistry, their argument seems to be that over the past forty years or so painting has survived the onslaughts of photography, installation, video, abject art, junk art and innumerable self-inflicted wounds, has never quite lost its place in the affections of the artist and is now on its way back from death's door. 'What's to be done about painting?' they asked of each other at the Jackson Pollock exhibition, seeing his work as a crisis for not only the big dipper himself, but for the whole of painting too, seeing painting as painted into a corner, trapped in 'a sort of iconoclastic cul-de-sac' from which it could find no escape – none, that is, until they thought about it and persuaded themselves that though painting may have been demoted to a category of medium instead of being virtually synonymous with art, it still exists and that its practice is merrily alive and kicking.

Looking back four decades – that is to more or less the point at which the practice of painting first fell into disrepute in the art schools of the West – they trace its Thesean thread from Bacon and Hockney in the Sixties to the present day, at which time, to perceptive critics, it seems at its most fragile, almost wholly dependent in the purlieus of Cork Street, the Arts Council and Serota country, on painters who reveal not the slightest talent and precious little skill. Do not for one moment suppose that we are invited to contemplate Bacon at his most heroic and Hockney at his most passionately homosexual (derived from the soft pornography of the Sixties, the invention very second-hand) – we are instead confronted with really very nasty little pictures that do them both serious injustice as representative works, pictures that tell us nothing about the ancestral traditions of painting, that invoke no ghosts of the great past even though Velázquez's portrait of himself at work on the Infanta and her maidservants is, as a frontispiece to the catalogue, employed as the touchstone for this exhibition. 'Velázquez's incomparable painting,' these curators say, 'set up a paradigm for the relationship between artist and viewer, artist and subject, artist and medium, within a complex choreography of spatial relationships' – and then they have the blind impertinence to assert that the pictures in their puerile exhibition perform the same function as 'a living and viable expression of painting today'. What then, one is compelled to wonder, would Velázquez, that master of discreet and delicate sensuality, have thought of *Love Is*, by Sue Williams, not a painting in any sense that even the Arts Council would seek to justify as art though the Curator of Interpretation at the Tate might manage it, but a primitive diagram of buttocks and phalluses demonstrating how two men may concurrently enter the nether regions of one woman's body; fit, perhaps, for the sad soul whose sexual fantasies are nourished by graffiti in the lavatories of slovenly publicans, the curators see it as a 'bitter-sweet message', poignant and sincere.

In terms of image, with this picture the curators plumb the depths of irrelevance if their purpose is to reassure us that painting is not dead. In other pictures, not pictorial in any sense other than that paint of some kind is their material and they are intended to hang on a wall, we have the printed message, sometimes hortative, sometimes enquiring, sometimes enigmatic, most times meaning-less – mere words on canvas, nothing else. 'Heavy Industry' is the bald statement on one canvas, and the curators tell us that this is to its painter as intensely felt an image as any view of Mont St Victoire was to Cézanne. What are we to make of, as painting, the *FEB.29.1992* of On Kawara in white on a black canvas? If it is in any sense a painting, then every signwriter in the trade is an old master.

These curators are a little nearer the mark when they quote Philip Guston's account of his conversations with the canvas, his unpreparedness, his solutions discovered during the progress of a painting – but this is what painters have always done since the discovery of oil paint and canvas, assessing their own work and often altering it extensively, and he speaks as though Titian and Cézanne had never existed and he himself was first to let his canvas inform him of the next stroke of the brush. When, how-ever, the curators urge on us the notion that 'Paint on canvas is instantaneously identified as art' we have the measure of their idiocy – as with this syllogism they accept rank amateur rubbish by a hypothetical grocer as art and tell us that we may only question whether it is good or bad – we should not be surprised to find so much dross in their exhibition.

There is an intolerable smugness about these curators; they tell us nothing of the nature of the material of paint, its obstinacy and fluidity, translucency and opacity, its sensuality; they draw no distinction between oil and acrylic paint, or between canvas of different qualities and tooth, or between supports of board and timber; we learn nothing of the brush. They claim, however, that they recognise painting as a thing of forceful compulsion going from strength to strength, driven by invention and improvisation – and so it always was – but if they see in their tawdry collection of contemporary artists any who match Michelangelo, Titian, Rembrandt, Géricault, Degas, young Picasso or old Freud, then they delude themselves and us.

A serious side issue arises from this miserable exhibition. How, if such a collection of unpainterly pictures – and most hardly deserve even the definition picture – is presented by a pair of well-paid and influential curators as demonstrating the resurgence of painting, can the demands of those who wish to learn the true traditional skills of the painter now be satisfied? The rot set in some forty years ago with the student generation of Hockney and Jarman: Jarman was intelligent enough to know it at the time, but Hockney was not, and Hockney, who has never known how to handle oil paint (or, for that matter, acrylic), is always quoted as one of Britain's greatest painters when he is no more than a whimsical illustrator, a filler-in between the lines. Students emerge from their schools and colleges in almost total ignorance of the craft they pretend to pursue, without technical knowledge, without handling skills, bemused by every subtlety and without the foggiest idea of how to paint a glaze or achieve a desired finish with a varnish; the simplest procedures of their trade defeat them. Every week letters reach me from would-be painters who are damned by the teachers in their schools for wanting to pursue the tradition of putting paint on canvas – I have one at hand that speaks of his tutor's apathy and loathing for his work, of vehement attacks on it and him, of constant derision: 'She repeatedly asks why do I bother, why am I here in this place, what is all this shit you call art? There seems to be a philosophy here in these places of art that skill, attention to detail and natural talent are to be crushed. They fear it.'

This letter must stand for many; it is from a student at one of the major London schools of university status and I must protect the writer by not naming it, but students at others in London say much the same and seek my help, complaining of the Slade, for example, that it is dismissive and oppressive, and at the Royal College students have for years told me that they must 'unlearn' what has been dinned into them there. Until the mid-Nineties I trawled a number of schools each year and occasionally did a little teaching, and am thus aware from my own observation of what is terribly wrong in so many of them. I have seen natural talent cruelly crushed and aptitude frustrated; I have seen staff hopelessly incompetent, indifferent and lazy, and even been shouted down by politically motivated teachers (I speak of art politics) and witnessed their downright hostility to students who hope for a measure of technical competence. The situation is even worse in Teacher Training Colleges, where paint on canvas is old hat and drawing based on scrutiny is utterly condemned as irrelevant — drawing must now, it seems, be 'non-objective' — what idiotic jargon.

If the curators of the Whitechapel exhibition had answered their question 'What's to be done about painting?' with the battle cry 'We must teach it again before the old skills die out,' and their pictures (the very same) had been chosen to demonstrate the urgent need, I could understand the wry point of exhibiting such wretched rubbish, but that they should believe these fashionable canvases to be robust examples of fine painting is incomprehensible. With such curators in power, determining what we must regard as great painting, dictating the hyperbole that we must use for it, the death of real painting is inevitable.

BRITISH CONTEMPORARY ARTISTS

Frank Auerbach

Evening Standard, 17 November 2001

The most damaging thing that his friends can do for an artist with a reputation for greatness as 'a leading painter of our time', is to give him a retrospective exhibition. The retrospective, in surveying the work of half a century or so, in prying into rudimentary beginnings and ill-considered ends, is a cruel scrutiny of the most rigorous kind and, if it leaves no stone unturned, lets loose a legion of doubts, dissents and disbeliefs.

Against these doubts his friends can, in advance, erect formidable defences. Well before the exhibition opens, the public, pusill-animous critics and news hounds are conditioned by persuasive promotion. The painter may be interviewed by a notable critic, the hapless answers of the one to the banal questions of the other spread wide across the front page of a cultural broadsheet – in such a context one is inexorably reminded of the King of Hanover who observed of experts that professors and prostitutes can always be had for money. Better still, the artist may be interviewed by a writer who knows nothing about art and has therefore un-questioningly swallowed what he has been told is the consensus of opinion – that the artist in question is 'living proof of the stubborn reality of painterly genius'; thus compelled to strike the attitude of the low kow-tow customarily adopted in deference to Ivan the Terrible and other early Czars of Russia, such a writer will with ease fill two pages of a broadsheet with such tales of Bohemian bliss and tribulation as to make of the artist's life the libretto of an opera. And best of all, for it is so expensive that it will sit for the buyer's lifetime on his bookshelves, the exhibition's catalogue will be laden with essays that, with lubricious and deceitful ease, liken the painter's work to that of Titian and Tintoretto, Watteau and Chardin, Constable and Van Gogh, implying that he is their equal.

So great is the weight of propaganda in these circumstances that the dissenting word is rarely heard or seen, and yet the visitor who does not read the broadsheets and cannot afford the catalogue is likely, through the exercise of an eye uncluttered by their influence, to make a more shrewd and accurate judgement of the painter's achievement. The Royal Academy, however, has taken an unprecedented step in attempting to distort the plain man's view of a contemporary painter, Frank Auerbach, by exhibiting his work concurrently with that of Rembrandt, not tucked away in the bleak attic, but in the same great suite of exhibition galleries, its President prominently remarking on the 'apposition of a show devoted to an intimate aspect of Rembrandt's rich career and an equally eloquent testimony to the searching spirit of a living master'. There we have it, by rather more than implication – Master Auerbach is the Rembrandt of today.

Is he? Even in this Rembrandt exhibition, limited to a single theme and less enriched by splendid loans than impoverished by their refusal, the sense of a self-critical and constantly observant genius is ever-present, the sense of a painter always developing and never hacking in a rut or obstructed in a cul-de-sac, but with Auerbach we have a painter who half a century ago developed a mannerism with paint that set him apart from his contemporaries and to which he has since clung with the dogged perseverance of the intellectually blind. The mannerism was the use of exceptionally thick paint applied layer upon layer in a synthesis of paint and painted object that is just short of three-dimensional modelling.

It is not unfair to say of Auerbach that his paintings of 1951 have, though the brush trembles with hesitation and the undecided images are flawed by uncertain drawing, all the characteristics of his paintings of 2001, and that the hesitation and uncertainty had, through gestures repeated daily, been trained out of him by the later 1950s, his confident wallowing in paint by then unthinkingly habitual. There have been odd brief periods when perhaps some self-dissatisfaction has caused him to thin his paint a little – but then it took on a thoroughly unpleasant slick and greasy quality – or to muddy his paint a trifle less, or to adopt an altogether brighter palette in which a particularly vile yellow gains sudden prominence, or to scribble over his townscapes instead of constructing a semi-abstract scaffold of long strokes to lend a little logic to confusion, but in essence his early and late pictures are very much the same, his sensibility as much arrested in a muddy mire as a child who does not respond to potty training.

Few painters were more transparently derivative and the art historian can easily do his duty with Auerbach in his formative years, pointing out that he was in debt to some of the brighter lights of the School of Paris in the decade after World War II, to the paintings of Giacometti, Nicolas de Staël and the now thankfully forgotten Fautrier for the thickness of his paint, and to the sculptures of Germaine Richier for the gross physical forms he used as nudes – all exhibited in London at the time by the many more commercial dealers than there now are, all illustrated in art magazines, a point that must be made for Auerbach hardly ever left inner London. Some art historians surmise that Auerbach also borrowed from Soutine, a more than slightly mad Russian painter who died in Paris in 1943, for their work shares something of the same attack, but he was virtually unknown in England until the Arts Council exhibition of 1963 and Auerbach cannot have seen the great Paris exhibition of 1949. If American Abstract Expressionism played any part in his development, it could only have been through images in magazines.

One thing is certain – that Auerbach's dense handling of paint was not derived from David Bomberg, as is so often asserted and assumed. He spent a very short time as a painting student under Bomberg at the Borough Polytechnic, in the spring and summer terms of 1948, before joining the St Martin's School of Art, where he studied for four years. If Bomberg's bravura use of paint was indeed a formative influence, then Auerbach betrayed his master, for even in Bomberg's very late paintings, in which, to some extent, he betrayed himself by going so far beyond the bold structural painting that he had developed in the 1930s and into a looseness with which he sought to communicate a less definite, more atmospheric, sense of form, the sense of structure and aerial perspective was never smothered by an accumulation of dense paint. If there is a connection between Auerbach and Bomberg it is that both responded to visual experience with paint and gesture, but there is no common character to either and resemblance is entirely superficial. Nothing in Bomberg's work was ever as dense, opaque or muddy as Auerbach's, nothing was ever so thick that it had as much physical presence as a sculptured high relief and cast deep shadows on itself, nothing so closely resembled a calamity in a cake shop, the wreckage of cream buns, chocolate sponges, *mille-feuilles* and Battenbergs.

Auerbach is held in awe for painting without pause, every day of every week, every week of every year, for over and over scraping paint from his canvases and rebuilding on the shadowy stains, for demanding hundreds of sittings for his caricatural portraits, for grunting, groaning and throwing paint about, for all this psychotic behaviour is interpreted as genius. It is nothing of the kind – it is no better evidence of genius than the obsessively repeated behaviour of animals confined in zoos, but the confinement in Auerbach's case, to the bailiwick of Camden Town and Primrose Hill, is self-inflicted. Would he have been a better painter had he, like Bomberg, travelled to see the dry harsh light of the Holy Land and the rich colours of southern Spain? I doubt it, for Auerbach sees only Auerbachs. Auerbach does not paint Primrose Hill, Mornington Crescent or Camden Town, nor does Auerbach paint portraits – Auerbach paints only Auerbachs. Even in the National Gallery to which, it seems, he has access in the dead of night, he sees painters as diverse as Rembrandt and Rubens, Titian and Constable, as feeble amateurs best reinterpreted as yet more Auerbachs. In this there is an obscene vanity.

Compare Auerbach with Freud and we compare him with an honest painter who has almost always known when he has exhausted a particular vein of inspiration or technique, who has had the intellectual and technical virtuosity to invent new ways of seeing and interpreting, who is, to some extent, still capable of the excitement of a young man just setting out and not in the least inhibited by an old man's melancholy and the weight of habit. Of this there is not the slightest sign in Auerbach. An Auerbach is an Auerbach, and that is that, the product of a hidebound eye, not 'living proof of the stubborn reality of painterly genius'.

Frank Auerbach, Royal Academy 2001

Head of Catherine Lampert **(1986)**
http://www.culture24.org.uk/asset_arena/3/11/28113/v0_master.jpg

Reclining Head of Julia **(1995)**
http://www.culture24.org.uk/asset_arena/5/11/28115/v0_master.jpg

Frank Auerbach

COURTAULD INSTITUTE

Evening Standard, 29 November 2009

Frank Auerbach, at 78, continues to be presented as, if not quite a 'grand old man of British painting', then certainly as one who has been 'a leading painter of our time'. At his dealer, Marlborough, his latest selling exhibition demonstrated yet again the falling-off in power and originality that was already obvious at least a quarter of a century ago. I forbore to review it rather than do both him and them commercial damage and it is now over. At the Courtauld Gallery, however, there is now a longer-lasting exhibition, severely art historical (though larded with unremitting reverence), of the earliest urban scenes on which his fame was founded, the memory of which still colours the way we see his current etiolated offerings.

Bryan Robertson, one of the few sane and reasonable critics of the day, described these early paintings in glowing, if general, terms: 'There is no hysteria in Auerbach's work, no grotesque excess, no falsification whatever of the essential integrity of the subject . . . (his) work is full of strong feeling, marvellously disciplined by his artistic intelligence.' I too thought I could see this then, but with much repetition I eventually began to doubt, and eight years ago, at Auerbach's retrospective exhibition at the Royal Academy, deliberately held concurrently with a Rembrandt exhibition in the same suite of galleries so that we should see him as the Rembrandt of this new century, it seemed to me that all that Robertson had observed had been degraded into mere habit by a painter clinging desperately to comfortable formulae. Of these, the principal mannerism has been the use of exceptionally thick paint. Put very simply, after the first short burst of near originality Auerbach relinquished the business of painting portraits and townscapes for the easier discipline of painting Auerbachs of Auerbachs.

His Marlborough exhibition perfectly made this point, though his once confident luxuriating in the depths of paint is now reduced to defiant kicking in its shallows. It was the victim of another unfortunate comparison – this time not with Rembrandt, nor with Constable (with whom the V&A compared him in 2006) nor with Titian, Tintoretto and Van Gogh to whom so many feeble critics liken him – but with himself as a young man. I now know exactly what Wordsworth meant in *Intimations of Immortality* when he argued that 'Shades of the prison-house begin to close upon the growing boy' (true of us all), for Auerbach's prison was of his own construction and its foundations were laid in his paintings of London's post-war building sites, now reviewed and reconsidered at the Courtauld.

Born in Berlin in 1931, Auerbach as a boy just short of eight found himself uprooted and in England, his Jewish parents left behind to die in Nazi concentration camps. German by birth and early education he had to learn not only a new language, but new loyalties. Iris Origo, a distinguished writer of the day, paid for his keep and education – a matter of pure chance – and he was sent to a short-lived boarding school run by a Jewish Quaker on very un-English lines, co-educational and idealist yet sexually restrictive, disciplined as a self-regulating community. Auerbach was thought to have the makings of an actor. In Shropshire throughout the war he saw nothing of it until it was over, and then, at sixteen he came to London, where assorted relatives clubbed together to give him £4.50 a week – a by no means miserly amount on which to live – and the slow business of becoming a painter began, first at Hampstead Garden Suburb Institute, then in the Borough Polytechnic where he was taught by David Bomberg, the tutelary genius who continued to be the boy's inspiration when, in September 1948, he joined St Martin's School of Art. In 1952 he transferred to the

Royal College, graduating in 1955 after seven full years of training as a painter.

It was precisely at this point of transition from one school to the other that he discovered what he could do with thick paint: a quasi-naturalistic painting of a bombed site in Earls Court Road in which rebuilding had begun, had for months defeated and confused him at St Martin's but returning to it at the end of his first day at the RCA, raging over some petty episode to do with the rationing of paint, he attacked it with angry fervour, disrupting its colour with oranges and yellows that were very much the flavour of the period, and its realism with the mass of paint. With the smothering of all that had earlier been descriptive, the painting 'began to operate by its own laws' – but isn't that the alchemy of all great paintings? – and he 'felt that it was the beginning of my life as a painter'.

It was exactly so. The paint was still thinner than it was to become in the evocations of building sites that were to follow over the next decade, the touch was still tentative, the drawing desperately uncertain, the identifiable elements unrelated in anything that could be described as command of space, height, depth, distance, light and shadow, but some of the possible impastose textures of paint were exploited and Auerbach had begun to establish his simple personal language of tension between aggressive lines and submissive inchoate form; the material of paint was about to become more than the material manipulated by the brush to represent a subject – it was to be the drawing, the painting and the subject itself. Paint was the mud and spoil that lay about in mounds waiting to be carted off as superhuman foundations were dug deep; paint was the concrete and cement; paint was the girder, scaffolding and crane.

Auerbach was not quite alone in painting bombed sites so long after the war – Eliot Hodgkin did so too, recording the last in King's Road, Chelsea as late as 1976. During the war many were recorded by artists or enhanced as romantic ruins, but after it – and long after they had been made safe and tottering ruins had been demolished and carted off to make humpy hills on the old parade ground of Wimbledon Common – Londoners had grown fond of them as open spaces where wild flowers bloomed, saplings sprang, rural birds flourished and butterflies were born. We were accustomed to them as reminders of nature and Ozymandias – so much so that we resented their redevelopments; where Auerbach, safely isolated from the war, saw the energy of creation in the diggers and the cranes – for that is what he jubilantly painted – we saw another Blitz in the work of the developers, another destruction of what we had, over a decade or so, accepted affectionately as a status quo. I, much the same age as Auerbach but in London throughout the war, felt very differently about these gaps in the teeth of the metropolis and would have left many as they were; I am glad to have seen St Paul's from the river with almost nothing to obstruct my view of that great edifice. I hated the destruction by developers of townscapes that war had made so beautiful.

On this matter of post-war planning and rebuilding the exhibition's catalogue has a remarkably lucid, factual and flannel-free essay by Margaret Garlake on the pre-fabs and the stubby skyscrapers with which London was dotted between 1945 and 1960 – the best that I have ever read. Two other essays deal with Auerbach in these early years, with his relationships with Bomberg, Kossoff and Parisian existentialism, with the looming presence of Melanie Klein, Georges Bataille and the ubiquitous and irritating David Sylvester – admirable, no doubt, but neither Barnaby Wright nor Paul Moorhouse seems to have looked enquiringly enough at other painters of the period in London and Paris to see if Auerbach's textures and palette were quite so original and unparalleled. My recollection of the *Zeitgeist* is that students were encouraged to trowel paint onto canvas, to treat it almost as a clay in which to model reliefs, and that only at the Slade School under William Coldstream was this actively discouraged.

Did Wright and Moorhouse ever ask themselves if Auerbach's

early work was really as perfect as Bryan Robertson proposed; or is connoisseurship irrelevant in the new history of art? Half a century on I now see only evidence of hysterical activity in the frenzied surfaces, of grotesque excess in the excrescented depths of paint, and of the essential integrity of subjects falsified for the sake, not of artistic intelligence, but of Auerbach's artistic identity, a thing to be immediately recognised in every painting since.

Visitors to the exhibition may not see even this. These paintings are hung in such a way as to make them impossible to see; under steeply raking spotlights every bristle-line of every brushstroke gleams and glisters, and from every nugget and blob of ragged paint cast shadows reach, disrupting our perception. Rarely have I peered into so many canvases only to see far less than can be seen in the catalogue's reproductions; rarely has there been so little point in going to an exhibition. The gallery is the instrument of the Courtauld Institute, once the finest school of art history in the world (coincidentally in the very decade of these paintings); is this the best display of paintings that its current luminaries can manage? Are they smug or blind?

Frank Auerbach, Courtauld Institute 2009

Maples Demolition Site (1960)
http://www.curatedmag.com/news/wp-content/uploads/
2009/11/frank-a-2.jpg

Shell Building Site from the Thames (1959)
http://www.theartkey.com/photos/news/7/3/
Fig.3AuerbachShellBuildingSitefromThames.jpg

Rebuilding the Empire Cinema, Leicester Square (1962)
http://www.curatedmag.com/news/wp-content/uploads/2009/11/
frank-a-1.jpg

Anthony Caro

NATIONAL GALLERY

Evening Standard, March 1998

'A strange idea, you might think, to show sculptures in the National Gallery . . . ' muses Neil MacGregor in his introduction to the works of Anthony Caro now exhibited there. To this the answer is 'No, not at all,' for there are indeed many of us who have long thought that sculptures might greatly assist our comprehension of the paintings, and have seen in our mind's eye the Donatellos and Berninis of the V&A transferred to Trafalgar Square to keep company with their Renaissance and Baroque equivalents by Mantegna and Giordano. If we treat sculpture and painting as clinically separate arts, then we are in error; Michelangelo made a not incompetent attempt at both (and architecture too), Tiepolo combined them in the convincing illusion of his painted ceilings, and even the refined and finicky Canova painted pictures that were by no means bad; put antique Roman sarcophagus reliefs with Poussin's pictures and they are immediately illuminated by these sources; put the ice-cold perfections of Neo-classical sculpture with the paintings of their day, and each is marvellously, if unappealingly, informed by the other. No, Mr MacGregor, it is not in the least a strange idea to show sculpture in the National Gallery, but it is more than slightly aberrant to offer us the heaps of industrial detritus that Anthony Caro combines in borrowed compositions, and then claim that he has sharpened our perceptions of Rembrandt, Goya and Van Gogh.

Caro has for many years been internationally celebrated, his position as the grand old man of sculpture proclaimed by Clement Greenberg, an American critic preaching in language of convoluted obscurity the gospel of irreducible purity and the renunciation of all that is explicit in visual references. This position was immediately confirmed on this side of the Atlantic on the death of Henry Moore in 1986, and truth to tell, there was a laying-on of hands of sorts at the beginning of his career, for in the years 1951–3, when Caro was in his late twenties, he worked as Moore's assistant; whether he was any use or not in this capacity, we are never allowed to forget the fact, just as the Tudor usurper, Henry VII, though five generations removed from John of Gaunt, and by a bastard line, claimed legitimate descent from the Lancastrian kings. Look back, however, to the work of Henry Moore, a man of wide-ranging and erratic genius, and we will discover not the slightest connection with Caro, whose independent work in the Fifties suggests not only a man who learned nothing from his master, but one whose aesthetic sense was dangerously close to the Royal Academicians who then (and now) exhibited engaging female figures doing what females do, and from whom he could separate himself only by deliberately adding to their conventions an element of humorous ugliness; conjure the languid girls of Caro's contemporaries Ralph Brown and Sidney Harpley, make them grotesque and fat, and we have an adequate notion of his early work, often omitted from 'official' books on Caro. Those who cannot suppress this aspect of his work seek to protect his reputation by likening it to the paintings of Bacon, de Kooning and Dubuffet, but to see how aesthetically and spiritually meagre it is, we should look instead to the bronzes of Germaine Richier, made in Paris a year or two earlier, of which Caro cannot have been ignorant.

Born in 1924, Caro belongs to the post-war generation of young Englishmen who realised, whatever their professional field, that transatlantic experience, however banal, would distinguish them from their peers and give them a professional lift – an absurd deception, but it worked. In 1959 he went to America for the first of many times, and there met not only the inane Clement Greenberg, but David Smith, a sculptor of visual puns on a large scale, in metal painted, polished or rusty; his head quite turned by such intoxicating influences, he abandoned the gross charms of his female figures and became the man of the chopped girder, the brightly painted agricultural machine, and the capricious assemblages of old iron that have ever since marked him as another arrogant lost soul. Few exhibitions could be less rewarding, less exhilarating, and less spiritual than a Caro retrospective.

For the past decade or so Caro has been toying with the student exercise of making three-dimensional tableaux from the paintings of old masters. In terms of understanding what painters can do on a flat plane of canvas to give it the perspective space in which to set the elements that make the subject, and a formal examination of these elements themselves, this has a serious purpose; one learns, if nothing else, the different natures of form and the abstract structures that are the cores of the least abstract paintings – it is, indeed, the exercise by which one learns that all art is abstract, no matter what its subject, and that abstract art, per se, is quite superfluous. Caro, however, is long past the age when he could care tuppence for the formal qualities of Rembrandt, Goya, Manet and Van Gogh, and is incapable of conceding to them the primacy; he is, instead, wholly concerned with the supposed wit of taking discarded pieces of metal from his stockyard, his off-cuts from other sculptures, his rusting *objets trouvés*, and making from them a three-dimensional collage that in some distant way resembles a *Descent from the Cross*, *The Third of May*, *Le Déjeuner sur l'Herbe* and the most famous chair in the history of painting. This is the stuff of the tiresome adolescent, even the tiresome infant, crying 'Look at me, look at me.'

Caro may be a popular sculptor in the sense that his work is to be found in a thousand galleries and public places, but this in itself should make us pause when we hear him acclaimed as a significant genius leading a new generation of sculptors – as Greenberg put it, more or less. The sheer quantity of his work suggests that it is dashed off through habit and at whim, and is entirely whimsical, with not even himself knowing whether it is what he wished to achieve; and the vast extent of his influence suggests that work in his style and mannerism is far too easy to make (the required skills require brawn, not brain), and thus is far too easy to imitate. The critic must argue, indeed, that once Caro has hit upon a formula, he imitates himself until the meagre notion is so exhausted that he must move on; he must argue further, that as Caro has found a formula only once every decade, five works are enough to get the short measure of the man; and arguing further still, the critic is justified in suggesting that Caro's new dependence on old art for his ideas marks the end of any small aesthetic initiative that he may once have had. Looked at in this light, we can only see his picture-sculptures as the wretched end of a career that was never promising – other than as a fashionable hack.

Why are his sculptures now in the National Gallery? Mr MacGregor's Beatrix Potter ancestor could well have seen some virtue in the Rembrandt as a scarecrow, but Van Gogh's *Chair* and Mantegna's *Triumph* would have served no purpose in his bed of lettuces. These crude abstractions tell us nothing of the art they imitate, offer no insights, heighten no perceptions, identify no fundamental truths; they utterly miss the dramatic, emotional, religious and political points, and even the formal points, made by artists far, far greater than Caro, and do damage in the sense that their cluttered ugliness diverts us from them. These sculptures wholly lack the humility of the homage, the imitation of one painter by another seeking to learn – Rubens after Caravaggio, Turner after Titian and Claude, Picasso after Congo barbarism, Moore after some ancient Mexican; Caro does not learn – he arrogantly rearranges the original and presents it as his own.

Mr MacGregor suggests that these unpleasant pranks rescue the paintings in his charge 'from the dulling of a false familiarity'. They do not, and nothing could be more dully familiar (and not falsely so) than the empty arid works of Caro. The only explanations for their presence in Trafalgar Square are the weary political correctitude that museums must constantly strive to make themselves more popular (and the National Gallery hardly needs to do that), and the stale business in which art historians indulge when they seek to prove that the arts of the past and the present are united by an unbroken thread – contemporary artists are favoured by the Arts Council and the Serota Tendency only when they demonstrate that they have cut that thread.

Exhibiting such junk as Caro's – literally junk – and before his work, drab pictures by Peter Blake and Frank Auerbach's infantile scribbles, is a pointless exercise in the National Gallery. If it proves anything, it is that contemporary artists, celebrated though they may be in the London art market, are ignorant, insensitive, incompetent and vain, their offerings irrelevant. Stop it, Mr MacGregor, you have no need to toady to the contemporary arts, even if the chairman of your trustees thinks himself a modern painter. Borrow old sculptures that are relevant – it is not a strange idea; borrow old masters by the dozen, invite comparisons between versions (as you so successfully did with the Caspar David Friedrich), involve us in problems of connoisseurship, teach us iconography and meanings hidden and forgotten, and take us seriously, respecting our capacity to make an intellectual as well as an aesthetic effort, but don't play silly games with us – none sillier than Caro's crude reinterpretations.

Jake and Dinos Chapman

SAATCHI GALLERY

Evening Standard, 3 October 2003

Hell changed my mind. In 1994 I felt only indifference to the Chapman Brothers' reinvention, on a life-size scale, in three dimensions and full waxwork colour, of a print from Goya's *Disasters of War*. The title of Goya's version is *An heroic Feat with dead Men*, of the Chapmans' *Great Deeds against the Dead*, but by both we are left with the suspicion that the victims were perhaps not dead when the feat and deeds were done – otherwise, why do them?

What could be the point of stripping prisoners naked, tying them to a dead tree and slicing off their genitals if they are dead? And where is the joke in decapitating the man hanging upside-down if he does not see the intent in his executioner's eye, does not see the drawing and hear the whistling of the sword? Is the deep shading under Goya's hanging man (lost in the Chapman revision) not more amusingly interpretable as the gush of exsanguination from the severed neck than as the cast shadow of his neighbour? Is the whole image not better seen as dying fast and slow, an event of calculated cruelty, than as the mere wanton mutilation of the dead?

How could I be indifferent to a sculpture nine feet high and yet so moved by an etching not much bigger than a post card? It was something to do with Goya's skill as a print maker, the bite of the etching acid, the tone of the print, the sense that to the impetuous anger of the drawing his printing methods had added another, more subtle, beauty that, without diminishing the violence of the image, elevated it and gave it the irresistible power of aesthetic seduction, whereas the Chapman Brothers had done no more with it than suggest mayhem among the models of Harvey Nichols' windows. Even so, it has become an iconic masterpiece of the 1990s, a match for Hirst's shark and Emin's bed, and with those it is presented in the holy of holies of the Saatchi Gallery as one of the dozen to which even the unbelieving are compelled by circumstance to bend the knee, a truly seminal work in that *Hell* was its progeny.

The other seminal work of 1994 was *Fuck Face*. This almost engaging life-size fibreglass figure of a confident four-year-old is so realistic that the mind at first refuses to accept what the eye can see — that his nose of Pinocchiesque proportions is the erect penis of an adolescent boy and his mouth the extruded rim of an anus too much abused in sodomy. This was the first of many such imaginings, the most notorious of which is *Zygotic Acceleration . . .* a zygote, I must remind you, is a living cell-nucleus formed by the fusion of two other such bodies — in which more than a dozen pre-pubescent girls and boys are siamesed together in appalling conjunctions, some of them the siblings of *Fuck Face*, others conventionally pretty. It is as though Rodin's *Burghers of Calais* had conjugated with the Tiller Girls and sired a multiple monster. Again the horror of it is diminished by the waxwork and window-dressing references, with a nod to the dildo and inflatable sex doll, the skins repellently untactile surfaces, but so numbed are we by exposure to such images that the more we see of them the less we react — nothing is so transitory as the frisson of distaste.

When the Chapmans dismantled, as it were, the zygotic mass in 1996 and reverted to the Siamese twins of their *Tragic Anatomies*, haunting creatures as furtive as deer set in the lush sub-tropical garden of the artificial pot plant, most of the irony was lost on most of the spectators; and when Saatchi exhibited them in his *Sensation* exhibition at the Royal Academy, compelled — as he was — to arrange the plants to conceal the genitals, the irony was altogether gone. Now, in 2003, when Saatchi is mounting a retrospective exhibition of the Chapmans' work in his own new gallery and he could have reconstructed this extensive piece as the artists intended it to be seen, not as a tableau but as figures with which visitors could mingle, he has merely repeated the Academy's presentation as a peep-show seen through an open door. This does not recover and renew the impact that it had seven years ago. Then we talked of shock; now we are inured to it. Goya shocked too when we first saw his work – but he shocks still.

And then, in 2000, came *Hell*. Gone was the life-size scale, gone the waxwork finish, gone the window-dressing reference, and in their stead we had nine tableaux in vitrines arranged in swastika formation. In each of these, hundreds of tiny figures are frozen in the apocalyptic finale of a World War, all lovingly engrossed in psychotic violence that embraces not only every act imagined in the Nazi concentration camps, but every act of cruelty devised by men from the crucifixion and impalement of antiquity to the blood-spattered torture chambers of Saddam Hussein, from the slow choking of piano-wire hangings reserved for those who attempted to betray Hitler's regime and the Japanese decapitations of prisoners of war, to the mass killing in south-east Asia and the Balkans that are fresher in our memories. Obsessively, determinedly, the Chapman Brothers spent more than two years dismantling model-makers' figures and, with fastidious attention to detail, reconstructing them so that they far exceeded the manufacturers' purposes. Often it is impossible to distinguish between victor and vanquished, tormentor, murderer and victim. The abiding sense is that roles have been reversed and will be interchanged again; with the passage of a minute it will be the brute who is without his trousers, he who is garotted, shot, decapitated and dismembered, he who is fresh flesh for vultures, he whose head is stuck upon a pole.

Astonishing though the variation is in these single figures – engaged in every conceivable act of a chaotic war, with the gloss of sadism and sodomy, leather chains and bondage, the ovens and the soap factory, the God-invoking and the hopelessness of surgery in field hospitals – it is the grand operatic scale and scope of the Chapmans' joint imagination that horrifies. Here the petty vision of the model railway fanatic is extended and transmogrified to trap in a glass box the cinematic gruesomeness of *Apocalypse Now*, the mass slaughters of the biblical, historical and recent past, the industrial disposal of unwanted people and their conversion into useful commodities. As in the opera house, it is the scene within the scene that gives the telling detail, while in the scene itself every member of the cast and chorus is on the stage to blast the audience.

Three years have passed since I first saw *Hell* and – unlike *Tragic Anatomies* – it is not one whit diminished in its impact, even though, wrongly reconstructed in the Saatchi Gallery, its inexorable logic is unforgivably disrupted. It should be in the rotunda there, but instead of its swastika layout, it is arranged in unequal blocks in the long transverse entrance room. The limitations of the Saatchi Collection's new premises are apparent too in the two rooms where the Chapman's spoofs of ethnic fetishes are appallingly displayed – as badly as though in a private provincial museum undisturbed since Livingstone's day. These pointed mockeries of McDonalds – of Christian missionaries and imposed American democracy too, as well as of all other forms of global commercialism – deserve, indeed need, to be free-standing and seen in the round in more sympathetic light.

Talking to the brothers, their disappointment with the insensitive and uncomprehending display of their work was evident – with the labels too, the texts of which plumb greater depths than the banalities of Tate Britain and Tate Modern. Of all the things of which Saatchi should be beware – and I wholly support him in his outburst against the bleak white cliché that is now the worldwide commonplace of gallery display – it is of the jabberwocky of the contemporary art world, for it belies his own innocent and impetuous enthusiasm.

Not entirely to my surprise I liked the brothers, sceptical about politics, religion and the art world, their sometimes solemn pessimism enlivened by a sense of mischief. Asked if their prize-winning contribution to the Royal Academy's Summer Exhibition this year had been, as it were, a Duchampian insult to that devious institution, they chuckled, confessed and went on to say that its President, with nod and wink, had told them that they will soon be elected Academicians. Astonishingly, they seem not to have recognised the Academy's capacity for unscrupulously exploiting anything that gives it free publicity – and giving the brothers its £25,000 prize for 'the most distinguished work' in the exhibition was an example of exactly that, for to the brothers their exhibit was a wilful affront to the institution and to the rest of us a test of its integrity. 'As Academicians, shall we,' they pondered, 'be Jake and Dinos Chapman RA, or RARA (which they fancy), or Jake RA and Dinos RA?' 'We have a problem too with the MBE and OBE,' murmured Dinos, 'though for myself I'd much prefer an HRH.'

Both have considered changing their name to Goya, so weary are they of the inevitable comparison. It would put an end to half the stuff written by the critics – they could hardly say that the Goyas are influenced by Goya. Weary too of being photographed with any of their zygotic images, they briskly remove themselves when they see a camera approach – 'Penises just excite editors – the photographs do nothing for the work or us.' They are burdened with a bad-boy reputation, yet they have moved so far from anything that justifies it that the later work is scarcely recognisable as coming from the same imaginations, the same hands, as the early root on which the present flower flourishes. The Chapmans are infinitely more various (the word Gainsborough used admiringly of Reynolds) than Hirst, more profound than Emin (not difficult) and, by far and over a far wider range, technically more skilled than both – I dare say that their recent etchings will eventually be judged a homage to Goya and at least the equal of any made by Klee.

There is in the brothers no hint of the aesthetic and intellectual exhaustion so evident in their contemporaries, nor the urge to turn aside from art, make films, run restaurants and succumb to the sad need to be celebrities, to expose and exploit their private lives.

They strike me as men with a firm philosophical base: the pessimism of Heraclitus and the humour of Democritus, artists who will do, not what their dealer wants, not what the public has been misled to expect, not what the gossip-mongers hope for, but what, as artists, they feel driven to do. They are that rare thing in our contemporary art world – genuine.

Jake & Dinos Chapman, Saatchi Gallery 2003

Tragic Anatomies: Doggy (1996)
http://www.saatchi-gallery.co.uk/artists/artpages/
jakedinos_chapman_doggy.htm

Tragic Anatomies: Fuck Face (1996)
http://www.saatchi-gallery.co.uk/artists/artpages/
jakedinos_chapman_fuck_face.htm

Hell (2000)
http://www.moolf.com/amazing/vision-of-hell-by-jake-and-dinos-
chapman.html
or
http://arts.guardian.co.uk/pictures/image/0,8543,-10804932875,00.html

The Chapman Brothers' Second Hell

WHITE CUBE SW1

Evening Standard, 6 June 2008

Hell has become *Fucking Hell. Hell*, you will recall, was the great last work of art of the twentieth century. Revealed in 2000, after two years of drudgery by Jake and Dinos Chapman and a legion of assistants, it was a summing-up of all the mass inhumanities of man to man since that century began with the Halcyon days of the Edwardian era. Its focus was on the Nazis and the solitary decade of their Thousand Year Reich, their exterminations and their Holocaust, but all-in-all it was a synecdochism standing for the First World War as well as the Second, for Stalin's purges of the rural peasantry and the Spanish Civil War, for the Sino-Japanese War and for Korea, Vietnam, Rwanda and the Balkans.

The nine vitrines in which 30,000 tiny figures performed their hideous guignols were placed in swastika formation to remind us of what we conventionally believe to have been the worst of these atrocities, but once, noses to the glass, we were engrossed, the logic of their sequence faded and each became a self-contained performance of minutely imagined horrors of advance, retreat, defeat and Armageddon. Every one of them was an *Apocalypse Now* seen from a viewpoint calculated to give each of us the sense of hovering low in a helicopter, helpless to help friend or foe in the mass of human figures struggling to flee, the dying mutilated in their death throes and the dead defiled. The nature of so many deaths, not merely from the accidents of war but from decapitation, flagellation, crucifixion and exsanguination from ingeniously lethal wounds, all deliberately inflicted in the Blitzkrieg of defeat, implied that in every single vitrine we had come upon the scene too late, that the monstrous, time-absorbing violence of vengeance had delayed withdrawal and that while a thousand desperate figures might still scramble to escape, others, resigned to the inevitability of their own deaths, meticulously engaged in the duty and enjoyment of inflicting inventive deaths on the few victims still left to nourish such a ghastly sense of purpose.

When this *Hell* was destroyed in the fire that in 2004 consumed the Momart warehouse in which it and so many other works of contemporary art were destroyed, my regret was profound. As a boy during the war of 1939–45, an addicted spender of pocket money in the News Cinema in Baker Street Station, I had been, at a remove, a witness of the events that inspired the Chapman Brothers, none more telling than film of the British Army's arrival at the Belsen Concentration Camp. The material seen then in black and white, seered into my visual memory, was powerfully evoked in colour by the Chapmans' operatic exaggerations of a past of which they themselves, born in the 1960s, can have had not even a remote experience. Quite how they became inspired, and quite what research they pursued to inform their inspiration, has not yet been revealed; critics have been far too anxious to root *Hell* either in the irrelevant history of the toy soldier (thus reducing its high seriousness), or in the equally irrelevant cod-philosophical jabberwocky of contemporary art theory, rather than ask the how and why of the Brothers' apparent obsession with a Götterdämmerung two generations after the event.

For me the how and why of it were vitally important, for my view of *Hell* was that when all the sharks have rotted, all the butterflies turned to dust and the Great Bed of Tracey been consumed by moth, the Chapman Brothers will be the only artists of their generation to deserve more than a wry footnote in the history of art.

Hell has now been re-born as *Fucking Hell* and can be seen at White Cube in Mason's Yard, an ideally bleak and oppressive torture chamber policed by many guards. *Hell* proved to be an exhaustible resource for *Fucking Hell*, for the latter not only expands the many narratives of the former but adds to them with tortures and torments so vile that I wonder what such imaginings may do to the Brothers, for in thinking of such things they have become the executioners and torturers. Have they acquired the indifference of the professional hangman who argued that his was only a job like any other? Have they, like workers in an abattoir, become inured to the fear and suffering of animals, even sneakily enjoying it? Or do dark demons lurk in the minds of Jake and Dinos, as I am certain that they did in Goya's brain? To what degree have their assistants in this great endeavour been affected by what they have had to replicate, vary or invent, for one might not unreasonably argue that much of *Fucking Hell* should have been beyond the imaginings of all but the most troubled minds? *Fucking Hell* employs the same idioms as *Hell*, the heads on poles, the gorging vultures, the Nazi uniforms and the conventional leather, bondage and other fetishes of sadism. The zygotic figures that most of us remember from the 1990s on a life-size scale as children siamesed together in variable, even multiple, conjugations, many of them suggesting two trunks permanently engaged in sodomy, standing on only one pair of legs, reappear in small, and so does one of the pre-historic monsters that stood in the forecourt of the Royal Academy a year ago, reduced to the size of a new-born newt. The model railway engines and the dinky Volks-wagens again play their parts as the vehicles to Hades instead of Charon's boat, and it seems that the Brothers, like Rubens and Ingres, discard nothing from their accumulated baggage of ideas, inventions and borrowings, never hesitating to re-use them.

But there are too, new ideas; I cannot recall a significant role for pigs in the earlier version, swine snuffling corpses (as they will), swine as beasts of burden, swine as substitutes for human victims (as in warfare and medicine they so often are), nor a role for horses; nor do I remember so much water, turbid with blood, through which to glimpse, tinged red, even more corpses and the detritus of war. The outstanding novelties are the inclusion of Anne Frank in her attic, Stephen Hawking ironically isolated on the tropical island of Dr Moron with zygotic women in bikinis, oblivious of the post-nuclear chaos all about him, and Adolf Hitler, not as Alexander the Great or the Duke of Wellington, but as an *à plein air* landscape painter, seeing not this landscape of the dead, but working on a canvas that depicts a peaceful Bavarian Bauernhaus at sunset of just the banal kind that he used to paint in watercolour.

Fucking Hell seems clearer than *Hell* in, if not definite references to great predecessors in the cult of the terrible, then at least to their digested influence. Behind these nine tableaux lie a myriad precedents reaching back to Greek antiquity, to the Pergamon Altar, to Roman Triumphs, to medieval Gates of Hell, to souls in Limbo and Hellfire, to the martyrdoms of saints – particularly to northern European depictions of the Ten Thousand Christian Soldiers crucified on Mount Ararat or thrown from its supposed peaks into the forests below, there to be cruelly pierced by the breaking branches of the trees on which they fell. Here are the *Bad Government* of Ambrogio Lorenzetti, the surging regiments of Altdorfer's great *Battle of Issus*, of Bruegel's *Triumph of Death* and *Suicide of Saul*, here are the fantasies of Bosch. Here are all the Hells of theological imagination, even of Michelangelo, brought into and beyond the killing fields of the twentieth century, beyond Warsaw and Stalingrad, beyond the Rape of Nanjing in which 100,000 Chinese civilians were massacred by Japanese troops, beyond Pol Pot's reign of terror, beyond the internecine slaughter of the former Yugoslavia.

Fucking Hell is not an elaborate toy for the Chamber of Horrors in Madame Tussaud's; it is instead an unrelentingly concentrated work of the imagination, a commentary on war to match any of the past, and if *Hell* was the greatest work of art made in Britain at the end of the last century, then *Fucking Hell* can claim to be far and away the best made so far in this.

Fucking Hell's Hitler as artist is the tenuous link to the very small section of the Chapmans' exhibition that gives it its title – *If Hitler*

Had Been a Hippy How Happy Would We Be. It consists of thirteen small (some very small) watercolours attributed to Hitler in the years 1908–14 when he hoped to become a professional artist and scratched a living in the pretence; one of them is improbably dated 1916 when, wounded, he was in hospital and away from the front line for the only time throughout the First World War. The Chapmans bought their collection as a parcel for a reputed £100,000 and have made them their own work through significant alterations and additions of which most are not easily identifiable.

Hitler's drawings have no value as works of art and only some distasteful value as curiosities or fetish objects; I should therefore argue that the Chapmans have increased their value, but in this I am confounded by near conviction that the originals are not by Hitler. I first saw his work in London in 1958 when no one would buy or sell it and, worthless, no one would forge it; during the Sixties I saw more of it in Munich and Vienna (exactly where it could be expected) and it was still worthless; all three batches were consistent in style and incompetent execution. I last saw a batch in Vienna in 1991, of the same consistent style, and by then a market for them had developed, sufficiently robust to make forgery or forged signatures worthwhile. Not one of the drawings exhibited at White Cube conforms to what I know of Hitler's work, nor are they stylistically consistent within the group. If they are not by Hitler, what was the point of the Brothers' interventions?

The third exhibit, on the ground floor – and I advise the visitor to see it last, for it will lighten the glooms of *Fucking Hell* – is a gathering of seventeen nineteenth-century portraits of dismal anonymity and provincial quality, dirty, damaged, punctured and unframed, bought for £10 each in boot sales. The Brothers have reworked them, their interventions technically subtle in that the division between old paint and new is far from immediately obvious and these once complacent middle-class sitters are now convincingly disfigured. I suspect that Jake and Dinos had some fun consulting textbooks on maxillofacial surgery, so frightful are their improvements – but amusing too, as they brighten the eyes with cat-like replacements, widen the smiles to accommodate a thousand teeth, elongate the noses to dissolve in snot or burn them off to leave a charcoal scar. The lips of one unfortunate woman are stitched together (a mistranslation of de Sade, perhaps?), another is a cross between a werewolf and St Wilgefortis Uncumber, the original bearded lady, and the skin disfigurements are vile. All this is, of course, no more serious than painting spectacle frames on the Mona Lisa, but even so, I wish I'd thought of it myself.

The Chapman Brothers' Second Hell, White Cube SW1 2008
http://www.jakeanddinoschapman.com/exhibitions/hippy-hitler

Tony Cragg

WHITECHAPEL GALLERY

Evening Standard, 23 January 1997

The Whitechapel Gallery is, to anything pretending to be a work of art, the most flattering space in London. The architecture of the lower room is irregular, anonymous, unselfconscious and retiring, and yet, by means of which the visitor is unaware, he is welcomed and drawn in. He senses an underlying proportion and geometry in the simple interlock of cubic spaces, opening a vista from door to the far wall, the divisions marked, as it were, only by subtle variations in the intensity of light and the directions of its fall. With nothing in this room, it, the space and the light are beautiful; with masterpieces on view, both they and the room are heightened in effect; and so effortless are its enchantments that even the second-rate and worse (common enough in Whitechapel) are lifted beyond their ordinary limits and made to seem considerable. So it is with the sculpture of Tony Cragg which, in essence, offers nothing more than the demanding decorative whimsy of clever window-dressing, and would do very well for Harvey Nicks or Harrods.

The work of Tony Cragg, winner of the Turner Prize in 1988, has not been seen in large in any public London gallery since the Tate's celebration of that event with a sad little exhibition of symbolic works – sad because the faint indication of promise that some of us had sensed in the very latest sculpture included in the much larger exhibition at the Hayward Gallery in 1987, seemed already to have evaporated. In that show it appeared that a new maturity was at last emerging among the confusions of ill-digested borrowing from hither and yon, the haphazard inspirations carried through in trial and error, and the schoolboy whimsies from which, with prodigious productivity, Cragg contrived his various floor pieces, installations, and what it is now fashionable to call 'object-based sculpture'. Now, ten years on, in Whitechapel, we have the opportunity to judge whether that briefly glimpsed maturity was real or a mirage amongst the rubbish, and see whether the ageing *enfant terrible* has indeed abandoned the pretentious provocations of his long student years in favour of greater intellectual rigour and self-criticism.

Richard Cork, Arts Council panjandrum off and on for ever, so it seems, and one of the judges who awarded him the Turner Prize, has described the sculpture of Cragg in this exhibition as on a par with Michelangelo. It seems that critics specialising in contemporary art now have a historical perspective of no more than five years; they have, one supposes, a cut-off valve in their memories, enabling them to hail as great, new, shatteringly iconoclastic, boundary-breaking, barrier-leaping and utterly innovative, everything that the rest of us have seen many times before and, lacking that valve, remember. In the case of Cragg it has functioned very well, for by limiting the years covered by this exhibition to 1990–6, the organisers present us with a show of work that they believe, no doubt, to be of recent invention as well as recent manufacture, everything seen in the 1987 show (a decade being twice the length of memory) conveniently forgotten. The work on view, however, is new neither in spirit nor in idiom, but is all reversion, self-cannibalism and hack repetition in image and material. When today's art students exhibit lavatory pans as works of art, we can tell them that we've seen it all before, but to Cragg we can say not only that he has done it all before, but that it is not one jot improved in the re-hashing.

Born in 1949, Cragg's earliest ambitions were to be a farmer or a sailor, but he spent his late adolescence as a laboratory technician in rubber research, before becoming an art student in 1968, and remaining one for nine years. As a student he exhibited pieces of crushed rubble and stacks of discarded rubbish in the galleries of fashionable dealers, and was given an MA by the Royal College. By the early Eighties he had a pan-European reputation as a sculptor working in 'non–art materials that one could claim for art' – shards of bright plastic crockery for wall drawings, broken furniture, building materials, driftwood, stones, shattered glass, assemblages of tools, boxes, saucepans and other household objects, and indeed anything that readily came to hand or foot, as long as it cost nothing and was not the conventional stuff of sculpture. These *objets trouvés*, which a generation earlier might have been used to stimulate their translation into art, themselves became art, though Cragg occasionally coated their surfaces with alien particles of plastic, both to reduce them to material anonymity and thus concentrate on shape and volume, and to give them a disturbing hint of Surrealism.

As he moved away (though not very far) from the childish affront of asserting that this and that are art because he said so (he called this 'a time of heroic gesture'), and became interested in rotundity and volume, he developed a taste for the forms of urns and vases, and, like the very earliest potters on the wheel, discovered anthropomorphic implications, at the same time, with rings of texture or colour, emphatically asserting the pottery origin of the conceit. He cast urns in white plaster on a monumental scale, disposed them in compositions with ancillary props, and for no good reason drilled close regular patterns of deep holes in them. He took to sandblasting the gloss from glass bottles, and assembling them in posses on the floor. The pestle, mortar, retort and other glass containers of the alchemist then came into play, as did the plumbing of the main drain and the air–conditioning system, and with the rings, hubs, cogs and wheels of industrial machinery piled high, he invented spires fit for fantastic gothic churches.

It all seemed ingenious, and still does, but art must surely be more than mere ingenuity? Now, with so much repetition so much later, it seems little more than the safe exploitation of proven formulae that will find unquestioning support among those of the

Serota Tendency and the Arts Council. The name *Administered Landscape* given to an assembly of giant rubber stamps cast in beeswax, lends it the momentary humour of a newspaper cartoon, but it very soon wears thin and has all but lost its point in *Sub-committee*, a bronze variation on the theme. It is, perhaps, amusing to screw hooks and eyes into old furniture and a piano so densely that they seem as whiskered as a mouldering carrot forgotten in the fridge – but at base this is schoolboy whimsy, not the imagination of a wise and world-weary adult, and Cragg is all but fifty.

The one sculpture that seems in any way fresh in idea and manufacture is *Boy*, of 1996, but even this is a reversion to Cragg's youth in a world of rubber, for in colour and texture it resembles, gigantic though it is, nothing so much as a floppily inflated condom, even to the teat end, twisted here and there to make it swell and bulge. Some may argue that *Secretions*, too, is new, because it is covered with a mosaic of thousands of large dice, but its underlying forms in styrofoam and fibreglass we have seen many times before, smaller and cast in metal, and they are not improved by inflation and the ingenious (but here and there ill-fitting) carapace.

'The most renowned British sculptor of his generation?' A modern Michelangelo? A leading member of a new Renaissance? What nonsense critics and curators talk, seduced, no doubt, by the beauty of the Gallery.

Michael Craig-Martin

WHITECHAPEL GALLERY

Evening Standard, 30 November 1989

In the months of theological dispute that prepared me for my Confirmation, the two prime problems with which I had to contend were the rampant sexual nature of the adolescent boy that seems so much at odds with the spirituality required of him for this occasion, and the vexing question of the Transubstantiation of the Host. No matter how much I wanted to believe that through the ritual words the wafer and the wine became the real body and blood of Christ, I could not. Confessing to my parish priest, I received advice by which I still abide – 'Bring everything to the bar of your own judgement.' It seemed a trifle sibylline at the time, but it not only allowed me to accept religious observance as a discipline full of hope but it opened the door to the agnosticism that eventually overwhelmed the will to believe.

I regret my departure from the church, but no other course was intellectually justifiable. Bound with that regret is a deep respect for those to whom the observances of the church present no dilemma, and the sense that their beliefs are to be protected and nurtured even by outsiders.

This must seem an irrelevant beginning to the review of an art exhibition, but it explains the rage that informs my response to the pranks, whimsies and pretentious assertions of Michael Craig-Martin and his absurd apologists. Craig-Martin, recently appointed a Trustee of the Tate Gallery (and very much the shape of things to come in that benighted institution), is the subject of a retrospective exhibition at the Whitechapel Gallery. He is forty-eight, was born in Dublin, educated in America, and has lived in England more or less continuously for the last twenty years or so.

He is a Conceptual artist. His most notorious work is a glass of water accompanied by a text asserting that it is an oak tree. 'It's not a symbol,' he maintains, 'I've changed the physical substance of the glass of water into that of an oak tree . . . the actual oak tree is physically present, but in the form of a glass of water.' Congratulatory critics see in this a parallel to the mystical performance of the priest at Mass, and with this Craig-Martin concurs. I see it as a blasphemy.

Q: When precisely did the glass of water become an oak tree?

A: When I put water in the glass.

Q: Does this happen every time you fill a glass with water?

A: No, of course not. Only when I intend to change it into an oak tree.

Q: Do you consider that changing the glass of water into an oak tree constitutes an artwork?

A: Yes.

Craig-Martin maintains that art can be found anywhere and made of anything – he merely has to assert that the contents of his chamber-pot constitute a landscape and the Whitechapel Gallery will put them on view in the odour of sanctity. Perhaps he should add that by his tokens art can be made by anybody, and if he regrets and resents 'the destruction of art education under the present Government' (as he does), then he has only himself and other teachers of his ilk to blame for the Government's hostility to art.

The Whitechapel Gallery looks like a barn or garage half prepared for a bring-and-buy sale or a country dance, with uncomfortable wooden boxes for seats and a row of trestle tables waiting for refreshments; on the walls are reminders of another function – the counterweights of up-and-over doors, clipboards on hooks, pencils hanging from strings, glass shelves with tins of paint and brushes, milk bottles partly filled with water (shades of the glass harmonica), galvanised steel buckets, spaghetti trails of wire to a neon arrow pointing to a lavatory, and bits of mirror in which the garage hands may amend their Mohican hair.

Alas, the Gallery is not waiting for the ancient worthies of the

Women's Institute to arrive with jams, jellies and an overgrown leek – everything that is standing on the floor or hanging on the walls is a work of art.

We may recognise most of it as bought from MFI, B&Q, Do-it-All and Texas Home Care, but because the purchaser was Craig-Martin, we are compelled by this self-declared artist to perceive these banal objects as works of art, and himself the intellectual equal of Michelangelo (to whom he bears as much comparison as do the execrable Beatles to Hindemith and Beethoven).

By those who contribute essays to the catalogue this exhibition is recognised as a religious experience. They assure us that only civilised human intelligence can grapple with the dilemmas of Craig-Martin's work, and that 'a conscious reconstruction of the self (of the spectator) as a responding participatory subject' follows from this grappling. They tell us that plain wooden boxes of which the lids do not fit or close are thus established as works of art, that the clipboards 'disengaged' Craig-Martin from making sculpture, that his outline drawings in narrow sticky tape are disembodied, ambiguous, and have 'a resonant presence but no actuality', and that his games with little bits of mirror are a match for the complex mysteries of Velázquez's *Las Meninas*. The *Laudate Dominum* reaches a climax when this bulk purchaser of buckets, bottles, blank canvases and Venetian blinds is described as an 'elegant fastidious wit' and the author of work that 'galvanises faith and through it restores a sense of wonder'.

Faith and wonder play no part in this arid exercise in implausible cod philosophy, to which scorn, contempt and sad astonishment that any of it could ever have been seen as art, are the reasonable responses. Some of Craig-Martin's visual trickery might be amusing in the Human Biology rooms of the Natural History Museum; some of his clipboard sequences might be useful as therapy for patients recovering from strokes; given an acorn, even the glass of water might make sense as a botany lesson for infants; but as an artist he deserves only derision.

Tracey Emin

HAYWARD GALLERY

Evening Standard, 19 May 2011

A lazy journalist might inform his readers that Tracey Emin's exhibition at the Hayward Gallery has for many months been eagerly awaited. A scrupulous art critic, on the other hand, must admit that it was with a groan that he greeted the first news of it, with a groan that he read the subsequent press releases and premature ejaculatory articles, and with a groan that he wandered through this retrospective celebration of unmediated autobiographical relics and self centred sentimentality. In the years since Charles Saatchi brought her to the fore in his *Sensation* show at the Royal Academy in 1997, I have said very little of Miss Emin; at that he exhibited her Tent to the interior of which she had patchworked the names of *Everyone I have ever slept with*, a thing of puerile simplicity, and two years later he acquired the tumbled bed that was her notorious installation for the Turner Prize, a squalid relic of concupiscence and misery reconstructed in self-pity. Neither had much to do with art, both justified my contempt for the paradings of herself that were the works of her earlier hang-out years promoted by Jay Jopling, and I thought that even our insane contemporary art world would have enough common sense to let her fade into obscurity. When she did not, but instead became, largely through the amused but sceptical interest of the popular press a very public figure, I dubbed her art's Jade Goody, seeing kinship not only in wretched background, but in their cunning exploitation of ignorance, irascible emotion and raw sex to draw attention to themselves. In unholy symbiosis, the more Miss Emin played the drunken slut, the more attention the press paid and the more she became the creature of the art establishment, nationally and internationally, promoted by the Serota Tendency (ever Mammon's mate) and the Arts and British Councils, with Jay Jopling ensconced in his White Cube quietly making fortunes for himself and her. It was, and is still, an unspoken but consensual conspiracy.

Now held in awe by men as sage, sibyl and Margate's thaumaturge, women, I am told, see her as some sort of heroic victim, raped as a child, ravaged as a teenager, sweetly sentimental towards her miserable self, yet still full of longing for the status of adored princess (part fairy tale, part working-class mythology) and still in need of the adulation and attention of men. Two such women are to give talks during the course of the exhibition and have contributed essays to the catalogue. Half way through hers, Jennifer Doyle, a Californian professor of literature and gender studies, is so moved by her exploration of abortion (twice Miss Emin's experience – '1992 Became pregnant again – had another abortion – didn't give a damn. Just did it – dealt with it without heart.'), the sweetness of children, the tenderness of mothering, the body in trauma and the emotions in revolt, that Miss Emin fades from her narrative and is replaced by Miss Doyle herself. Perhaps, however, this is exactly what Miss Emin sets out to achieve with her wearisome concern for her body and emotions – the requirement that all women should respond to her abject predicaments with such powerful but essentially feminine empathy that by transference they assume Miss Emin's miserable self-concern.

This is all very well, but it eliminates half her potential audience. As a man, I do not feel excluded from the distress of Madame Bovary, Madame Butterfly, Louise, Violetta or Isolde, but as a witness of Miss Emin's self-examination I remain an uninvolved outsider and feel not the slightest sympathy. When asked by a *Guardian* interviewer with whom I would least like to be trapped in a lift, I answered 'Tracey Emin with a full bladder,' for I knew from her many drawings that she would not hesitate to empty it without a thought of modesty, but in truth I feel nothing for her relaxations of that sphincter, nothing for her masturbation, nothing for her sexual conjugations, nothing for her abortions and nothing for her current apparently denatured state of dry old stick no longer capable of bearing children. I am utterly unmoved by all the means that she ineptly employs to mirror or narrate her various experiences; her silly patchwork blankets, her feeble scratchy monoprints and drawings, her Kodak Brownie photographs, her neon signs, videos and records of futile live performances, and her variations on the shed I see only as clear evidence of an arrested infantile craving for the aedicule – she should indeed have seen a psychiatrist in 1981, as was advised when she dropped out of the Medway College of Design.

I do not recognise the almost mystical status conferred on her as an artist whose life, art and being are so interrelated as to be inseparable (surely the case too with every artist of any weight), when her life and being so greatly outweigh the very little that might (but only with extreme generosity) perhaps be classified as art. Being Miss Emin is her core activity, 'Look at me, look at me!' she whines to get an audience, and then, like some fraudulent medieval marketeer of relics, she gulls us into venerating the trivial keepsakes of herself that she now exhibits in glass cases.

The other woman contributor to the catalogue, the writer Ali Smith, whose essay was reprinted on two whole pages of the *Guardian* ten days before the exhibition opened, promotes Miss Emin as a major literary figure 'really good with words', her misspellings, as with PICASO, offering 'a whole new possibility of the notion of Picasso . . . the missing letter makes you look twice . . . ' If her essay demonstrates anything – apart from the folly of encouraging writers who know nothing of art to write ekphrastic bilge – it is that Miss Emin likes to be frank with words that are, for the moment, largely not to be said or printed in polite society. To some extent I agree – I have in the past written in favour of *fuck* as verb and noun, its loveless, selfish, gleeful and trophy note so much more truthful than the common euphemisms; and I am inclined to argue for *cunt* in the context of Lucian Freud, again because it is more fitting for his blunt and loveless imagery, with nothing of the coyness of Augustus John's Romany references to *cunnie*; but Miss Emin seems to employ the word for the small shock value that it may still have.

Is any of us now really shocked by MY CUNT IS WET WITH FEAR, a neon sign that can only have meaning over the door of a brothel, or by *A Rose is a Cunt is a Rose* (a play on a cunt by any other name), a carefully posed photograph of Miss Emin enthralling us with legs wide apart stuffing banknotes into her vagina? For this there is a classical precedent in that Danaë, consequently mother of Perseus, was seduced by Zeus metamorphosed into a shower of gold – a not uncommon subject in Renaissance painting, an allegory of prostitution and an opportunity for mild pornography tinged with wry male humour – but as Miss Emin shows no evidence of education, it is to be doubted that she knows of it and the kinship of imagery is mere coincidence. Blake, Van Gogh, Munch and Klimt have been claimed as her antecedents, but I doubt if she knows in any depth anything of the arts and cultures of the past that, until a century ago, used to inform the arts and cultures of the present. But to return to *cunt*, surely D. H. Lawrence, if his use of it in *Lady Chatterley's Lover* failed to elevate it into the polite conversation of our grandparents in 1928, must posthumously have inspired its resurrection after the famous obscenity trial of 1960, when the literary lions of England closed ranks against the censor; when in 1977, two decades before Miss Emin's scattering it hither and yon, Gilbert and George trounced the taboo with their *Dirty Words Pictures*, hardly an eyebrow moved.

The last words of Miss Emin's interview with Ralph Rugoff, Director of the Hayward Gallery, are 'What's it all about? What am I doing? And I'm still asking those questions now.' And so are we. How has it been possible for Miss Emin, once notoriously drunk and abusive, formerly 'Mad Tracey from Margate', now moaning with self-pity, to have become, as the Hayward's panjandrums put it, one of this country's 'most renowned and celebrated artists'? How have our definitions of art, and even more preposterously, sculpture, been so elastic as to include crudely patchworked blankets, crude images of bladder-emptying, masturbation and abortion, crude neon messages to FUCK OFF AND DIE YOU SLAG or PEOPLE LIKE YOU NEED TO FUCK PEOPLE LIKE ME, and crude life-size dilapidations of the beach hut? Far from being 'really good with words', she is illiterate, witless, turns the alphabet topsy-turvy and employs the language of graffiti boys. Miss Emin's words and images, laden with catharsis, are less art than bullying demands for empathy.

Skill, if she ever had any, has been usurped by celebrity; celebrity has been nourished by deliberate outrage and offence; and now, in the constant public parading of private distress, she has developed a tiresome arrogance that conflicts with what is left of the instinctive self-abjection that has always been her home-made muse. The title of her retrospective, so tediously repetitious that neither shock nor distaste survives it, is *Love is what you want*, its emblem a neon sign with these words contained within a heart, bathetic, silly, sentimental, the stuff of the teenage girl besotted with boy bands rather than the serious business we might reasonably expect of a famous woman of forty-eight. Weighed down with self-expression, producing it has, no doubt, been therapeutic for Miss Emin, and we, simple wanderers through the circles of her hell, now know the answer to her question 'What's it all about?' You, dear Miss Emin, you – but you have never been enough.

Tracey Emin, Hayward Gallery 2011

http://www.guardian.co.uk/artanddesign/gallery/2011/may/16/tracey-
emin-exhibition-hayward-gallery?INTCMP=
ILCNETTXT3487#/?picture=374654163&index=0

Lucian Freud

TATE BRITAIN

Evening Standard, 21 June 2002

It is with a heavy sense of duty rather than enthusiasm that I write, yet again, of Lucian Freud, no Michelangelo, no Rembrandt. For more than fifty years – since the Festival of Britain in 1951, to be precise – I have been aware of him, increasingly intensely, if my bookshelves are a record of my interest, since 1972, when, at the age of fifty, he deserted the Marlborough Gallery for Anthony d'Offay's more lively efforts as a dealer. There was a whiff of excitement about that change, something of the scandal of a celebrity divorce – though Freud was not then nearly so well known as now – and though he later deserted d'Offay too, it cannot have been mere chance that with that dealer nurturing the market for his work, together with his professional eminence, his private persona leaped into the public eye. Exhibitions burgeoned, the first enthusiastic retrospective was given him by the Arts Council in 1974, international and transatlantic interest accelerated, and writers, few qualified to comment, began to take him to their bosoms.

He has been their subject ever since and the current exhibition has for past weeks engendered orgasm in the broadsheets. Over the past thirty years Freud has been mad, bad and dangerous to know. His pictures pitiless, ambiguous, violent and aggressive, he has been a man of twilight lives between the gutter and the Ritz, mixing with the most rich and socially eminent, yet a man of privacy and mystery whose telephone number no one knows, and who inhabits houses without doorbells, flitting like Dracula from one to t'other, to work on sleeping models through the night. He is as Bohemian as Puccini, as much a ruffian as Caravaggio (I once witnessed his stealing a girl from Peter Langan without plunging a dagger into that clumsy lecher's groin), and as much a creature of the ivory tower as Vermeer. All this lends gloss to his pictures and pushes up the price – the truth is probably much less fabulous.

What I have said of Freud in reviews of other exhibitions I must say again in this, for though Tate Britain concludes its retrospective with some very recent pictures, they provoke nothing new to say of him, for all the flaws of drawing and construction, the angles of vision, the tricks, quirks, mannerisms and subjects were more or less established forty years ago and have developed only in the size of canvases and the thickness and opacity of paint. He is still the painter that he was at previous retrospectives, still the painter of successive exhibitions devoted to then recent work. There must be, however, a new young audience since the British Council retrospective of 1988, and just as those who arrange the programmes at the Proms should remember that, no matter how familiar Mozart and Beethoven must seem to them, to the young they may be thrillingly new, so the weary art critic must think of Freud and be prepared to reinterpret him.

A minor painter, a footnote in the history of art, Freud is, and always has been, 'capable of producing horrible paintings' – as Grey Gowrie, an aesthetic polymath writing for *Modern Painters* (that most influential of art magazines), put it some years ago – and horrible paintings a-plenty dominate this exhibition, oppressive to the visitor. It is, nevertheless, his biggest and most important retrospective yet, with more than 150 exhibits spanning the more than sixty years that reach from his late schooldays to the present.

Born in Berlin in December 1922, the grandson of Sigmund Freud, Lucian came with his family to England in 1933, was educated at Dartington Hall (an expensive private school for intelligent delinquents, with the American Mark Tobey, a dramatic draughtsman of the nude, as art master) and Bryanston (a conventional public school), and was naturalised in 1939. He studied at the Central School of Art and, at Dedham and Hadleigh, with Cedric Morris, an eccentric old dear whose relish for thick dabs and stabs of paint is still, in Freud's dotage, evident. From 1942 to 1944 he attended Goldsmith's School, largely to draw from the live model, encouraged to do so by Graham Sutherland and Peter Watson, his first patron. Though his work was tentatively exhibited as early as 1942, the year in which he was introduced to John Craxton, an equally young but better trained and more experienced artist under whose tutelage he began to mature, it was not until a decade or so later that he began to emerge as a painter whose style and vision were in any way distinct. Thereafter, 'preoccupied with a kind of painting now widely regarded as disreputable' — the comment of a distinguished critic in 1965 — his life was an unremarkable slog until d'Offay took him in hand in 1972.

Those of us who know something of the painters fashionable in Berlin when Freud was a child and perceive their influence in his very early work, are damned as 'aesthetic weasels' by the author of Tate Britain's catalogue. The fact remains, however, that the early work resembles nothing that he could have seen in England and is redolent of the fierce caricatures of Otto Dix, the stylish linear quality of Hubbuch and Schad and, particularly, the flat, dry glooms of Lenk who had five one-man shows in Berlin between 1929 and 1933, and took part in twenty-eight mixed shows in that period. Freud was only ten when he left Berlin but if he was as precocious and proficient a draughtsman as he claims, he may well have been aware of so popular and much reviewed a painter — I, at that age, was well aware of Dürer and Murillo.

I am content to be an 'aesthetic weasel' for another reason; when Lawrence Gowing wrote his slim and illuminating book on Freud in 1982, much based on conversations with the master, he told me that beyond recalling his childhood home to have been hung with woodcuts by Hokusai and that his grandfather, Sigmund, had given him reproductions of Bruegel's *Seasons*, Lucian absolutely refused to discuss all other possibilities of influence and thus 'We know nothing of how it was that by 1933 . . . Lucian was drawing all the time.' In dismissing this early chapter of his life and in glossing over the years in which his close relationship with Craxton was so significant (there are common drawings in which their lines are indistinguishable), Freud the myth-maker, preferring the image of the self-made artist, has reconstructed his biography.

The lurking presence of Craxton in Freud's work was much diminished by 1950, replaced by paint as thin and pale as tempera, the planes of modelling conscientiously constructed with delicate strokes of small brushes, engagingly finicky on a small scale, laborious on a large canvas. In *Interior in Paddington*, his Festival of Britain commission from the Arts Council, the walls and carpet must have taken infinite patience in their dry similitude; the yucca too is dry, dying unwatered in its cracked pot, an eerie and cruel monument of diligent observation. The high point of his transition from essaying amateur to austere professional is embodied in this picture, and though it is very different from his later work, a period with the clearest demarcations, it shares with them one constant – that Freud is a painter without imagination, a painter utterly dependent on whatever is under his nose and the perspective sweep through which he sees it. This perspective sweep, short-sighted, explains all the distortions and disruptions of his sense of space, all the disjunctions and distortions of his naked bodies.

In the mid-Fifties Freud moved on to a broader manner, the underlying work still delicate, but the surfaces and modelling disrupted by unrelated fatter dabs of paint, as though he had to reassure himself that he was a painter, not a dexterous embroiderer. By the beginning of the Sixties his technique had broadened further, the delicacy gone, replaced by broad gestural sweeps of hog-bristle brushes that left their mark with every lazy stroke, and the iconography of the portrait in all his favourite forms tentatively established.

After this his mannerisms became a matter of thick paint or thin, high viewpoint or low, drawing not quite bad enough to be noticed, and drawing so bad that the spectator could see nothing else – Freud indeed bids fair to be the worst important draughtsman of the later twentieth century. As a painter he occasionally reverted to earlier ideas, as in the portrait of himself seen through the leaves of another yucca minutely observed, and in a jug of buttercups, the background of both as delicate as tempera, but gradually such subjects were overwhelmed by ugly and contorted female nudes, the ugly ugly in themselves, the pretty deliberately uglified, the modelling as wooden as a broomstick, the brushstrokes running with perceived form rather than constructing it, the genital obsession mounting in importance as his focus. When the male nude entered his iconography it became, and remains, evident that he cannot solve the intellectual and aesthetic problem of including testicles and penis, specifically depicted, without letting them compete for attention with the face and, often, dominate the canvas. The most sensitive and desirable painting of the monstrous Leigh Bowery is not of the two hundredweight of lardy flesh, nor the study of the proportionate penis that went with it, but the tiny canvas of his head, much the same size as the notorious portrait of the Queen and infinitely more successful. Women are his trophies; in his paintings of men he mixes rapport with the curiosity of the locker-room. His finest portraits are invariably of himself; the early examples are posed to conceal rather than reveal; in the later, the paint, thick and deeply troubled by reworking as he struggled to arrive at a truth acceptable to his self-esteem, he is an ancient hero, an Odysseus returned to Ithaca.

By the standards of today, Freud is a great painter, his handling of paint painterly, the scale of his figures old masterly, but if we think of his pictures in the context of Rembrandt, Hals, Rubens, Velázquez, Titian and Goya, and his obsessional interest in female genitals in the context of Rodin, Courbet and Degas, he is indeed no more than yet another footnote in the history of art. This is a melancholy exhibition, but we must be grateful for it; against the tides of fashion, hard edge, soft edge, bucket and slosh, and against the slough of abject art in which the body fluids and faecal matter of the artist are his base materials, in Freud lies the only evidence that the Serota Tendency has any respect for ancestral figure painting. He approaches eighty; who will take up the baton when he dies?

Lucian Freud, Tate Britain 2002
Room guide, contains paintings of each room in the exhibition:
http://www.tate.org.uk/whats-on/tate-britain/exhibition/lucian-freud/
lucian-freud-room-guide

Lucian Freud

THE WALLACE COLLECTION

Evening Standard, 16 April 2004

My notes on Lucian Freud's current exhibition are headed 'Freud in the WC', by which is meant the Wallace Collection rather than the water closet – and yet, by chance, there is an odd accuracy in the confusion, for it is an exhibition of much raw and uncomely nakedness. Freud has not trodden where Tracey Emin and Picasso dared to tread with the emptying of bladders, but he has inexorably moved towards an imagery of the human form, both male and female, that is stripped of sensuality, of warmth and comfort and tactility, and certainly of self-regard. These naked bodies lie on beds that they were never in; no sheet warmed by their flesh has been thrown aside – the bed in every case is merely a support for poses that speak of nothing immediately past and nothing in the immediate future.

These are pictures of an empty present, the human figures reduced to the unloved objects required daily by an unloving painter who is as much driven to paint as a vampire is compelled to suck life-blood from his victims.

Freud is, of course, the greatest living painter, magisterial – a claim made so often by silly interviewers claiming to have been granted exclusive interviews that even he and David Hockney now believe it, and art critics repeat it as the mantra of the day. One of these last, a man who has turned curating Freud into his particular cottage industry, compares the old boy's current work with the late quartets of Beethoven – the perfect shibboleth, for we all know that these are unquestionably wonderful, extending the medium, expressing mystical exaltation (were Freud's pictures more lyrical in subject and happier in mood, the comparison might well have been instead with Verdi's *Falstaff*). Another critic, less adventurous, falls back on the convention of the roll of great earlier painters to whom we habitually bend the knee – Freud, it seems, shares a 'precious quota of awkwardness,' with Van Gogh, Cézanne, Matisse; Constable and Corot, with Courbet, of whom more anon, with Rembrandt, Hals, Titian and Watteau; and some years ago, at the Dulwich Picture Gallery, the comparison was made with Rubens. Sharing the same breath with these, Freud immediately becomes their equal in the blind scales of greatness; say 'great' of him often enough and not one of the mass of us will dare to question it.

I persuade myself that visitors to the El Greco exhibition in the National Gallery are there to question as much as to revere, to resolve the puzzles of elongation and distortion by taking the intended positions of paintings into account and the consequent perspective, as well as the emotional requirements of their narratives, to be the intellectual equivalent of ratting terriers with rotten pictures and spiritually exalted by the best – in short, to see, analyse and understand. But that is not what I witnessed at the Freud exhibition in the Wallace Collection.

Let me explain the circumstances there. One of the rooms that for a century or so has been hung with old Dutch paintings of the cabinet kind, has been cleared of these and, in their stead, it is hung with Freud's productions of the last two years or so, the very latest still drying on their canvases. They are destined for Freud's dealer in New York and there can be no doubt that their having been exhibited in the Wallace Collection to a plethora of adulatory reviews will increase the pressure on demand and inflate the prices – for a common dealer to be able to write in his catalogue (on sale in the WC for £15, but free to his clients) that his stock has been flown in from 'one of the greatest repositories of old master paintings in the world', must in every case be worth much more than the odd dollar.

We are led to believe that this exhibition has come about through grace and favour, that Freud was anxious that the great British public should not be denied the opportunity to see the latest work of the greatest British painter before it is utterly lost to the shekels of Mammon in New York. There is grace and favour too in the Wallace Collection's showing it, breaking all the traditions, even the rules, of the institution in disturbing the permanent collection – but then Freud perhaps insisted on this, rather than the poky temporary exhibition rooms downstairs, as proof of his 'long-standing affection for the Wallace Collection'. At this prospect the eximious directrice, Rosalind Savill, no doubt behaved like a Labrador puppy having her tummy tickled; she should beware of Freud's reward, the suggestion that he might paint her next, for she too will be just another unloved slab of ample flesh displayed on unwarmed sheets.

Positioning the exhibition so has, in their circulation, resulted in a gross interruption of the galleries, for so many visitors want to see the Freuds and care not a damn for the permanent collection that they queue to get into the room like sheep waiting to be dipped. Once in, they slip into the trance-like state of visitors to the Rothko room in Tate Modern and, as Roger Fry once put it, vibrate in harmony with the exhibits – and very little could be more ridiculous than a gaggle of white-haired readers of *The Oldie* transported into Never-Neverland by contemplation of the more than life-size penis and raw red testicles of David Dawson, Freud's once sheep-farming model and assistant.

The proper response to this exhibition is not awe, not reverence, not veneration, but melancholy – melancholy that a man who throughout his long working life has shown flickers of promise among much dross, should now show none. In his earlier seventies Freud painted interestingly enough and with occasional fumbling insights to suggest that by twice that age he might become a consistently and modestly good painter; but now it is clear that, even if he were to match Methuselah in years, this can never be so.

Far from being at the top of his form, these are among the worst pictures that he has ever painted. How is it that men and women who earn their livings as art critics are so blinded by his celebrity that they cannot see what an unself-critical old blunderer he has become, that he cannot draw, that he has lost what little eye he had for composition, that he has abandoned all interest in space, proportion and perspective, and that with his curdled and murky paint he drifts from small frenzies of acned detail into small acres filled with the dead long strokes of the lazy man who has lost interest.

For the past two decades or so Freud has been only partly interested in what he paints and even in the initial drawing has rarely been able to sustain coherence in the subject as a whole — even with quite small canvases. He has almost managed to keep control in the portrait of his friend, Andrew Parker-Bowles, fussing thickly over the face, the hands, the braided cuffs and collar, the medals and, to a lesser extent, the feet — all pockets of interest and absorption distributed about the canvas in much the same way as an abstract painter might lend interest to the surface of a picture by varying the nature of his stroke — and the uniform of the Household Cavalry has proved a useful camouflage for what would have been the bored and boring treatment of the long legs had they been naked. But the sceptic must surely see how crude and coarse the details are, how clumsy the corrections and adjustments, how Freud's courtiers mistake crass fudging for bravura. Do the Brigadier's eyes really look in different directions?

In *The Irishwoman on a Bed*, bare legs, absurdly elongated, bridge two thirds of the canvas, paint dragged along their wooden lengths, silhouetting lines defining their limits, not their form — indeed their form is utterly abandoned and they are unconnected afterthoughts to the torso to which they barely belong — this is Freud at his downright laziest, at his most vain too if he cannot see how obtrusively bad it is. With the legs of David Dawson there appears at first glance to have been some effort on Freud's part to suggest bone, musculature and overall form but, at second glance, the dabs of paint, unrelated and misleading, break down into incoherence — desperate dabs and nothing more.

To put no fine point on it, this is an exhibition of wretched pictures by a vain man incapable of self-criticism. He can, it seems, talk persuasively of his own cleverness and can convince his interviewers that he is sensitive to imperceptibly subtle changes in the unfortunates who are his subjects when they have 'eaten different things, read different books, woken with a different person in a different bed . . . ;' he even sees a common hen's egg as so individual that he claims to have painted a clutch as four portraits quite distinct — and if that is so, then he should bother himself to look at the still lives of Eliot Hodgkin and bow his head in embarrassment. I do not believe a word of his boasting. I see only a man who can no longer draw, who will not see when he has made a mess of things, whose brushwork is predominantly crude and whose paint, a material for the translucent and subtle qualities of which he has no feeling, is turbid and opaque.

There is a painting that achieves Freud's intentions — but it is by Courbet, and it does so so wonderfully that one gasps at its beauty, even at the transparent warmth of the brown background and the translucency of rumpled sheets that are pure paint. Courbet reduced a woman's torso to an object of nipple, belly-button, hirsute rima and plump thigh, headless, legless and armless, but it is a painting of such exquisite sensibility that it elevates what some mean minds of 1866 and since insisted was obscene. It is not a thing of crude enquiry and observation, not a thing of erotic invitation, but a thing so exalted by the painter's response with paint, by his understanding of both flesh and the material with which he must represent it, that it is, very simply, beautiful — a word impossible now to use of Freud. *L'Origine du Monde*, in the Musée d'Orsay, is a painting to which Freud should pay a weekly pilgrimage and genuflect. Conjuring Courbet as an antecedent and justification for cold Freud invites a devastating comparison.

Much more Freudian enjoyment is to be had from a too small exhibition at the National Portrait Gallery of photographs taken by his studio assistant of the last twelve years, the David Dawson whose face and nakedness we see at the Wallace Collection. These are a thousand times more interesting than Freud's paintings — more expertly composed, more mysterious, more mischievously surreal, and yet informative, recording low jinks in the studio. Freud stands on steps to paint a large canvas; when The Queen sat to Freud she did so in a chair of giltwood and red damask; with David Hockney, Freud and he wait in long silences for Godot; with Hockney under his nose, how could Freud so elongate the portrait head that hangs cheek to cheek with the photograph? And what on earth is Neil MacGregor doing in Freud's studio — is even he, past master of the National Gallery, seduced by all the pro-Freud propaganda?

Lucian Freud

HAZLITT HOLLAND-HIBBERT SW1

Evening Standard, October 2008

To enthusiasts for the Epsteinian vulgarity and texture of Lucian Freud's recent painting, a small exhibition of the work with which his career began some seventy years ago may be a disconcerting surprise. That the curator is his studio assistant, confidant and occasional model, should give it authority, but David Dawson, in his choice of drawings and paintings, none large, some very small, executed in the years 1939 to 1954, merely repeats Freud's authorised version of his carefully reconstructed early life. It is yet again the tale of a boy who, protesting that he had no natural talent (blatantly false modesty to counteract his mother's boasting of his genius), was cunning enough to develop successive styles that fitted his limited abilities as they developed, styles that were not so much unfashionable as outside all English conventional parameters of fashion, quirky and singular enough to be immediately identifiable as his and to draw informed attention to him.

To those who have watched Freud from the beginning, the obsessive concentration with which early, but not first, he examined, close-to, his subjects, is familiar, the consequences, particularly in his smaller paintings, almost hallucinatory, and I have always wondered what the benign panjandrums of the Arts Council expected of him when they commissioned a significant painting for the Festival of Britain in 1951 – that they did so was a measure of his celebrity at the age of twenty-nine. This, *Interior, in Paddington* at five feet by four, was the first serious break in his chosen mould, both in its new scale and in Freud's stepping back from the close intensity of his gaze, replacing the immediate proximity of the magnifying glass with the skewed perspective that has ever since lent his subjects an unnerving space in which to have their uncomfortable being.

At the end of the period covered by the exhibition, Lucian, bearer of that awesome and internationally famous name, son-in-law of Jacob Epstein, pensioner of Colin Anderson and protégé of Peter Watson (both extravagantly generous patrons of young painters at the time), was, with Bacon and Ben Nicholson, chosen to represent Britain at the Venice Biennale of 1954. This was the year in which he said that a painter's tastes must grow out of such obsessions that he never had to ask himself whether a subject is suitable for him to paint. His use of the idiom *grow out of* was a Freudian slip; I suspect that he meant grow from, but grow out of his obsessions was what he immediately did, making 1954 the perfect year in which to end this exhibition.

The beginning is imperfect. From many paintings and drawings not included the shrewd observer must construct another life with very different roots. The first soil for these lay in German traditions, less the grandeurs of Dürer and Grünewald than the various realisms of Freud's immediate predecessors, Grosz and Dix and the now forgotten generation of Hubbuch, Schlichter, Lenk and Raederscheidt. I know that he left Germany at the age of only ten, but I cannot believe that in the sophisticated circumstances of his childhood he was wholly ignorant of fashionable painters such as these. In 1982, when Lawrence Gowing, my sometime tutor, published the first serious monograph on Freud and remarked that his first figure paintings 'were remembered or invented or imagined', I accused him of evasion. 'Not so,' he answered, 'Lucian forbade me to discuss his German sources.' The absence of these other early paintings makes a nonsense of this exhibition as a record for posterity.

Gowing also told me that the tale so often told of Freud's signing-on as a merchant seaman in 1941, repeated yet again by Catherine Lampert as obedient author of the adulatory essay in the catalogue, is in error: his three-month jaunt across the Atlantic was impetuously undertaken so as to keep company with an infatuated boyfriend. That a merchant seaman should, after so little service in the second full year of what seemed then a hopeless war, be invalided-out for tonsilitis is intrinsically improbable, and that he should be released in order to become an art student at Goldsmith's even more so. Credit for some of Freud's imagery and invention should go to John Craxton, his immediate contemporary, with whom, between 1942 and 1947, he shared rooms in St John's Wood (the rent paid by Peter Watson), tuition at Goldsmith's, an exhibition and long post-war months in Greece and Crete; it was Craxton who, after staying with a country vet, introduced him to the notion of painting dead animals in 1944; and it was with Craxton that he jointly worked on drawings in which their hands are indistinguishable. Craxton has, however, virtually been written out of Freud's life by the official spokesmen, and when Freud said of himself, 'My method is so arduous that there has never been much room for influence,' it was what he wanted us to believe. I am with Craxton: 'Freud,' he said in 2002, 'is a mimic. He must see, constantly, what it is he has to paint.' In the beginning he saw with the eyes of other men, and there were influences. In the end – that is now – he sees only with his own, so firmly concentrating on his models that it is they who become the influence, they whose surfaces he mimics, utterly without imagination.

At some point between the completion of the catalogue and the exhibition's opening, five paintings and two sketchbooks were added to the hang. An unfinished *Self Portrait* and a dully characteristic *Man in a Mackintosh* add nothing to our perception of Freud – they are merely typical of the transitional phase in the late Fifties when his brushwork was becoming broader, looser, more broken and less certain, and the paint was beginning to put on weight. The other three, however, are early, two from 1939, a year before the exhibition's earliest catalogue painting, and to some undramatic extent they demonstrate the German influences; the third, *The Village Boys*, of 1942, is (but for an absent picture, *The Refugees*, of the year before) the most powerful picture of his belated Berlin phase. This could not have been painted by anyone unaware of contemporary art in Germany between the wars. The little that we are allowed to see of the sketchbooks – one page of each – hints at a sympathy for boys perhaps too scabrous for further revelation.

Were the earliest of these additions made because the curators recognised that they had failed to tell the whole truth, or are their owners shrewdly jumping on the bandwagon of commercial opportunity offered by the exhibition? To the Jesuit they so enrich and transform the exhibition that it hardly matters, but I would like to think that the curators had a twinge of conscience and recognised that a truth that is not whole is not a truth at all. The pity is that there is no illustrated addendum to the catalogue, for catalogues should always be the truthful records of events.

Lucian Freud, Hazlitt Holland-Hibbert SW1 2008
http://www.hh-h.com/artists/lucian-freud/exhibitions/

Lucian Freud: L'Atelier

CENTRE POMPIDOU

Evening Standard, 20 May 2010

'It is an honour and a great pleasure for the Centre Pompidou to welcome on its walls the painting of Lucian Freud, an artist not well known in France because too little exhibited and rarely collected here. One small portrait of 1946 hardly represents so profoundly individual a development that runs counter to all the current orthodoxies of contemporary art, taking the human model for its subject.'

'The painting of Lucian Freud intrigues, disconcerts, irritates, fascinates. How should we see this man? Is he a great creator or a supernumerary, a towering rock or a flat plain? Empathic, ironic, or cynical? . . . Are we attracted or repelled? Is the work realist or caricatural? Obscene? Provocative? Or is it harrowing, close to the truths of the body, its flesh and the human condition?'

These opening sentences of introductions to the catalogue of Lucian Freud's paintings currently exhibited in the Centre Pompidou, written by two of that museum's panjandrums, represent the Parisian response to the phenomenon that is Freud, prolific painter of the naked body in its ordinary unloveliness. One implies regret that France, fecund melting-pot of European art between 1850 and 1950, has paid so little attention to a painter whose work is so much in demand in England and America that every one of his brush-strokes is now worth at least a thousand pounds, all of whose major paintings have passed into collections and museums at prices beyond those paid for the great patrimonial painters whose oeuvres the French authorities so vigorously protect and retain. The other launches into a confusion of visceral responses until, with sudden recollection of Freud's celebrity and worth as the holder of the record for the highest price ever paid for the work of a living painter, it is supplanted by cool-headedness. It is as though the French regret their neglect of Freud, not because they judge him to be a great painter, the Rubens of our day, but because they sense that they have – both publicly and privately – let slip all opportunities to acquire his work and are now envious. Perhaps, by granting him the flattery of this not particularly impressive show, they hope for an impulsive donation of the masterpiece that they otherwise will never have.

The Pompidou is a gallery that makes many things seem better than they are. It once displayed as a work of art the body shell of a Renault 14 – one of, if not the ugliest, the most uncomely cars ever to come from the usine up-river at Billancourt – yet in the sober classical circumstances of the old Tate Gallery its dull monstrosity would at once have been apparent. In the Tate Britain retrospective eight years ago Freud's more recent work looked raw, but in the architectural anonymity of the Pompidou (and its very different light), it seems altogether more comfortable and less assertive and aggressive. The exhibition is not a retrospective – even if it covered every decade since 1940, its forty-nine paintings would be far too few for that – but concentrates on the work of the 1990s, with some familiar support from the previous decade, and a dozen or so earlier things. A small handful of later canvases does nothing to expand what we see in these and demonstrates only a marked falling-off in every quality; nothing wet from the easel is included. The uneasy addition of ten etchings and seven drawings, all mere trifles bolstering my view that Freud, in infecting his drawings with the crudeness of his painting, has become the worst draughtsman ever to be acclaimed a great painter, do nothing to make this a representative or overwhelming show. The few accomplished paintings are diminished by the ill-chosen company they keep.

I fell to wondering what French critics have made of it – but long ago, translating for the Arts Council, I learned that French art criticism is what David Lee, editor of *Jackdaw*, might dub high-octane artbollocks – that is the self-indulgent blethering of pseuds in the obscure jabberwocky that has developed among cod-philosophers who pretend an interest in art. It was more informative to watch my fellow visitors. They did not stand in awe as they might before a portrait of papal villain by Titian, or his *Death of Actaeon*, Giorgione's *Tempestà* or the *Atelier Rouge* by Matisse – all of which are reproduced in the catalogue to imply that Freud shares their position on the heights of Mount Olympus.

Instead, they are slowly on the move, showing little sign of any engagement with the paintings. Occasionally they stand for a moment, but only to pursue some genital enquiry, as with the almost life-size awkwardly recumbent Leigh Bowery (*Nude with Leg up*) whose largely tumescent penis is pretty well dead centre in a canvas seven feet wide – for Freud is nothing if not thorough in his depiction of the penis, testicles and cunt. I use the C-word quite deliberately, though aware that many will be offended, because it is the word written so indelicately in paint by Freud himself; for him there is no polite euphemism, no anatomical correctitude – just the brutal Middle English or Teutonic radical – and it is extraordinary that he can, in paint, strike precisely that same bleak and shocking note. Freud's naked figures do not continue the academic tradition of the nude as metaphor for an ideal; they are so far from beautiful as to suggest that he cares nothing for sensuality; they represent a tenth circle of Dante's Hell occupied by those who have never been desired.

I am inclined to argue that Freud's crude unloving note extends to all areas of the naked body, but is less noticeable away from the erogenous zones – we are barely aware of it in arms and legs to which he has given no more attention than he might to a broomstick, the long strokes of the loaded brush following the straight forms rather than rounding and constructing them. He is, indeed, at his most uncomfortable and tentative with heavily rounded forms, reduced to fumbling. In his *Evening in the Studio* the gross bulk of the torso flows and sags and the thrusting legs are bent at the knees to condense them into short and matching forms; with these his brushwork seems almost haphazard in the struggle to communicate the shape of the body's various features. He implies weight and volume, but of structure he communicates nothing – breasts, belly and thighs are considered separately, not as a whole, and the tone of flesh is utterly lost in the flurry of conflicting pale opacities applied by a hapless brush. This is great painting?

Yet again I was struck by how consistently bad a painter Freud has been since he got into his painterly stride in the early 1960s – the flaws of his *Red-Haired Man on a Chair* painted then still dog him. Earlier paintings, his intriguing juvenilia (some of it very Twenties German) and his emergence as a painter under the influence of John Craxton, are all but omitted from the exhibition; this is not surprising, for since he forbade Lawrence Gowing to explore these in his attempted biography of 1982, Freud has reconstructed his life without them. Only *The Painter's Room* of 1944 offers a hint of how things then were, as well as how they might eventually be, for even then the interior with a couch, fallen drapery and a yucca in a pot were gleams in his immature eye. There is nothing of the refined and meticulous drawing of which he was capable as a young man; there is no image of his mother, the one being in whose company he revealed himself as capable of respect, sympathy and even love; there is only an occasional glimpse of the whippets for whom he seems to have had much the same feelings. No English enthusiast for Freud will be in the least informed by this exhibition and the French are being deceived by it; they deserve more paintings and a wider span if they are to judge how much the old man has fallen off.

As for what the curators made of it, this is most clear in the Analyses at the end of the catalogue, for it is in these that Freud is compared with Matisse, Giacometti, Dürer and Bonnard, Titian, Watteau and Picasso – a common curatorial conceit to convince the unwary innocent that their subject is of equivalent substance.

The folly of such nonsense is immediately apparent in their pairing Freud's *Irishwoman on a Bed* with Titian's *Venus of Urbino*, the one a desolate Hispanic broomstick ten feet tall, the other a deliciously sensual Venetian courtesan dishevelled after coitus but mischievously inviting the spectator to join her in her rumpled sheets. Only from the illustrated Chronology will the French be able to divine Freud's German ancestry as a painter, see that as a young man he had surreal abilities, and absorb, if they will, tantalising glimpses of an orderly studio.

I raise this last point because, in his old age, the studio has become disorderly, beguiling, romantic, picturesque, and the word *l'atelier* (the studio) is emphatically part of the exhibition's title – no fewer than thirty-two pages of the catalogue are devoted to it and Freud's activities therein. As with Francis Bacon's studio we feast on extravagantly discarded brushes and emptied tubes of paint, reproductions pinned to the walls, piles of material on the floor, drips and splashes of colour everywhere, and whole walls encrusted with paint as deep and rough as pebble-dash – a texture that must have taken years to grow and which appears as the backdrop in *The Painter surprised by a Naked Admirer* of 2004–5, a painting that is, but for one garden scene, the latest in the exhibition. Should we attempt to preserve this atelier when Freud is dead? Should we make a shrine of this house without a doorbell? Should we do what Dublin has done for Bacon's, deconstruct and reconstruct it in a public gallery, Tate Britain perhaps? Or shall we be sensible, take yet more photographs, let the house go to anyone prepared to suffer Freud's ghost and stick a blue plaque on the wall? The preservation of Bacon's studio is a precedent we should ignore, but with *l'atelier* attached to Freud I fear that we shall not – and then whose premises will become a fetish? Auerbach's, Kossoff's, Hodgkin's, Hockney's and the house of Gilbert and George?

Should one make the effort to see *Lucian Freud: L'Atelier*? In the spirit of devout pilgrimage of course one should – but, like hearing Tosca for the twentieth time, it will be a wearied pleasure.

Lucian Freud

Lucian Freud, Centre Pompidou 2010

Exhibition poster
http://www.centrepompidou.fr/Pompidou/Manifs.nsf/0/
57C293CB2BD5E0CFC12576E3003A4771?
OpenDocument&sessionM=2.2.2&L=2

Lucian Freud

NATIONAL PORTRAIT GALLERY

Evening Standard, 9 February 2012

De mortuis nil nisi bonum

Of the dead speak well or not at all (*Latin tag*)

It is rare for the death of any man, other than senior politicians, to be headline news and honoured by obituaries that occupy two full pages in our intellectual newspapers, but this was so when Freud died last year. He had been, it seemed, 'the finest painter of the human form in the second half of the twentieth century', one of our greatest painters ever, an artist of extraordinary skill and, driven by a fierce unyielding determination, he not only redefined British art, but his work stands comparison with any artist of any period anywhere. Critics, curators and friends, far too many for any bandwagon, clambered onto the replacement juggernaut to ululate their grief from telling tales, revealing personal experiences and reiterating the party line that this great man was the Raphael, the Rubens and the Rembrandt of our day. I, who had known him from the mid-Sixties, but on no more than nodding terms and an occasional exchange of letters, took no part in this, refusing to say or write a word, for this was no time to express the scepticism that will soon enough chip away at Freud's celebrity. That Latin tag makes better sense as 'Of the *recently* dead speak well or not at all'.

Let us now praise famous men . . .

(*Ecclesiasticus, Book VII of the Apocrypha*)

There is no doubt that Freud was, in his last three decades, regarded as the world's greatest living figurative painter, though he himself would never have made that claim – indeed, I am inclined to think him, if not modest, then engagingly reticent, seeing himself so much apart from other painters that there could be no such competition. It was competition with himself that drove him on to so often change his style, develop and discard it, settling comfortably in his fifties into a use of paint that was thick enough to jut from the canvas and spiky enough to prick the finger, features that jarringly disrupted the surface of the painting and the representation of the subject, as though the texture of the paint must have absolute primacy. It seemed impulsive, intuitive, undisciplined and immature, as though Freud were still a student in an experimental phase, uncertain of his judgement; when he painted himself naked in 1993, full-length, full-frontal, based on an ancient Roman sculpture of the suicide of Seneca, I thought it formidable, so imbued with the profundity of sentiment that it outweighed all else that he had done, and wished him another three score years and ten in which to reach his full maturity.

Let us now praise . . . our fathers that begat us

(Ecclesiasticus, Book VII of the Apocrypha)

'He is survived by many children' – so ends his obituary in *The Times*; some put the figure at forty or so and this seems entirely possible, so many were the women, older and younger than himself, taken without emotional involvement to his bed. In later life, when not quite so capable, he talked openly of his earlier seductions, his view of them not the least sentimental but physical to a degree I have encountered in no other man; his clinical studies of the rima are exactly that, not beautiful, but life-size unloving observations.

A legend in his lifetime

(common saw)

Painter, gambler, Bohemian, night-hawk, lone wolf, Lothario, Freud was understood neither by the critics and curators who eventually paid sycophantic, grovelling court to him and, self-interested, made him their cottage industry, nor by the gossip columnists who pried into his life. All contributed to the legend, but with Freud a name of immediate frisson, wild good looks and an enticing aura of random sexuality when young, notoriety and celebrity came first; rank came at fifty when created Companion of Honour, then international fame and legendary status, neither of which seemed to have the least effect on him.

The deed is all, the glory nothing

(*Goethe, Faust*)

To Freud it was not reputation that mattered (though occasionally he called his lawyers to protect it), but the deed, the doing, the act of painting, and this he did almost to his dying day. The memorial exhibition at the National Portrait Gallery includes the portrait of David Dawson, naked, with their whippet, Eli (perhaps the two beings who, at the very end, meant most to him), the last of all his canvases, unfinished, unresolved, yet both figures are encrusted with the scabby, scabrous and ultimately pointless piled-on paint. Seated on his high chair before the easel Freud looked down on them – and on so many other sitters – just as Goya looked down on his Majas, an awkward and even vertiginous perspective for a portrait, sometimes compelling astonishing distortions and extensions on his subjects.

Some critics have it that all Freud's paintings are portraits, be the subject human, animal or floorboard; but to me he reduces the human body to still life – the still life of the butcher's shop from Carracci and Rembrandt to Soutine and Bacon, but as slack bags of bones or blubber rather than the blood and muscle of the flayed ox, their faces uniformly unsmiling, blank-eyed, melancholy and even disagreeable, distanced by the tedium of posing, all intellectual and emotional energy internalised. Some sitters are victims of intensely physical and genital enquiry, often ugly; some paintings are gauche, so badly composed that their glaring flaws blind the spectator to small virtues; and he who looks for form will find only formula – formula for the muscles of the trunk, formula for fat and faces, formula for skin and scrawn, formula for walls and rags and floorboards.

It is an honest exhibition. It begins with youthful paintings that, were they not known to be by Freud, would be attributed to the German painters of *c*.1930 whose influence he constantly denied (much of his early life as we know it is a carefully adjusted reconstruction). Paintings of *c*.1950, imbued with English Neo-Romanticism, are as delicately done with tiny brushes as many tempera masterpieces of Quattrocento Florence (go next door to the National Gallery and compare them with Botticelli), compelling, frozen, pale, with not a hint of brushwork or impasto, but a powerful sense of form. In the later 1950s, when his imposed pallor is tentatively replaced by colour, the thin paint thickening, the brushes broad, their strokes swirling and sweeping, the faces enlarged far beyond life-size, we sense the fracturing of a brilliant beginning and the intrusion of dead formula. From the early 1960s on, that formula is steadily developed until, two decades later, the *Large Interior (after Watteau)* surveys his past, establishes a present and foretells the now overwhelmingly familiar future of monstrous nudes and other ruthlessly ugly paintings, their surfaces so scabrous as to seem, as in *Ria* of *c*.2006–7, hideously diseased.

I am told that Freud loved to hate me. I did not hate him; nor do I hate his paintings — it is only that I share neither his lust for ugliness nor his taste for furfuraceous paint, and wish that he had found a different escape from the trap of beautiful Neo-Romanticism. I wish that he had always painted sheets and wiping rags in the white paint in which he clad his mother in 1982–4, when Sargent and Pontorno seem to have held his hand, and given us more such exquisite details as the rat in the hand of a naked man and the fringed blanket in *Flora with Blue Toenails* of 2000–1, the hand of the octogenarian not trembling. When all is said and done, for all his perversity, Freud was perhaps as great a figurative painter as is now possible, and he is well served by this exhibition.

> *In perpetuum, frater, ave atque vale* –
> *Hail, dear brother, and farewell for ever*
> (*Catullus, Carmina CI*)

Lucian Freud, National Portrait Gallery 2012
http://www.guardian.co.uk/artanddesign/gallery/2012/feb/08/lucian-
freud-national-portrait-gallery#/?picture=385691837&index=0

Gilbert and George

With Tracey Emin's bed, Hirst's shark, the infinity of moulds of Gormley's naked body, the blood and placenta sculptures of Marc Quinn and Tate Britain's lights switched on and off by someone quite forgettable, who here now remembers G&G, Gilbert and George? The problem with outrageous art is less the outrage in itself than that each outrage obliterates its predecessor and the eye and mind are numbed by the speed and frequency of the succession. To be an aficionado of contemporary art is to be a happy masochist, but to be a sceptical spectator of the kaleidoscopic scene is to be, intellectually and aesthetically, the victim of the birch and bastinado, the strappado and the thumbscrew, the iron maiden and the boot, the rack, the wheel and peine, each agony dulled by its successor. In such a list of torments G&G now rate as teasing with a feather.

The last time I heard mention of G&G was before Tate Modern opened, when it was widely presumed that the blank wall of the hideous bleak entrance would be hung with their vast works, but it was not – a disappointment even to those who think the pair pretentious frauds, as near to serious art as the Beatles, their near contemporaries in fame, were to serious music. G&G who must have been aware of this expectation, now abuse Tate Modern and Tate Britain too, seeing racism and isolation in the division, where others see only intellectual confusion in Serota's desperate desire to ride two circus horses at the same time, a foot on each saddle as he races into what he thinks is the future and the rest of us see as the futility of riding in a ring. Now, in something of a huff with the Serota Tendency, G&G have chosen to celebrate this current

Jubilee with an exhibition at the Serpentine Gallery of a set of pictures that were first seen piecemeal at the last, taking some small pleasure in so sylvan a setting for subjects so profoundly urban – the twenty-six *Dirty Words Pictures* of 1977. One of these, some years ago, was removed from the very same gallery when its patron, Princess Diana, was about to visit, though I am reliably informed that most of the words were well established in her informal vocabulary.

A quarter of a century ago no four-letter obscenity could be uttered on radio or television, printed in a newspaper or said in polite society – whatever that is. G&G, who were then in their early thirties but had adopted the persona of the middle-aged bachelor bank clerk, had already established the formula with which, ever since, they have expressed what I suppose we must call their ideas – the regular grid of upright rectangular photographs, in black and white at that point in their career, or tinted with the red of Hammer Horror blood. They had been a brotherly twosome since 1967 in their days as student sculptors at St Martin's School of Art; as neither could sculpt in any conventional sense, they changed the definition of that ancient skill to embrace crude drawing, photography, collage, postcards and, above all, themselves in the carefully honed and demandingly conspicuous identical twin presentation that has ever since ensured the interest of scribblers. Carefully nurtured by their dealer (now retired), their image as well-washed, carefully groomed and buttoned-up, low church and lower middle class, antimacassar and paper doily, William Morris and Clarice Cliff, they became an endless (I am tempted to say bottomless, but they were far from that) resource for any journalist at a loose end with an interest in tittle-tattle, so much so that G&G were almost as familiar to the British public as Bruce Forsyth and Cilla Black, and on much the same level.

With so much literary exposure, their work was swiftly familiar to a public that never set foot in galleries, but by the same token, it was censored. The public knew that the two seemingly fastidious old dears had a passion for including themselves in most of their work and divined, but rarely said, that they were probably queer, but nothing that might upset the prudish or attract the attention of the police, was risked in illustrations. Did G&G in 1977, lose patience with their images as maiden aunts? Did they look back with fond nostalgia on 1970 and their self-portraits as *George the Cunt* and *Gilbert the Shit* and wonder what happened to the brave new world in which they made their first assault on the taboos of society and art? Was it a sense of frustration and failure that drove them to renew that assault and take it much further with the *Dirty Words*?

Poof, Bollocks, Bent, Bummed, Wanker, Queer, Cock, Prick, Ass (not Arse), Shag, Piss and Bugger, as well as Fuck and Cunt, may now be nightly the vocabulary of comedians and the American Cinema as seen on television, but in 1977, even as art, they were too challenging. Odd small groups of pictures with these titles might be shown here and there, but the whole series could be exhibited in neither London nor New York — Moscow might have taken them then as evidence of western decadence and degradation, but the fame of G&G was not to spread so far until 1990. A small group, however, courts misunderstanding and, then as now, risked interpretation as a deliberate affront to bourgeois sensibilities, the cutting edge that cuts in a way not intended by the artist, and one is forced to wonder how the images would have been received had G&G not given them these titles but merely numbered the series under some such bland heading as *Spitalfields 1977*, for that way no catalogue, no reviewer, no reporter would have been compelled to print the word and an intelligent audience might have interpreted the pictures differently. The group as a whole has a cumulative effect that invites, not hostility and disgust, but a benign interpretation, and some of us who have long held G&G in undiluted contempt feel moved to make tentative amends and suggest that, among their vast and vacuous output, these are the only pictures that have some sincerity and merit. In immediately subsequent work, the sincerity was diverted to an infantile interest in their own genitals, their anuses and, particularly, their turds, and to images that implied an almost certainly 'don't touch' idealism embodied in the adolescent boy – sincere, no doubt, but of interest only to the analyst; the merit evaporated without trace.

Had G&G, like Raphael, died early, their *Dirty Words* their final work, we might hold the twins in high esteem as social commentators and these pictures as examples of profound pessimism and protest against the tenor of their times. To understand them we should recall what the mid-1970s were like under the faltering Labour administrations of Wilson and Callaghan, inflation rampant, the pound shrinking by the hour, industry debilitated by strikes, immigration the cause of discontent, the streets rubbish-strewn and graffiti-stricken and the nation depressed by the sense that it was drifting towards doom-laden oblivion. In the light of their subsequent adoration of Mrs Thatcher, the only woman to break their male gender barrier, this seems to have been exactly their view of Labour's socialism, and with an unrelenting *Daily Mail* approach to political comment, G&G expressed it. The wry thing is, of course, that such papers as the *Daily Mail*, representing their readers' views, were precisely those who protested most against such images as art.

Perhaps they were right to do so, though the fire in their bellies was against the dirty words, not in defence of art and, diverted by the words, they missed the pictures' point. What G&G had developed was indeed not art in any ancestral sense, but merely a confusion of photography, advertising, the glossy magazine and the kaleidoscopic rush of television stilled – an ingenious technique of easy appeal to the semi-literate and those with short attention spans, but in the *Dirty Words Pictures* there is a depth, a passion and a protest. Seen as a whole we realise that the dirty words have no relevance to the particular images with which they are framed and their importance fades, giving primacy to the derelict drunks, largely melancholy blacks and references to the continuing campaigns in south-east Asia after the American withdrawal from Vietnam.

As despairing political comment these pictures have their point and are, as it were, the hopeless and angry shouting of a dirty word as a helpless response to the condition of the world – we have all done it in our time; considered in terms of technical competence, however, they are a clumsy disappointment. The individual panels are largely out of focus, the subject often set against the light, their details lost, their silhouettes hazy, and when they are in the light their modelling is bleached flat by it. Overall the impression is of blur, over-enlargement, fuzziness; this gives the pictures a certain tonal unity and at first glance we see black and white in abstract terms rather than as specific images; at second glance, as sources of specific information, the images are all but useless. Even so, together, the twenty-six panels begin to take effect – the dirty words don't matter, but the images do, for they perfectly encapsulate our lives a quarter of a century ago.

What G&G have done since has undone the high despairing seriousness of these pictures. They have become technically better; they have introduced a wide range of garish colours; they have elevated themselves and their turds to icons and toyed with morality and God. In their way they have become the Testinos of Spital-fields, flashy and shallow, utterly without significance. Taking the subsequent oeuvre of G&G into account, I am probably in error in finding anything worthwhile in the *Dirty Words Pictures*; perhaps now, seeing them retrospectively and for the first time as a whole, I am mistaken in interpreting them as a grim and gritty commentary on their day, as observation at a remove, of the underdogs of society, as a formal expression of despair.

Perhaps they are no more than a development of style, transitional works between the tedium of their earlier self-portraiture and the flamboyant banality that within three years was their accomplished idiom and is so still. Even so, I have a nagging doubt. Perhaps . . .

Gilbert and George, Serpentine Gallery 2002

Cunt Scum (1977)
http://www.tate.org.uk/art/artworks/gilbert—george-cunt-scum-t07406

Exhibition poster
http://www.artnet.com/galleries/
artwork_detail.asp?G=&gid=107047&which=&aid=
6964&wid= 184308&source=inventory&rta=http://www.artnet.com

Gilbert and George

TATE MODERN

Evening Standard, 15 February 2007

Gilbert and George – these names alone are enough to make the heart of the sane man sink. Gilbert and George – no, not again, please not again, so soon, so soon. Yet Tate Modern tells us that more than a quarter of a century has passed since last they had a retrospective exhibition. How can this be? Over these empty years have I not gathered on my bookshelves a yard of catalogues devoted to stagings of their work, a yard of books by the obeisant critics, curators, historians and novelists who have turned praise and propaganda into a cottage industry? Have I not seen the work of G&G, as they are fondly known, en masse in Tate Liverpool, in the Whitechapel Gallery, the Serpentine and in the premises of their erstwhile dealer, Anthony d'Offay? Have G&G not scraped the barrel of exhibition space with shows in the South London Gallery and Milton Keynes?

How has it been that in journeys to Düsseldorf and Cracow, Vienna and Budapest, indeed almost everywhere between Aarhus and Zürich, searching for Rembrandt and Rubens, Dalí and Delacroix, I have encountered the vast banalities of these apparently neglected artists? Wealthy crones who winter in Palm Beach have had to share their pleasures with this pair, so too any who have ventured to Moscow and Peking; no gap year traveller round the world is safe from them, for they are as readily exhibited in Shanghai and Los Angeles as in Rome, Paris, Dublin and The Hague; and this new retrospective at Tate Modern is destined over the next two years for Munich, Turin, San Francisco, Milwaukee and New York. Beware, oh villagers of Little

Piddlehinton, G&G and all their works to you may yet be on their way.

And what are these works? These are pictures Democratic, Cosmological and Rudimentary (their words), pseudo-sociological and hectoring with cod-theology (this time the words are mine), of supposedly Bad Thoughts and certainly of Dirty Words. These are icons on panoramic scale, as big as the painted ceilings of baroque churches, bigger by far than the painted chapels of the earlier Italian Renaissance; in the company of G&G, Giotto, Masaccio and Piero della Francesca, Gaulli, Pozzo and Pietro da Cortona shrivel into insignificance. But there is more than vastness to their work – they not only execute it but in the beginning they *were* it, singing, dancing and standing still, until they discovered that they could photograph themselves; then they became their own icons – they are God the Father and the Virgin Mary, they are Christ and the Holy Ghost, they are the angels and shepherds of the Nativity, they are the Magi of the Adoration and the gifts they bring are not Gold, Frankincense and Myrrh, but Shit, Nakedness and Bum Holes – again their words, not mine, for these are the titles of their images and with G&G we are compelled to abandon delicacy and politesse. The Shit, Nakedness and Bum Holes are, of course, their very own.

A kindly critic might argue that theirs is the ecstatic innocence of Blake, developed for a naughtier world than his, and that just as he sat naked in his garden, a new Adam before the Fall, G&G too are visionaries who see a company of angels in a Peckham tree and esteem nakedness as virtuous, sinless and immaculate. Just as Blake declared in *Jerusalem* that he 'must Create a System or be enslav'd by another Man's', so G&G, in their sweetness and sensibility, have imposed a system on the streets of Spitalfields, their adopted bailiwick. Again like Blake, their belief seems to be that sin is the creation of law and the immediate consequence of prohibition – thus what is natural in man, God's inborn gift, the freedom to do this and that, is made sinful by the negative rules that men impose on other men. While Blake restricted his rebellion to a continuous attack on chastity, G&G extend theirs to all functions of the body, sexual and lavatorial, demanding the liberty to empty bowels and bladders without the imposed constraints of modesty, to rejoice in worship of the buttocks and the orifice between, to wallow in ejaculated semen, to savour the extruded turd with the lubricious anticipation of the coprophage, and to revel in their own uninhibited nakedness and the more sheepish nakedness of boys.

But perhaps, in raising the familiar ghost of Blake and the forgotten ghost of Swedenborg, his sometime mentor at a distance (the eighteenth-century philosopher who believed – put very simply – that the true order of Creation had been disrupted by man's misuse of his free will), I search in G&G for a philosophical explanation of work that in no sense can I see as art and is devoid of all aesthetic merit. There seems throughout their imagery a crude yearning for things spiritual among the physical and, to make the point, a very recent picture of two pseudo-voodoo figures crucified bears the legends – 'Jesus says forgive yourself' above, and below, 'God loves fucking! Enjoy,' as well as a label with the date, the signature of G&G and the question 'Was Jesus heterosexual?'

Have they been reading *The Da Vinci Code* or is it that G&G see themselves as in the long tradition of Christian enquiry into the nature of Christ's manhood, usually outside canonical authority? Was he capable of erection, coition and ejaculation? – from the drapery gathered in his groin it is clear that many Renaissance painters thought that of the first he was. Is it possible that G&G see themselves as the fathers of the last of such religious sects as the late medieval Brothers and Sisters of the Free Spirit, who believed that pre-destination made what were deemed by the Church to be sexual sins irrelevant to their spiritual salvation, and therefore to be indulged as much as they chose with orgiastic variety and enthusiasm? Certainly they have constantly offered their nakedness for adoration, often enough in the company of the cross and forms and layouts cruciform, and in their incarnation in Tate Modern that uncomely building seems less a series of galleries than of basilican cathedral halls where bright images of G&G unrelentingly assault us with a wearying certainty better suited to a Happy Clappy sect.

The exhibition reaches back to 1970; George the Cunt and Gilbert the Shit, as they then called themselves, at twenty-eight and twenty-seven had dispensed with surnames and become a single entity. Everything they did they recognised as sculpture, whether it was buying a post card, standing still in the street or pouring their energies into enormous feeble drawings that hang like faded ancient tapestries, deliberately creased and crumpled to divert us from their technical incompetence; a photograph was sculpture, a printed pamphlet was sculpture, and they too were sculptures that produced more sculpture – yet sculpture in any ancestral form was quite beyond their capabilities, so too drawing and painting. Their only accomplishments were that they could point a camera and scrawl like uneducated adolescents unwillingly at school. In 1971 they made the first of their photo-pieces, as disjointed and irregular as any random collection of petty memorabilia haphazardly accumulating on the walls of ordinary mortals with nothing better to display and no sense of relationship or interval, and from these sprang the regimented grid patterns that were to be the armature of their ever-extending images of skewed sex, skewed religion and quotidian banality. Only once since 1970 have I felt inclined to take G&G with any seriousness and then not as artists, but as social commentators on the bleak world of urban degeneration, and that was five years ago when the complete set of *The Dirty Words* was shown at the Serpentine. Twenty-six photo-pieces headed with graffiti scrawl spoke trenchantly of London in the year that they were made, 1977, to confront the comfortable middle classes with what was ubiquitous beyond their leafy purlieus. Had we seen them in 1977 when G&G were still a new phenomenon, they, like Hogarth, might to the sensible have seemed to venture properly beyond the conventions of taste and manners, and to have an angry message worth supporting. Unfortunately, for the sake of public morality and taste, for a quarter of a century the most usefully aggressive works ever made by G&G remained virtually unknown. Alas, even in this retrospective exhibition their presence is reduced to seven panels, their impact minimal.

What have G&G done since *The Dirty Words* of 1977? The sad answer is that they have been frivolous. Their work has grown larger — the four-part *Death-Hope-Fear-Life* of 1984 more than eighteen metres long, the current monster, *Named*, a phalanx of advertisements by homosexual hustlers pieced together in 2001, a little less at more than fifteen metres. They have explored the bodies and bright faces of adolescent boys, Martin Clunes among them, and a young actor once given to policeman roles, and explored their own less comely bodies and faces more lugubrious; they have tiptoed into the delicate fringes of homosexuality that might have appealed to desiccated Oxford dons half a century ago, even into the *Physique Pictorial* world of Hockney in the Sixties, and they have plunged into the darker areas of divergent sexuality that were the prurient interest of the Surrealists between the two World Wars and are now the preserve of specialist pornographers in the United States and Germany.

Their output has been prodigious, the 200 exhibits in Tate Modern no more than a sample, and yet too many, for their cumulative effect is one of tedium, of sameness, uniformity, monotony, leaving us with the impression of two shallow minds with ideas too meagre ever to merit inflation to such gigantic scale, but this is the idiom of the day among their fellow sculptors — witness those equally trivial and limited darlings of Serota, Gormley and Kapoor. That G&G were ever sculptors is, of course, the fundamental nonsense of their work, their addle-pated notions and themselves.

Gilbert and George, Tate Modern 2007

England **(1980)**

http://www.tate.org.uk/art/artworks/gilbert—george-england-t03297

Fates **(2005)**

http://www.tate.org.uk/art/artworks/gilbert—george-fates-t12168

Naked Eye **(1994)**

http://www.tate.org.uk/art/artworks/gilbert—george-naked-eye-t07493

Andy Goldsworthy

THE BARBICAN

Evening Standard, 15 September 2000

In 1977, Andy Goldsworthy then aged twenty-one, made some 500 works of – for want of a better classification – sculpture. They were ephemeral. He has since estimated that of the one or two made every day throughout the year, perhaps a dozen were worth a second glance, saying of all, 'My sculptures can last for days or a few seconds – what is important to me is the experience of making. I leave all my work outside and often return to watch it decay.' It is significant that he made no mention of years or centuries.

This is a subversive view of sculpture, the most durable of arts, often outlasting even architecture, as did the legs of Ozymandias when all else was desert. Permanence, however, has never been of interest to Goldsworthy, and if permanence there has been, then it lies not in bronze or stone, but in the photograph of something done that could not last, some aesthetic notion too fragile or futile to resist the force of sea or wind, gravity or even change of temperature. It has been, and still is, enough to throw a handful of sand, splash water in the sun to make a private rainbow, make a path of holes or stones leading directly towards an in-flowing tide, draw a Klee-like line in seaweed strands, stack sheet ice or coat a snowball with mud as though it were a gigantic and exotic chocolate truffle – and all the time be certain sure that someone is there to witness the action with a camera.

All this has been here today and gone tomorrow, ephemeral indeed, except in the idea, which in some cases has recurred as often as a Wagner *Leitmotiv*. In 1977, for example, he made his first snowball as an art form, in 1979 another, and more still in

1982, 1987, 1989, 1992, 1995, 1997 and last winter, then for the memorable occasion – because the media were so well prepared for it – when on midsummer day this year smart city bankers on their early morning way to work were confronted with a baker's dozen of them messily melting to reveal the detritus hidden in their cores, pine cones, barbed wire and the like, as emblems of their place of origin. Can there be a significant difference between a snowball made at the dawn of the millennium and one made a quarter of a century ago?

Snowballs in Summer was an exhibition of sorts, although there was no private view, no gathering of Arts Council, Saatchi and Serota groupies to guzzle wine, nibble canapés and massage each other's *amour propre*, no catalogue in which Goldsworthy could make the fashionable 'artist's statement' and explain this act of urban terrorism. It brought him formidable publicity, consolidating the OBE awarded in The Queen's Birthday Honours (and how did that come about, one wonders? – did he make a garden pond for Tony Blair?), but the snowballs were, like his ice and icicles, his leaves floating in a shallow stream casting shadows on its bottom, his shards of slate thrown in the air, his pinnacles of balanced stones, his drawing in seal's blood in the snow, his grass stalks caught in cobwebs, transitory, all gone within the shadow of a second, with nothing to show of them but videos and photographs – but it was with the sale of photographs to the Arts Council Collection that he found his first apologist and his first step on the ladder of state patronage, eventually including a National Lottery grant of £340,000.

We forget when we look at these photographs that they have some considerable independence as works of some kind in themselves. Some very early photographs were taken by Goldsworthy but when, as early as 1976, other hands began to hold the camera, other aesthetic sensibilities came into play and with these the original work can only be seen at two removes – the first its transference from the performance act to the photograph, and the second that it must be seen through the mind and eye of the photographer. We must not forget that photography is now officially an art form, as is video, the equal if not the superior of painting and sculpture; on the other hand, as all sensible sceptics know, the camera is a plausible and inventive liar, a creature of contrivance and deceit that if not kept on a short leash as an instrument of documentation, gives meaning and presence to the frivolous as well as permanence to the fleeting trifle. With rock and stone and slate, Goldsworthy has produced a scattering of work that will last longer than sand thrown into the wind, but photography reduces them to the same idiom.

Almost everything that Goldsworthy has done is in some sense touchingly whimsical, redolent of Hans Anderson, Peter Pan and the ghastly Arthur Ransome, and he seems to plead for applause in much the same way as does a brain-damaged adolescent who achieves something worth encouragement when done by a child of three. We treat the Goldsworthies of this world as Holy Fools, as vehicles of divine or revealed wisdom and utterly innocent of guile – that is why we accept the Emin bed and the Hirst shark. Whatever such artists say is given oracular status, whatever they do is perceived as having the authority of inspiration beyond our understanding, and we must stand in awe, unquestioning. We do not give politicians, theologians, economists or policemen such authority over us without frequently contesting it, but with artists we do not dispute – it is as though we harbour some superstitious fear of them.

Consider Goldsworthy's current exhibition at the Barbican, *Time* – supposing that so well hidden an event can be discovered in that hostile labyrinth – where, for £4, four works will numb you into submission. One of these is all that remains of the fourteenth Summer snowball, held back so that it could melt here – now no snow, only some fragments of ruddy rock and a dry spread stain of ruddy dust from it. How its peers looked last June we are reminded by videos nearby, blurred, fidgety, amateur, tedious beyond endurance and wretched as emblems of Time. Were sane men dismayed by these snowballs, disturbed, discomfited and sent on their way thinking of the Four Last Things, of Time itself, Eternity and Messianic Hope?

What are we to make of *London Wall*, 'another new sculpture commissioned specifically for the Barbican . . . 11,850 kilos of London clay bound with human hair collected from local hairdressers . . . '? This is the largest of such exercises, as cracked and fissured as the skin of Ivy Compton-Burnett, twenty-five metres long and the height of three tall men, but none the better for such scale. To open the door of a room in an Edinburgh house onto such a wall rather than a space, as was the case in 1998, was to realise a painting by Magritte and suggest that the corpse of Surrealism is capable of a post-mortem (and Postmodernist) wriggle, but in the year 2000 to cake a Barbican wall with eleven tons of mud when, for the past decade, this conceit has been Goldsworthy's party trick in many museums and commercial galleries, mud on the floor as well as walls, suggests a crippling loss of inventiveness and aesthetic energy.

But what are we to make of mud as the material of art? What as clay and terracotta has played an essential role in European sculpture throughout its history, the thinking man's material for three-dimensional drawing, has become flat and two-dimensional, joining chocolate and faecal matter as another instrument of shock – but as with those, its limitation is that it can only shock once; as with so much contemporary art, the idea is shallow and manifestly more so the more overblown its exploitation. Two days after this exhibition opened, the *Guardian* published a photograph of a car covered with volcanic ash as deeply fissured as Goldsworthy's mud and looking much the same. Nature's imagery, however, seemed infinitely more significant.

At first sight the big room with a random arrangement of thirty or so big blobs on its floor, seems either to represent an apprentices' disaster in a *Sachertorte* bakery, or an assortment of gigantic turds.

But these are not the evacuations of diarrhoeatic elephants to delight dear Chris Ofili, these are not made of rich Viennese chocolate, they are not even made of mud – they are boulders taken from the sea's edge and fired in a kiln at more than 1,000 degrees centigrade, just to see what happens. Some are sundered, resembling Lucio Fontana's *Natura* series of solid objects (1959–60), others melt, all lose their nature. Was any of this the artist's intention? Has he contributed anything to these transformations other than, as it were, to put a bun in the oven and play King Alfred? Have the random consequences any aesthetic significance? Why must we believe that these coprolitic accidents are art?

The last work, *Stone Melt 2000*, is, of course, the related video – three screens in a dark room showing what a man with the mildest of pornographic minds might take to be the Götterdämmerung of the vagina.

Goldsworthy at his most wistfully charming might be a great success at the Chelsea Flower Show, for he is a man to make follies in the gardens of the rich, the ruined arch, the broken pavement, the rough-hewn obelisk, the man to turn your dead leaves and fallen twigs into a fairy fancy rather than a bonfire, and certainly the man to bury your dog under a cairn. But here is a man with whom not to walk a wilderness, for he will be for ever stopping to rearrange the natural fall of things, to newly decorate old surfaces with a conceit, to improve on the bird's nest, the rustic beehive and the ant heap for whom Nature's wild architects are not good enough. Here is a man who follows Stuart Brisley and Anish Kapoor in the exploration of the hole, who follows Richard Long in the use of mud and stone and wood and photograph, whose interest in snow and molten rock follows Helen Chadwick's in snow and chocolate. Here is a man whose 'sculpture' is less aesthetically substantial than good window-dressing. If Goldsworthy is indeed, as the Barbican asserts, 'one of Britain's most acclaimed artists', then we must be as mad as he for allowing ourselves to be so fascinated by a Perfect Fool.

Antony Gormley

HAYWARD GALLERY

Evening Standard, 25 June 2007

Those who admire Antony Gormley and those who do not must all, on one matter, agree — that the quality of his self-promotion is unrivalled in the history of art. Can there be a City-bound passer-by who has not in the last week or two encountered a cast of the sculptor's naked body in the streets or on the skyline? In his omni-present nudity his whole body is better known than that of Michelangelo's *David* or the warriors of the Elgin Marbles, his genitals and buttocks more familiar to millions than those of any porn star. Has any newspaper, free to all takers or overpriced and paid for, failed to publish photographs of both the eminent man and his images of himself? Is there a duke or dustman who has not read of him? Could any pensioner, slumped before a television set, have slept through all the cover that he's had? Has any critic (other than me) failed to review his latest show in terms of gushing adulation? And have not writers, poets and politicians, in their profound ignorance of all the visual arts, peddled without pause their praise of Gormley ever since the exhibition opened? Were Leonardo and Raphael ever so much interviewed?

This triumph of self-exposure is the consequence of hefty organisation and, no doubt, extravagant expense — and the sceptic, seeing little aesthetic merit in the work, wonders just how much public money has been poured into it, not just for the benefit of Gormley and the profit of his dealer, Jay Jopling, but even more for the aggrandisement of Ralph Rugoff, the new American Director of the Hayward Gallery, unknown to most of us and thus determined to make his mark. There is, of course, a sponsor, one of the world's largest law firms, but can it really have paid for all this – for *Event Horizon*, the installation of Gormley's body casts in thirty-one locations, as well as a semi-retrospective and a Gormley-now show in the gallery? If it has, then clearly its fees are far too high; and if it has not, then the accounts should be open to scrutiny so that we know exactly how much we, the tax-paying public that in one way or another funds such exercises, have put into the pockets of Gormley and Jopling. This exhibition is presented both as a 'public art commission' and as one of 'brand new monumental works specially conceived for the Hayward Gallery . . . ' – to whom then do they belong and by whom and how have they been funded? Works specially conceived for galleries and other public spaces (the fourth plinth in Trafalgar Square, for example) have in recent years had interesting histories; though paid for by the galleries in question, some, at the end of exhibitions, have reverted to the artists and their dealers and have then, with a little tinkering, been adapted to the premises of new owners who have paid for them again. My view of such chicanery is that the works, if not wanted for the permanent collections of the commissioning galleries, should be sold for their benefit and their benefit alone, preferably on the open market (Christie's and Sotheby's would surely oblige) and not entrusted to the artist's dealer.

This is a matter into which the Department of Culture should have enquired years ago, just as it should investigate the benefits that accrue to the very few artists (and indirectly their dealers) who receive most of the patronage in promotion and cash doled out by Tate Modern and the Arts and British Councils, with the immediate consequence of the Turner Prize or an international exhibition a hefty increase in the prices asked (and got) for every scrap of work. Year after year, through these public agencies, public money is pumped into artists – Gormley, Kapoor, Hirst foremost among by them – who are millionaires supported by (and supporting) even richer dealers; yet neither the artists nor the dealers need these subsidies. I know that this is not a clear-cut issue, that the public should be kept aware of major artists' recent work and that the country should be represented at great international events by the best artists that we have – but nothing of this is done without cost to the public and great benefit to the artist; there ought to be some kick-back to the public purse and, at the very least, the occasional gift by the artist of a significant work. At the moment, and for years past, the notorious artist and his dealer have by the rest of us been feather-bedded at enormous cost.

Twenty years ago, when Gormley was thirty-five or so and had for at least five years employed his body as object, subject and manufacturing tool on an industrial scale, I thought I could discern in his work an intense and melancholy talent, perhaps at a crucial moment of change, self re-assessment and burgeoning development. There was about his body casts something eerie and disturbing, all human qualities and characteristics smoothed, generalised and even neutered, the figure forced into enigmatic forms and attitudes that seemed, at the time, to suggest the spirit imprisoned. Human only in a symbolic sense, these simplified figures, ponderously limbed, asserted the nature of the iron or lead with which they were made, never Gormley's skin or features. My one misgiving was the sameness of them all, the suspicion that Gormley was, so like so many other contemporary artists, tied to one desperately thin idea.

Only my misgiving has been fulfilled. Gormley refers constantly to his own work and is perfectly happy to repeat it, as in the various *Fields*, without significant variation, the close reduplication of motifs a device to wring from them every possible slight shift of meaning. Once in a while the source of a new work may be an external borrowing; in his *Space Station*, fresh this year, he reflects the monumental ugliness of Paolozzi's public sculpture; his celebrated *Angel of the North* of the late 1990s had, a German curator suggests, a forerunner in the photography of Dieter Appelt, in which the artist used his own body (albeit naked only above the waist) with canvas wings to construct an image, published in 1980, of a disconcertingly Gormleyan Daedelus or Icarus. *Event Horizon*, a reworking of

Gormley's folly in Stavanger six years ago, ultimately reaches back to the baroque idea of sculpture as the terminal element of the constituents of traditional monumental architecture, but the random installation of his body casts atop the blank facades of London's office blocks has not exactly turned them into rivals to Rome's St Peter's or established him as a new Bernini. In such a comparison Gormley's single static figures, though they may add a point of focus for those given to gazing at horizons, seem wooden, mean and meaningless small things of scant aesthetic interest.

Even *Blind Light*, the work that has given so much perverse unaesthetic pleasure to visitors unable to distinguish a work of art from a circus side show, had a precedent in Westkunst, Cologne, in 1981 – a room filled with shredded paper through which the visitor, disoriented, had to find his way. *Blind Light*, a glass room within the gallery, is filled with cloud-like humidity so dense that visibility can be measured only in inches, and the cautious visitor, if he is to find his way back to the door, should keep a hand on the glass walls – this provides modest entertainment for spectators outside the box. Tessa Jowell is reported to have thought the jape a work of genius; I think it a silly nonsense and Gormley an arrant fool. No one with asthma or a heart disease of any kind should enter it; my immediate response was difficulty in drawing breath, followed by violent sneezing, then equally violent coughing and a crazily erratic heartbeat. As in so many galleries, there is nowhere in the Hayward to sit, so retreat to the loo was the only option for recovery.

In *Allotment II* of 1996 Gormley simply increased to 300 variations the single motif of his *Room* cast in concrete a decade earlier, an imprisoning box that at a height of over two metres might just have contained Gormley himself, with apertures for his mouth and ears in the small upper section, and anus and penis in the lower. In multiplying the number and varying the scale to accommodate human beings of every size and shape – in this case inhabitants of Malmö aged between eighteen months and eighty-five years – and then arranging them on a grid ground-plan, they resemble both a miniature model of a post-nuclear New York and a sale at B&Q of bat and bird boxes or council blocks for little furry animals.

Mother's Pride may suggest that Gormley is not entirely dour and humourless, for the medium is sliced white bread and the subject a foetal silhouette bitten from them by the man himself – but it is a feeble schoolboy joke. Dated 1982/2007, it is, I presume, a recent reworking of an earlier idea too puerile, the sane man must think, to be worth the repetition. Does the 1982 version still exist, I wonder? – I ask only because, when in 1988 in Liverpool I saw another work by Gormley in sliced bread, his *Bed*, of 1981, I noted the active presence of weevil and the menace of black mould. A Tate curator of the time (of pre-Serotan vintage) perhaps pulled my leg when he explained that Gormley, in eating his body shapes (fore and aft) in depth and volume into this Andrean spoof (the bed in some simple sense recalls Carl Andre's brick *Equivalents*), had for days consumed nothing but the bread and then cast his stools in lead, seeing some significance in the transformation of so much into so little. These stools, it seems, are to be found among the unidentified objects in *Natural Selection*, an immediately contemporary work now in the Tate's permanent collection; leg-pull or not, this conceit fits well with so much coprological art of the later twentieth century.

The so-called catalogue is useless; virtually devoid of the inform-ation expected in such a volume (and the very little that there is, printed very small in almost invisible grey ink), this consists of flattering photography (how the camera can lie), a sycophantic interview primarily by Rugoff and three ludicrously and ostentat-iously exhibitionist essays by American academics. Two of these do nothing but quote other academics and philosophers, pheno-menologists, Alberti, Winckelmann and even Diodorus of Sicily, the uncritical compiler of myths and history in Julius Caesar's day who means so much to most of us; the third must be credited with the invention of a word for Gormley's sculptures of himself, the clumsy fusion of his surname with the Hebrew golem, of which, apparently, the literal translation is cocoon – Gormlem. What fees, I wonder, were paid these American nincompoops? Could Rugoff not have found familiar English fools at half the price for twice the jabberwocky?

Gormlem? It is an ugly word even for Gormley's featureless figures. I hope it doesn't stick.

Antony Gormley, Hayward Gallery 2007

Event Horizon (2007)
http://www.antonygormley.com/sculpture/item-view/id/256#p8

Blind Light (2007)
http://www.antonygormley.com/sculpture/item-view/id/241#p1

Susan Hiller

Evening Standard, 3 February 2011

Susan Hiller was born in Tallahassee, Florida, on 7 March 1942, the day devoted to Sts Perpetua and Felicity, young mothers, obdurately Christian, whose martyrdom began with their being tossed on the horns of a maddened heifer. I offer her awareness of these female saints, suffering at the hands of men, in the hope that after much subconscious mulling of her mind and memory, prime nutrients of her work, they may provide her with a subject suited to her feminist sensibilities, surfacing from the undertow of half-forgotten recollection as a work of art expressed in the dreams she charts, in automatic writing and the ghostly palimpsest, or in recorded screams and prayers in classical Latin or ancient Carthaginian (she is in thrall to dying and dead languages), or some other favoured medium.

Hiller was first trained in the archaeology and anthropology of Central America but disillusioned with what she felt were the impossible limitations of this field of academe, experienced a 'crisis of conscience' that was resolved while making pictorial notes during a lecture on African art; at this she experienced an 'exquisite sensation' apparently akin to the orgasmic ecstasies of St Teresa of Avila, 'brim-filled bowls of fierce desire . . . with the draught of liquid fire'. She had already spent 1961–2 as a gap year in a self-plotted programme of training in painting, drawing, photography and film, with linguistics as a lollipop – a programme that for any ordinary mortal would occupy three years at the very least – and the transition from anthropology to art, exchanging 'factuality for fantasy', was thus accomplished in a trice. After two or three years of drifting and painting, painting and drifting, in 1969 she settled in London and abandoned both. The first of her countless artist's residences had been in 1968, and within a decade of her settling here she had had or had participated in some twenty exhibitions under the public patronage of the Arts and British Councils, the Royal College, the Camden Arts Centre, the Serpentine, Hayward and other galleries, and been taken up by dealers. In 1980 she was appointed Lecturer at the Slade.

From all this one might assume that she was brilliant (she has often been described as so), but I am inclined to think that formidable self-confidence and skills in networking combined to blind the panjandrums of these institutions to her evident lack of talent. She was too, very lucky – a feminist when the feminist movement was at its most exhaustingly belligerent, a conceptualist when the language of conceptualism was at its most obscure, its concepts most provocative and its supposed works of art absolutely à la mode, and concurrently a minimalist when minimalists sought to persuade us that in the purity of their forms and materials they were, in fact, maximalists. If this very small play on terms confuses, be assured that it is nothing compared with the flood of jabber-wocky generated by the makers, curators and other apologists in their strivings to invent a 'dialectical syntax of support' for con-ceptualism and minimalism. A dialectic, I should perhaps recall for those already confused, is, in philosophy, the process through which contradictory beliefs may be reconciled. In this, if the beliefs are that conceptualism and minimalism are and are not art, then the dialectic failed utterly in 1970 and, four decades on, fails still. I am resolutely on the not art side, and if in this I am perceived to be another Ruskin in another Whistler debate, an 'old pelican in the art wilderness', so be it, for I believe that the Hillers of this world have indeed reduced art to a barren waste.

Never mind the obfuscating language; if, as visual art, they are to be relished by the eye as much as by the mind, I do not believe that 280 photographs of Hiller's belly during her pregnancy in 1976–7, no matter how collated, framed, labelled and displayed, constitute a work of art. I am not to be moved from this position by those who write of the repeated image as having affinities with the harvest moon, echoes of landscape, and allusions to ripeness and fulfilment, or assert from it that Hiller 'understands that it is perfectly possible to forget who one has been and what one has accomplished'. The sequence of images in this installation may, perhaps, be of some small professional interest to a gynaecologist, but the rest of us must be content with the cleverness of their display – twenty-eight equal exposures in each of ten frames hanging in a descending diagonal to match the weight of her increasing gravity, so that we must bend double to inspect the last.

Five years ago, in 2006, Hiller contributed to a fat book on first works by artists; hers, she claimed, was *Dedicated to the Unknown Artists* inspired by finding in Brighton, in 1972, a hand-tinted postcard of rough sea. Elsewhere she found more, and intrigued by the 'sublime drama', and touched by the anonymity of the tinters in their repetitive sweatshop toil, she decided that we too, as dedicated followers of art, must share her responses and their drudgery. With 305 of these rough seas framed with pseudo-scientific observations and irrelevant linguistic statistics, looking is drudgery indeed. For her, however, mulling over these postcards matured into a Eureka! moment – the realisation that 'using cultural artefacts as basic materials could be a starting point' – and the following year, as artist-in-residence at the University of Sussex, she began 'the concrete work' (a foolish and misleading confusion with Concrete Art) of collation and categorisation that has ever since required a whole room to exhibit. Legitimised by ironic post-modernism, we all could make variations for ourselves, as she did with *Addenda* – more frames of postcards, but only of ten or so, as she continued to discover them.

The unshrunken *Unknown Artists* was not, however, her first work. There had been paintings, but these she had cut into little parcels that she called *Painting Blocks*, or had burned, storing their ashes in glass jars and the burettes of the chemistry laboratory, conserving and labelling them as might a forensic scientist, making still life sculptures of them, as in *Hand Grenades* of 1972, the reliquary of canvases painted in 1969. These cremated *Relics* too are ongoing, leading me to wonder if her own ashes will end in a burette as an exhibit – a by no means wild idea in a wilderness where artists are willingly cut, shot and crucified and sell their shit in tins.

Hiller, I fancy, wants her place in the history of art to be, not in the sub-section of Abject Art (mutilation, body fluids and other weirdo stuff), but as a thinker, a systematic scientist of sorts whose ideas have intellectual force. I see her as responding willy-nilly to her whims, irrational but imposing false reason of her own, convinced that she cannot be in error. I see her as an incapable romantic – incapable in the sense of having neither skill nor talent in any ancestral form of art, and thus compelled to express her angst in ways that are as obsessively deliberate as those of any manic collector rather than as scientific as the museum curator she half thinks she is. She collected shards from pueblos (an archeological discipline), numbered them, catalogued them by colour and exhibited them, not as might an archaeologist but as an artist romantically seeking a meaning in what she presented as Freudian transference, leading to what one of her many apologists defines as the science of sentience, the science of the invisible, a woman's thing in which men and their myths can play no part. In this she apparently formulates a challenge to 'the powers that, on the most foundational [patriarchal] level, determine the politics of our culture'.

What piffle, what a bore this pretentious woman is with her underlying feminism, her fey interest in dreams, and her extra-ordinary conviction that she has shamanistic power over very ordinary things. Reinforced by encounters with her work in mixed shows here and all over Europe, I have been aware of her since the mid-Seventies when I was foolishly enthusiastic about contemporary art and she twice exhibited at the Serpentine; I saw her ICA exhibition in 1986, another in 1996 at Tate Liverpool, yet another at the Baltic in 2004, and now, bigger than all these, a new but unwelcome, unnecessary and untimely survey of her work at Tate Britain, occupying rather than filling thirteen rooms and, had one the time to spare, requiring 2 hours, 51 minutes and 14 seconds to view her videos and other electronic offerings. These, more an offshoot of television than visual art, belong in a museum of flat-footed ideas.

Susan Hiller is not, as Tate Britain would have us believe, 'one of the most influential artists of her generation'. To all intents and purposes she is unknown in America, in Europe she is regarded, as are so many of her kind, as a feeble acolyte of Joseph Beuys, and here she is all but indistinguishable from a thousand others of her bent. Were one compelled to choose a single artist to represent the fatuity of the Arts Council–Serota–Saatchi orthodoxies in the last quarter of the twentieth century, Hiller might well be the answer, for she has embraced every addle-pated manifestation of departure from ancestral forms of art, though without ever achieving notoriety. She has toyed with automatic writing to document her mind, with light, language, sound and television sets, with provocative titles and objects in boxes, with photography, video wallpaper, Ripolin paint and the Twombling palimpsest. She may even have been first with some of these but all are now the stuff of students imitated from a score of sources, all are now jejune and stale. Can Hiller's shallow showing-off still be of interest in this new century?

Susan Hiller, Tate Britain 2011

***Monument* (1980–1)**
http://www.tate.org.uk/art/artworks/hiller-monument-t06902

***An Entertainment* (1990)**
http://www.tate.org.uk/art/artworks/hiller-an-entertainment-t06987

Damien Hirst's *In-A-Gadda-Da-Vida*

TATE BRITAIN

Evening Standard, 5 March 2004

To understand the title of Tate Britain's latest exhibition one must, I am informed by friends young enough to be my children, sing it as though slightly drunk and in the tone and timbre of Elvis Presley. It has nothing to do with that fat folk hero in tight white leather, but it is safe to assume that most of us have not only heard of him but, in some sort, have heard him too, and thus may understand the elision of consonants and distortion of vowels that in its written form make the exhibition's title, *In-A-Gadda-Da-Vida*, quite incomprehensible. To be accurate, this title comes from a record made in 1968, not by the divine Elvis, but by Iron Butterfly, a psychedelic rock band; of this, however, I had until now never heard, and uncertain as I am of the meanings of rock and psychedelic in the context of music, I found the reference too obscure. Having wasted hours working on the assumption that *In-A-Gadda-Da-Vida* is a Spanish anagram or some scrap of cockney wisdom uttered by a man with a heavy cold, I am grateful to those who supplied this information and, particularly, to the baritone who turned it into song.

To those of us who prefer spoken English, *In-A-Gadda-Da-Vida* means 'In the Garden of Eden', and is the concept of three artists who seem not only not to have read the opening chapters of Genesis but to know precious little of the pretty myth as it is told in Sunday Schools. The best known of the three is Damien Hirst, he of the shark, sheep, cows and pigs in tanks of clear formaldehyde, of dead and dying bluebottles, of the pinned-down butterflies and hearts of pink canvas beloved of Mrs Beckham. Sarah Lucas is the less successful twin of Tracey Emin with whom she ran a sordid 'art shop' in Bethnal Green, now made slightly less obscure by her proposal to dump a rusty Lada drowned in bird droppings on the empty plinth in Trafalgar Square. And the third triumvir is Angus Fairhurst. Angus who? Our response may well be blank – even Matthew Collings, the great guru of contemporary British art and the nation's annual apologist for it at Turner Prize celebrations, has nothing to say of him other than that he has been described as the art world's secret weapon and an unspecified 'they' say 'he is very clever and gives all the young London artists their ideas, including Damien Hirst.' If a wider public than the miniscule and self-regarding art world has encountered his work, it was probably his modest contribution to *Apocalypse* at the Royal Academy in 2000, that venerable institution's most desperate attempt to be 'with it'; he is a one-man Theatre of the Absurd, a Dada joker eighty years behind the time.

Born, respectively, in 1965, 1962 and 1966, *In-A-Gadda-Da-Vida* must have been for all three a cradle-song of sorts, as indelible a memory as Amelita Galli-Curci crackling through a wireless set became for me three decades earlier. Perhaps at this point, we need a turbid essay by a Freudian analyst for, without some such authority, how can we explain the joint infantilism of three adults in settling on such a title for their exhibition? They were together as students at Goldsmith's College in the later 1980s, where their heads, already brimful of rubbish, overflowed into what was immediately perceived as genius by those who grooved the grooves of British art. Now on the point of forty and a trifle old for naughtiness (male masturbation must surely no longer be a mystery of smutty speculation for Miss Lucas who has evidently hitched a hike too many), Tate Britain has offered them what it chooses to describe as 'a unique opportunity for collaboration', both as individual artists contributing individual works to this exhibition, and to treat the whole as a common installation.

The exhibition is very little more than yet another display of provocations (they can hardly be called original ideas) that range from the folksy and naive to the amateur theatrical, from the weird and nasty to the best that the Women's Institute can do, from the unmitigatedly silly to the shudderingly creepy, from the crass craft incompetence of infants to the severe professionalism of their employed technicians. It offers us the wearyingly familiar clash between the expectations of high art engendered by its being housed in an age-old national gallery associated in most minds with the somewhat detached position of historic British art, and the low art of popular culture and common artefacts that we have, like Pavlov dogs, been trained to recognise as art because self-styled artists and curators tell us it is so.

The informed sceptic, however, is compelled to ask why this exhibition has been mounted in Tate Britain, not Tate Modern. In short, the answer is that all three artists are British, but those of us who have for decades been spectators in a larger art world than that subject to the narrow orthodoxies peddled by the Tate's panjandrums and the gnomes of the Arts Council, can see nothing specifically British about the three contributing artists – they are, indeed, part of an international trend that has spread throughout the western art market and are as intellectually indistinguishable from their peers in foreign parts as they are from their peers here. This is not to suggest that they are stylistically indistinguishable, only that in their various ways they reflect the whims of international fashion as readily as any mainland European artist, any American or man from Xanadu, and that so internationally notorious has their work become that, were visitors to this exhibition suddenly transported to an art gallery in another land, they would be unable to tell from the exhibited works whether they were in Aarhus or Eindhoven, Chicago, Tokyo or merely Milton Keynes.

The first impression on entering the Tate's vast rambling space is that one is less in an art gallery than in the vestibule of Deutsche Bank or some other random institutional collector of contemporary art, or perhaps in a Blue Water showroom for lavatory tiles and wallpaper, or in some misbegotten setting for a party conceived by the giddy wives of footballers, or in a rumpus room for their rich-kid children. It is light, bright and very definitely decorative. A motorcycle, phalluses, a lorry-cab designed as what, when I was in the army, was called a wanking-pit, and a masturbating Zeppelin equipped with what, in a helpful note issued to uncomprehending critics, the Tate describes as a 'wanking mechanism', will, no doubt, enchant adolescent boys. For men of my age great black gorillas – particularly the beast echoing Narcissus in a pool – evoke the pathos of the original King Kong (black and white and 1932, or thenabouts). And for those who, again like me, are wistfully convinced that in the wayward intelligence of Damien Hirst there lurks something better than the prankster and the fairground show-man, there is a new aquarium piece in which tropical fish swim languidly between the plastinated halves of a butchered cow, loops of sausages and a black umbrella.

Described so, *The Pursuit of Oblivion* must seem preposterous but, homage to a canvas by Francis Bacon that it is (*Painting*, 1946, MOMA New York), it has an undeniable baroque splendour about it, as though to mock all the ancestral traditions and apparatus of the altarpiece, the martyrdom, even the Crucifixion, with the contents of a butcher's shop. Now rare with Hirst, whose ingenuity and inspiration have in recent years seemed deadly desuetudinous, this is a work that compels us to see him still as an artist of some sort. His *Adam and Eve towards the End* must also stop us in our tracks; a retreat into work of a kind on which he concentrated more than a decade ago in a notable exhibition in the ICA, glass and steel traps in which evidence of sometime human occupation lay deserted, this is a not unsympathetic evocation of the squalor into which the unattended old descend, the scattering of earth an indication of the final stage. As with Sarah Lucas's wanking-pit, its origin lies with Edward Kienholz, the distinguished American who half a century ago shocked us with such telling room-installations. Such dependence on distant originals has always been the Achilles' heel for those who argue that Hirst and his contemporaries are significantly more than followers and consolidators, or worse, the pilferers and cribbers of ideas, but the highest compliment that I can pay them for this exhibition is that Duchamp would have been enchanted by it and might well have claimed Hirst's *Pursuit of Oblivion* to have been inspired by his *Large Glass*.

Part of this showy show is loathsome. I can respond only with disgust to the fluttering deaths of butterflies with battered wings trapped in a glass case too small for the patterns of their flight, and a calf born with six legs is not a work of art but a medieval monstrosity fit only for the curiosity of alchemists. As for *Adam and Eve* gently breathing on a double operating table, shrouded by blue sheets but for their genitals visible through fig-leaf windows (oh the sparkling wit of it) – what is the point of this, other than to rouse the prurience of schoolboys? But then so much of this exhibition demonstrates the artists' immaturity and little else. Their apologists suggest that they are nourished by a profound vein of British humour, the slapstick and innuendo of the pantomime, the 'she sits among the cabbages and peas' of Marie Lloyd brought up-to-date. They suggest that this is working-class visual art to suit a working-class fondness for the fart. They tell us that a kipper is visual slang for a vagina, that spam – surely now a distant wartime memory for most of us – has associations with the penis, and that all this 'art' is a response to the middle-brow decorous humour of Monty Python and Peter Sellers. And then, they contrarily claim, it represents an epic sense of imminent collapse, disintegration and renewal.

What, I wondered, would Michelangelo have made in the half-ton of bronze that Angus Fairhurst used to cast a peeled banana as a dark and well-formed turd?

Damien Hirst's *In-A-Gadda-Da-Vida*, Tate Britain 2004
http://www.damienhirst.com/exhibitions/group/20041/in-gadda-da-vida

Adam and Eve Towards the End (2004)
http://www.damienhirst.com/adam-and-eve-towards-the-end

Damien Hirst and his *Murderme Collection*

SERPENTINE GALLERY

Evening Standard, 24 November 2006

Who now remembers Damien Hirst? I do – but then it is my job
to do so.

Artists in their early forties do so – but they are his immediate
contemporaries and as many have languished in his shadow,
remembrance is easy because it is also bitter. But to the very
young it seems that Hirst is no longer the fashionable hero whom
all art students want the opportunity to emulate; to many of them
he is as old hat as Hogarth and Howard Hodgkin, two other
ancient worthies who swim with him in the primordial soup of
half-forgotten recollection and half-remembered ignorance that
now, in art schools, passes for the history of art.

I have in the past week encountered an art student who could
neither name nor describe a single work by Hirst and whose view
of our much celebrated Brit Art was firmly not only that its day has
passed, but that it need not be remembered. I rattled off the names
of Sarah Lucas, Tracey Emin, Gavin Turk and the Chapman
Brothers, and of these only Emin was worth a derisive snort of
recognition; and he tried me with other names, not one of which I
knew – and I was not in the least abashed when I learned that all,
famous in his eyes, are well under twenty-five. To be, as Hirst is,
over forty, is to be as irrelevant to students half his age as were the
great grandees of the Victorian Olympus to Sickert, Steer and
John, though none of those would smugly have rejoiced in my
young interlocutor's dim and wilful ignorance.

Is Hirst within his lifetime just one more of a long line of fallen
giants to be recalled, like Ozymandias, for the boastful but ultimately

ironic inscription on the pedestal of a shattered monument? – 'My name is Damien Hirst, King of Kings, Look on my Works, ye Mighty, and despair!' A decade ago Hirst was the Leonardo of his day, draughtsman, painter, sculptor, cod-philosopher, author, playwright, polymath and God's gift to all mankind. This was a man of such and so many ingenious ideas that he must run a Renaissance workshop to achieve them, with assistants to construct steel cages, cut sheets of armoured glass, drain blood from slaughtered animals, cleave their corpses without losing an inch of intestine, and, in breathing apparatus and protective rubber clothing, wade with him in tanks of formaldehyde, for these were the constituents of his most famous works of art; no action painter of the Sixties ever provided so many and so various activities and entertainments.

Not a man of any serious education – indeed, as a schoolboy Hirst acquired the truant's customary skills of shoplifting and burglary and achieved only the grade of E in art (he could sink no lower and still pass) – it is we art critics and curators who elevated him to the state of genius, claiming, as we do, that anything and everything can be metamorphosed into art by the simple means of declaring it to be so – though the man who makes the declaration must first have declared himself to be an artist. The other easy means of metamorphosis is through the exhibition of banal objects in art galleries, for mere presence within the walls of these new cathedrals of belief and genuflexion is enough to turn things quite preposterous into icons thaumaturgical, the arrogant artist's turd a match for any masterpiece by Turner. To the question 'But is it art?' when confronted by the rotting head of a cow or a shoal of fish suspended in formaldehyde, was to invite Hirst's stock response 'It's in a gallery, ain't it?'

When Hirst abandoned the role of passionate exploratory artist and became celebrated as a wild and heavy drinker, nocturnal clubman and man-about-town in the stews of London and Berlin, it was easy to dismiss him as no more than a self-publicist and prankster, and even though he is much reformed, something of that characterisation clings to him. Do any but his closest courtiers now take him seriously? Have the welcoming embraces of the Royal Academy – that Vicar of Bray of the fine arts – lent him intellectual gravitas? Did he gain admiration and respect for the about-turn in his relationships with the two panjandrums who gave him his status as the great Brit Artist, Saatchi insulted as a man of no discretion, no taste, no aesthetic sensibility, but simply a man driven to possess, recognising art only with his wallet, and Serota as the organ-grinder of contemporary art, a player of the same old tunes surrounded by compliant monkeys, of whom Hirst is determined to deny that he is one?

How stands Hirst's aesthetic reputation now? In the shadows, I must argue, damned for the first of his great works, the now rotting shark – what else will rot, unhappy owners ask, my sheep, my calf, my cow, my sweet Empress of Blandings in formaldehyde? Damned for his gigantic sculptures too, their subjects and their imagery borrowed (some say stolen), their scale bleakly fascist, their modelling and surfaces deadly dull, the rewards for their contemplation trifling and transitory. Damned for his spot paintings, repeated and repeated, a stock workshop production – are they to be numbered in their thousands yet? Damned for the wealth gained from so much pointless labour by so many slaves, his huge country mansion and his determination to make of it a monument and memorial devoted to himself, his work and his possessions.

It is as connoisseur, collector and the curator of his possessions that Hirst has now emerged into the winter half-light to amuse us with a pantomime. He has, he lets us know, 1,111 paintings, sculptures, images, concepts and things in his collection – the sort of precise number that Salvador Dalí might have conjured for effect – but of these, only sixty-five are exhibited, the choice made, I suspect, to boast of his wealth, for his early Bacon and his Warhol *Electric Chair* cost the best part of £10 million between them, and at the same time to demonstrate his continuing support for such pathetic old friends as Angus Fairhead and Sarah Lucas, surely the most feeble-minded and vulgar of the Brit Art crew. With these and the least ingenious Jeff Koons pieces of the carpet sweeper genre and the protest work of the ingenuous and puerile Banksy, we have a glimpse of the range of Hirst's connoisseurship – range without depth but not without financial value, for the whole collection is insured for £100 million.

Hirst calls all these possessions the *Murderme Collection* – murderme because, it seems, his aged mother was offended by his intention that it should be buggerme and this specific selection from it he calls *In the darkest hour there may be light*, because these two phrases were the legends on the sleeves of a jacket sent him by New York friends (but then the titles of his works have never had much to do with anything). He is evidently still a man of puerile Puckish humour, and yet in *Murderme* there is perhaps the hint of a darker side to his nature, the pessimistic side from which stemmed his only serious and worthwhile work, the cage pieces that suggest inhumane laboratories, interrogations and prison cells, the bleak hygienic cupboards that make mute comments on surgery and the pharmaceutical industry. Serial murder long fascinated Hirst, and of Jeffrey Dahmer, whose biography was for years his bedside book, he once observed that this multiple killer had a 'terrible curiosity to find how living things work by taking them to pieces'. The same curiosity has driven much of Hirst's own work, and to some extent his collecting too, for his darkest hour is haunted by other artists' references to death, sex, mutilation and decay.

It is perhaps inevitable that my reaction to this meagre sixteenth of Hirst's vast collection should be that in one shape or another I have seen it all before, and that seeing it again has not a jot enriched my response to work that still seems shallow. Only the Bacon has intellectual, emotional and painterly weight – the grim Warhol is nothing better than a photograph tinkered into the pretence of painting. The rest of the exhibition is the transitory fashionable stuff bought by investment banks in the brief certainty of profit, the stuff that seems so familiar, ordinary and stale when promoted yet again by the Tate and the Arts Council, the monkey-see, monkey-do stuff of every would-be Saatchi – easy and empty sum it up.

Hirst has bought the whimsical at whim, and the whimsical is too often superficial or gratuitously nasty. There is no evidence of shrewd judgement in his choice, only of impulse immediately indulged by a man too rich to care. He is not much of a curator – but then, illiterate and inarticulate (for which, perhaps, much thanks), why should he be? Is his comment on the Bacon – 'un-fucking-believable' – a comment on the quality of the painting or on his ownership? Has he nothing more profound to say of his Warhol than that it is one of 'the greatest art works of the twentieth century' and 'I fucking need one of those'? And consider this of the prankster Banksys: 'I love that piece . . . he takes a found landscape and basically shits on it to make a great painting. Banksy is a great artist.'

With these opinions firmly held, what shall we eventually find in the 300 rooms of Toddington Manor, the rambling mansion that within a decade Hirst hopes will display permanently the whole murderme collection, by then, no doubt, numbering 2,222? If what we see now in the Serpentine Gallery is a true sample, then by the time Hirst reaches his three score years and ten, buggerme may well seem a better name for the collection. So far, I would not even grade it E.

**Damien Hirst and his *Murderme Collection*,
Serpentine Gallery 2006**
http://arts.guardian.co.uk/flash/page/0,,1946887,00.html

The Damien Hirst Sale

SOTHEBY'S

Evening Standard, 19 September 2008

For everyone and anyone in the art world, this week began with Damien Hirst's sale at Sotheby's – not the auction itself, but the exhibition that preceded it, for on show was an echo of everything that Damien has ever done, every idea that he has ever explored and exploited. At first glance it appeared to be a retrospective of the two full decades since 1988 when he sprang into celebrity, but at a second glance it was evident to long-term Damien-watchers that the sometime freshness had evaporated and that whatever it was that once caused outrage is now stale, for what Damien offered in this sale was not the urgent originality of his ideas when young, but their polished revision and repetition by the slave labourers on his production line.

For all its glitz and glamour it was a sad occasion, for here was the Damien who once seemed a sincere, if wayward, intelligence, selling his soul to the soulless. His exhibition at the ICA in 1992, four years into his career as a professional artist, was its high point, enough of its exhibits outweighing with high seriousness the frivolity of others. The cages, cabinets and fish in tanks, the spot and butterfly paintings, were all there, and they then had about them a craftsman quality of execution that is wholly lacking in the recent reworkings of these old ideas. In its place there is a new vulgarity and extravagance, a new glint and gloss and glister, a show of gold leaf and precious stones, a sense that everything has been redesigned with the wives of footballers in mind.

Wandering through Sotheby's it seemed transformed into the nightmare lobby of a would-be grand hotel in Miami or Las

Vegas – the pill-box pages and their brassy baggage trolleys were missing, but the harsh lights, glass cases, reflecting surfaces and celebrities were there. A nincompoop guiding a bevy of Dolce and Gabbana housewives through the masterpieces, waved towards some desperate scribbles and proclaimed them to be, at £30,000 or so, trifles that every one of them could easily afford, and a loudmouth pop star much given to troubling our charitable consciences proclaimed the whole show to be 'fucking marvellous'.

And there was the rub – all this was pop star stuff, not art. It was addressed to the moneyed with no taste, to the man with the Maybach or the Rolls, to the arrogant ignorant who have suddenly become the arbiters, not of art, but of what must be in and what is out in the households of the truly filthy rich. 'What are we waiting for, gathered in the marketplace?' asked the poet Cavafy, to which came the answer, 'The barbarians are to arrive today' – as, indeed, they did, laden with money-bags.

The Damien Hirst Sale, Sotheby's 2008
http://www.guardian.co.uk/artanddesign/gallery/2008/jul/29/
damien.hirst

Damien Hirst: *No Love Lost*

WALLACE COLLECTION

Evening Standard, 15 October 2009

The Laughing Cavalier, painted by Frans Hals in 1624, is one of the greatest treasures of the Wallace Collection. That this roguish anonymous gentleman is indeed laughing has been a matter of dispute since the title was coined in the later nineteenth century, but as it has become canonical and the image iconic, the questions 'why,' and 'at what?' have not been much asked in recent years. Now, however, almost four centuries after his depiction, he has a wry reason for his laughter, for it must be the sane man's immediate reaction to the puerile and maladroit paintings by Damien Hirst newly installed in neighbouring rooms for the next three months or so.

They are, for the most part, of human skulls. That Hirst, like Turner in his day has great paintings of the past in his mind with this display of his own very recent work, is not in doubt, for Poussin's *Dance to the Music of Time* now hangs in the Great Gallery so that it can be seen – though so distantly and dimly as to be inscrutable – as an adjunct to his skulls. This interpretation of it as a simple memento mori is naive – the subject, dictated to Poussin by Pope Clement IX is far more complicated than this. The Hals Cavalier is a far stronger image to be seen at such a range, but his imminent laughter might prove a subversive influence on everyone flanked about by Hirst's phalanx of skulls. These, I have no doubt, were painted with high seriousness, if for no other reason than that they must sell for millions, for as original works from the very hand of Hirst himself, each must surely rank higher as a work of art than any such multiple workshop offering as the notorious diamond–encrusted skull.

Alas, however, these paintings are shoddy, slipshod and derivative, not of Poussin or Frans Hals (the latter has a wonderful painting of a skull in the National Gallery), but of Francis Bacon, whose work he crudely mimics but does not understand. At vast expense Hirst has provided new hangings for the gallery walls, striped moiré silk in an aquamarine blue that conjures the spirit of dix-huitième France in an attempt to influence our opinion of his daubs. At vast expense he has framed his canvases as Bacon did, primarily in silver and gold, sheet glass both obscuring the images with reflections and lending mysterious depth. But, discounting these Baconian tricks of presentation and concentrating only on the canvases, we have nothing but the wretched incomprehensions of the first-year student cribbing from an acknowledged master.

As well as human skulls, the constituents of these still lives are Hirst's familiar idioms of the cigarette, the ashtray, the spot and the butterfly; the new elements are sharks' jawbones, the skeleton of an iguana, lemons, the hint of landscape and a composition with a vase of flowers that must be a gross enlargement of one by Bosschaert or Van der Ast early in the seventeenth century. All these are painted in white-toned blue on backgrounds of disturbed black that recall Derek Jarman's very late paintings. Were Hirst's canvases the work of a late teenager we might take the random lines around the skulls as a clever allusion to the measuring-points of a sculptor of Canova's generation, or as an illusion of cracked glass, and forgive the ugly clumsiness of inexperienced execution; but Hirst is nearing his half-century and should have a far higher level of skill than this rough daubing, with which he degrades his master, Bacon.

Is Damien his own worst enemy? He claims these caricatures of Bacon to be 'deeply connected with the past', but it is a past no earlier than the last quarter of the century in which he was born. He is vain enough to proclaim that his work as Bacon's shallow pasticheur belongs in the Wallace Collection with paintings by Rembrandt and Velázquez, Titian and Van Dyck, but one minute spent in the Great Gallery with these is enough to prove the arrogance of this delusion. Are then his uncritical friends, allies and advisers his worst enemies? – those who daily greet him with 'Oh King, live for ever' and tell him he can do no wrong. Has Ros Savill, directrice of the Wallace Collection, done him a great disservice in her foolish desperation to increase the number of the museum's visitors by exhibiting so notorious and filthy-rich an artist – the exposure should do no good to either herself or Hirst.

The exhibition is supported by the usual events performed by the usual lackeys who can be trusted to 'Praise him, praise him, praise him' – including Tim Marlow, a director of White Cube, the art dealership most closely associated with Hirst's huge commercial success (only in the arts could so crass a conflict of interest be ignored). It is accompanied by a catalogue in which all twenty-nine canvases are illustrated, but in no way illuminated by the text of a conversation in The Pig and Whistle between Hirst and John Hoyland, the grand old bore of British bucket-and-slosh abstract painting. In this the words most used and most superfluous are fuck and its derivatives – the fucking chair, fucking debris, fucking rectangle, fucking artist, fucking unbelievable . . . I take this as licence, for this occasion only, to declare this detestable exhibition fucking dreadful.

***Damien Hirst: No Love Lost*, Wallace Collection 2009**
http://www.guardian.co.uk/artanddesign/gallery/2009/oct/13/damien-hirst-art-wallace-collection#/?picture=354199037&index=11
or
http://www.wallacecollection.org/collections/exhibition/77

To own a Hirst is to tell the World that your bathroom taps are gilded and your Rolls-Royce pink

TATE MODERN

Evening Standard, 5 April 2012

Damien Hirst was born in 1965. At eighteen he took the year-long Foundation Course at what was then known as the Jacob Kramer College of Art in Leeds. After a two-year gap labouring on London building sites he started the BA course at Goldsmith's College. There compulsory drawing and every other discipline that might lead to his becoming a professional artist in the traditional sense had been abandoned; instead, wild theory, wilder ideas, and art history of the most erratic, shallow and misleading kind had absolute supremacy over all the ancestral skills of art in its ancestral forms. In 1988, two years into the course, he was the presiding genius of Freeze, the now famous three-part exhibition in a disused Docklands warehouse that proved to be the crucible in which the group known as the YBAs (Young British Artists) was formed. In 1991 the Institute of Contemporary Arts gave him, at twenty-six, his first solo exhibition in a publicly funded art gallery; the following year he was nominated for the Turner Prize; and in 1995, at thirty, he won it, trouncing the feeble opposition of Mona Hatoum, Callum Innes and Mark Wallinger.

He had by then been the subject, in whole or part, of some forty exhibitions (many more if we count all the venues to which some of them travelled) in Britain, Germany (the consequence of a year's fellowship in Berlin), Italy, America and elsewhere. He had also the support of the Arts Council, the Tate, Hayward, Serpentine and Whitechapel Galleries as well as the ICA, of several leading London dealers in contemporary art, and, most important of all because of the publicity attached to the relationship, of Charles Saatchi at his most flamboyant. Saatchi not only owned the notorious shark in formaldehyde, dubbed *The Physical Impossibility of Death in the Mind of Someone Living*, of 1991, but was rumoured to have had a hand in its conception and the organisation and costs involved in its making. To supply the work for so many exhibitions, patrons and collectors, Hirst must have had substantial financial support from the very beginning, even while still a student – how else could he have afforded the technical assistance required to construct the seventy-six leak-proof cases of formaldehyde for the fish of his *Isolated Elements swimming in the same Direction for the Purposes of Understanding*, of 1991, let alone the tank big enough to hold the shark?

Rapidly he became dependent largely on ideas first developed as a student and their industrial repetition. The ubiquitous *Spot Paintings*, for example – of which there are some 1,500, with the production line still working at full pelt – were first produced in 1986, more than a quarter of a century ago. Hirst himself now has no hand in them – they are the product of assistants given only the simple instruction to keep the colours of the spots entirely random with no perceptible sequence. To justify this workshop practice he raises the ghost of Rubens – but not even the most wretched apprentice in seventeenth-century Antwerp was still producing in 1635 precisely what Rubens had painted in 1610; nor would Rubens have charged so much for a painting not even touched by his hand – he charged according to a tariff that recognised the difference in value between work executed entirely by himself, by himself and assistants, by assistants with an improving touch or two by the great man, and entirely by assistants of varying levels of competence. Hirst charges as though everything is entirely by himself; this is only justified if we are fools enough to accept that the concept is the quintessential work of art and it is of no consequence who gives it physical embodiment; but from this it is possible to argue that in our postmodern art world we have every right to paint our spots ourselves – with a little practice they will be neither better nor worse than those marketed by Hirst, neither more nor less his autograph work.

The pharmaceutical cupboards and vitrines too reach back to Hirst's student years – the first, *Sinner* and *Enemy*, were produced in 1988 and ten more were made within a year, four of them exhibited in his graduate show of 1989. Assigned such non-pharmaceutical titles as *god*, *Pretty Vacant* and *Anarchy* (perversely, early spots were dubbed *Acetic Anhydride*, *Aprotinin*, *Calciferol* et al), they are essentially everyone's bathroom cabinet enlarged and every single one of us has from time to time done what he did – that is, lent order to disorderly arrangement. A decade later he was still stocking vitrines, but with skulls, bones, brains and surgical instruments, and some developments were homages to the seven-teenth-century Cabinet of Curiosities and to the medical models and specimens accumulated in the pan-European schools of surgery and medicine in the Enlightenment. Even so the basic concept of the cupboard or vitrine remained unchanged. In 2008, however, Hirst reverted to his earliest pattern and repeated, for his now notorious auction sale at Sotheby's, pretty well exactly what he had made twenty years before.

In the bottom left-hand corner of *Sinner* is a small medical model of a female torso with the belly skin and ribs removed. It is not the same as the gigantic *Hymn* of 1999–2005 that once stood in Charles Saatchi's first gallery, subject to accusations of plagiarism, but, apart from the overwhelming scale, is very like and again demonstrates that once Hirst has lit on an idea he keeps it on the boil for years, even decades, until he has exploited its every possible variant and purpose. Add to *Hymn* and *Sinner* the organs in specimen jars of 1991, the fish, the shark, the butterflies and the farm animals in formaldehyde, and it must seem to the enquirer that, with the exception of the *Spots* (though even for these he claimed a 'scientific approach'), all his ideas were borrowed from things seen as a boy on frequent prowlings in the university's anatomy museum before, at nineteen, he left Leeds for London.

If we compare the major works executed for the Sotheby's sale of 2008 (his last significant exposure in Britain) and the later works in the new but meagre retrospective at Tate Modern (only seventy-three exhibits), with the earlier examples, we see gestation and production periods of more or less a quarter of a century. Did any great artist's workshop of the Renaissance or the Baroque ever develop so little over so long? It helps to look at Hirst less as an artist than as a craftsman, a maker, even a manufacturer, of extravagant goods desirable to footballers' wives and cupiditous collectors governed by envy and social inferiority rather than connoisseurship. Why should Hirst, as a businessman (of which indisputable proof lies on his website, even at the market-trader level with trinkets and souvenirs), embark on serious development or fundamental change when he has identified half a dozen formulae that need only to be 'refreshed' if they are to sustain their appeal to his hedge fund, filthy rich, pop-star, monkey-see, monkey-do, done-thing clientele? To own a Hirst is to tell the world that your bathroom taps are gilded and your Rolls-Royce is pink.

In the exhibition at Tate Modern spin paintings revolve, a beach ball balances on an intolerably noisy jet of air and we wander from John Bell and Croyden into branches of Boots, John Lewis, Divertimenti and David Mellor. Though tedious, it is bearable. The butterfly room, however, is unbearable. I saw its first incarnation in the Woodstock Gallery in 1991 and was sickened by it then, for it knowingly involves the death of butterflies, probably tens of thousands of them by the time this wretched exhibition ends on September 9. Even before the exhibition opened these creatures were fluttering exhausted on the gallery floor, denied anything that resembles their natural habitat. How is it that they are 'only' butterflies? How is it that the RSPCA does not protest? How can any decent man or woman walk through this room – the *In and out of Love* – without the rise of anger at such cruelty? What an artist does at twenty-six one may perhaps attribute to the waywardness of his intelligence, but at forty-seven how could Hirst bear to repeat such vain cold-blooded inhumanity?

All who care for living things should boycott this exhibition. Disgust must be the response of the sane, not only to the use, abuse and death of butterflies, but to the exploitation of farm animals mercilessly slaughtered in the knacker's yard and, at an aesthetic level, to Hirst's taste for the ghastly glitter and glamour found in Miami's holiday hotels. I can sum it up as shiny shit. Bob Geldof, on the other hand, might repeat his estimation of Hirst's Sotheby's sale when, awestruck as he was by its garish glister he bellowed 'fucking marvellous' for all to hear.

Hirst himself will, no doubt, describe this show of his work too as 'epic'. It is nothing of the kind; a meagre third of the number of exhibits in the Sotheby's sale, it is a little more didactic. A handful of things tell us how Hirst began, another handful the state of his imaginings in 2006-9 – bigger, much bigger and much shinier, but essentially the same – and between them lie the sterile old familiars that, once seen, have nothing more to give. Put bluntly, this man's imagination is quite as dead as all the dead creatures here suspended in formaldehyde.

David Hockney

ANNELY JUDA, W1

Evening Standard, 8 May 1997

His sixtieth birthday upon him in July, David Hockney is soon to join the grand old men and pensioners of British painting – Carel Weight (his tutor long ago at the Royal College), Craigie Aitchison, Jefferey Camp and Lucian Freud, all in a sense academic painters, all painters whose work is received by critics with superstitious awe, and all painters whose eagerly awaited pictures are grist to the mill of those who would bring art to popular attention. In all these aspects they are the heirs of Stanley Spencer and James Gunn (a now forgotten painter of the formal portrait), in the days of my childhood the long and enthusiastically anticipated subjects of genteel controversy and blind adoration year on year as the Summer Exhibitions opened at the Royal Academy. David too is an Academician, but he has never served it well, sending it only the stale sweepings from his studio, keeping his new work for his dealers and his sentimental buddies, work that is carefully handled by specialists in press relations so that it is guaranteed to attract the veneration of the broadsheet critics – indeed a Hockney exhibition, anywhere of anything, be it drawings of dogs or photographs of his foreskin, is greeted with much the same emotion as a Mass said by the Pope.

The Tate Gallery honoured David with a retrospective exhibition in the winter of 1988–9, but London has since then seen virtually nothing of his paintings and is largely in ignorance of recent developments, though of prints, drawings and gouaches we have been kept aware by Cork Street and the Royal Academy. Now, at last, we are privileged to see the very latest work in a special exhibition at the Annely Juda Gallery – 'brand new . . . never exhibited before,' cry the press relation barkers, 'the largest ever commercial gallery show,' they shout, with 'an extensive 160 page, two volume, fully illustrated catalogue documenting all the new paintings'. Documenting? It does no more than illustrate the wretched things, and in two brief deceitful paragraphs conjures the support of Turner and Vermeer – Vermeer, it tells us, caught light within his paintings and used it 'to finely delimit the spaces that his colour described'. What bilge (and a split infinitive to boot) – and there is more; after spending many hours at the Vermeer exhibition (specially opened so that he could have it to himself), David 'mounted his own challenge to capture light and space'. David, I was privately informed as though vouchsafing information about the nature of the Holy Ghost, had never thought of looking at Vermeer until everyone else did so in The Hague last year; that does not surprise me, for there seems no end to the ignorance and arrogance of modern artists (Anthony Caro, an any old iron sculptor revered by the Serota Tendency, you will recall, paid his first visit to Greece, the fount of all European sculpture, only when well past his sixtieth birthday), but that Hockney should now claim that the vulgar cheap-jack daubs he offers as his latest work have even the most tenuous connection with Vermeer, is laughable – though anger and outrage are responses just as reasonable.

The exhibition is restricted to paintings of flowers and faces, though the word 'spaces' is incorporated in the title to justify the assertion that Vermeer inspired them. If Peter Blake were again on the Hanging Committee of the Royal Academy (which Heaven must forfend) we might discover primitive flower paintings of this kind there, but the proper place for them is on the railings of Green Park, where they might find a ready sale to visitors from Scunthorpe in search of souvenirs; they might also seem in some tawdry way 'robust' (the critic's jargon word for crass images painted with blind assurance) in the context of the amateur – at the annual summer painting school in Lower Scrotum, perhaps; but they have no business to hang in any circumstances where the credulous can be convinced that they are art within any acceptable definition of the word. The faces are no better – indeed they are so much worse that not even Peter Blake could argue that they have the naive peasant streak he finds appealing, and one is compelled to argue that they belong to the boiled baby school of portraiture. If David asserts that they challenge Vermeer, then we must assert that he is as blind as he is deaf – or just plain vain and stupid.

These banal flower paintings are lurid in colour, crude and insensitive in a handling of paint that, daubed, scribbled and scrawled, suggests the desperation of frustrated infancy, the oil denied its translucent nature and made as opaque as poster colour; the drawing (when there is any evidence of it) is uncertain, haphazard and insecure. The silhouettes of bright flowers against brighter backgrounds are crude, lacking any subtlety of observation, and the tones clash too, destroying the very sense of space at which he aims; shadows fall arbitrarily, and sometimes not at all; and the haphazard dispositions of pots, bottles, vases and blooms convince us that David is wholly unaware of the architecture that lies hidden in the compositions of the still lives of the past. He painted similar subjects in the Seventies with some finesse, but not much sensitivity; now, twenty years on and more, the evidence of steep decline is irrefutable.

Most of the portraits are small – roughly 14 × 11 inches – and twenty-four of them in a phalanx must be considered inseparable parts of a larger work, an iconography of sorts (in imitation of Van Dyck as well as of Vermeer?) recording himself, his family and friends. The flesh tones are those of prize nasturtiums, and the heads, most of them cut close across the brow or down one cheek, varying a little in focal length, are set against a common bright green ground that is harsh and dissonant (made worse when there are touches of blue in shirt, or hair or shadow) and helps to destroy the sense of volume. The caricatural likenesses are, to put no fine point on it, disconcertingly weak as portraiture, though the inadequate critic will no doubt aver that the awkward cutting of the images adds tension, and, seduced by the obvious brushstrokes, will mistake them for the gestures of brave purpose. They are, singly and together, the woeful stuff of adolescent student years, and remarkably unpleasant.

There are those who would have us believe that David in these latest pictures conjures the harsh light of Los Angeles as surely as Vermeer depicted the soft humiferous light of Holland – but this is arrant nonsense, the assertion of feeble critics too cowardly to acknowledge the consequence of disbelief in the cardboard maestro after thirty-five years of churning out images in which too many millions have been invested. It is, nevertheless, high time to reconsider David's work as a whole, to look back from these feeble offerings and ask if he was ever the skilled genius in whom we have been led to believe by his vociferous apologists, for decades the subject of unquestioning admiration. That he has been an amusing designer for the stage cannot be denied – but then so have hundreds of others (and better too) without at the same time claiming to be a Cork Street genius; but for a man who has never shown the least comprehension of paint as a subtle material with which a virtuoso can work miracles, who only uses it as the colour between lines or as a decorative texture, to claim that he is a painter, is absurd. As for Hockney the draughtsman who equals Picasso, Ingres and Michelangelo, whose portrait studies are unrivalled and not the tame caricatures with the wit excised that the cool spectator sees – why do we persist in deluding ourselves that, apart from a brief period in the Seventies, his work on paper was ever worth a second glance? Looking at this exhibition, and then the long retrospective view back to 1960, we are quite justified in damning him as a minor provincial talent, Bradford's only brilliant son – and brilliant only for as long as he was exposed to cosmopolitan influences, dexterously reflecting them.

David's fame is inextricably bound to the period of his emergence in the Swinging Sixties, when wealthy limousine liberals were happy to be seen supporting a deliberately camp homosexual as part of their right and proper protest against savage and restrictive laws. David became their mascot, their regimental goat, their banner with the strange device, and no one who was anyone, however desperately heterosexual, could risk his liberal reputation by not having his bedroom decorated with Hockney's Cavafy boys having their way with each other in fine Physique Pictorial style. Those liberals have aged and faded, and so have the Cavafy prints and all they stood for; the years of protest ended and came to all but nothing, the homosexual tide has ebbed and with it the driving force of David's work has gone. He did a great good in his way with the bigger bums of California – splendid propaganda for his cause – but now that he is no longer driven by a need, or has relinquished it, the force has gone from him, and without its purpose, all delicacy, skill, judgement and painterly integrity too are gone. For the best part of twenty years David has been in decline, and we have tolerated it; now, confronted by the poverty of this latest exhibition, we must weep at the falling-off.

David Hockney's Secret Knowledge

Book Review

Evening Standard, 21 December 2001

'Hockney strikes gold', proclaimed one ignorant reviewer, and such words as thrilling, fascinating, entertaining, revealing, delightful, stimulating and captivating flowed from the lips and pens of others. We are accustomed to such hyperbole in the context of Hockney the great painter, but this was in the context of Hockney the great art historian, scientist and man of letters, the writer of a book with such 'big new things to say' that it turns topsy-turvy the whole history of western art. Page after page of the intellectual broadsheets has been devoted this past autumn to Hockney's *Secret Knowledge* – 'an enthralling intellectual journey . . . an amazing detective story . . . about the lost techniques of the Old Masters . . . revealing secrets of the past . . . ' and even sceptical reviewers have felt constrained, recognising the whole nation's supposed affection for the author and, particularly, the power of the publisher to blight books of their own, to commend Hockney's wretched thesis for such vague reasons as 'it makes you see things too, in a way you may never have done before.' Indeed, it is intended to make you see things that simply are not there.

Put in a nutshell, Hockney's notion is that as soon as lenses and mirrors became more or less widely available in medieval western Europe, artists began to use them as a means of scrutinising the things or people whom they wished to paint, and that these scrutinies, caught in detailed drawings, were then pieced together like a jigsaw puzzle to construct a composition. If the junctions happened to be blurred by loss of focus at the edges, or details were taken from minutely different angles (thus disrupting the geometrical perspective that, until now, we have all assumed to be the underlying unifying element in paintings), or details were taken from precisely the same angle with precisely the same focus no matter whether they were for the centre or the perimeter of a picture, then these disjunctions could be sufficiently fudged by the painter to deceive the patron and the critic. In other words, all peculiarities perceived by Hockney, no matter how contrary (and no matter how much imagined or erroneously observed – many of the errors inexcusable from a man with a supposedly sharp eye), are proof that painters from the early fifteenth century to late in the nineteenth relied heavily on optical devices.

Apart from mirrors, flat, convex and concave, and lenses, convex and concave, two contraptions came into play – the camera obscura and the camera lucida. The camera obscura – literally, dark room – was known for many centuries for it is a natural phenomenon tamed, so to speak; essentially it was a small room, shed, or even tent, from which all light was excluded but for one small hole on the sunny side; by some seeming miracle, through this hole, the sunlit world outside projected its image onto the inner wall opposite it, but on a dull or wintry day there could be no image, for very strong light is essential; on a summer day, if an artist had pinned a bright white sheet of paper where the projection fell, he could follow with his pencil, pen, chalk or charcoal, the outlines of the projected image with, according to Hockney, an accuracy impossible to achieve by looking and drawing. To him, the fact that the projected image was upside-down is neither here nor there, nor the fact that the artist himself was working in darkness made more blinding by its contrast with the bright light outside.

The camera obscura could be rigged within any house, or in tent form could be carted about the countryside by every landscape painter wanting to achieve topographical accuracy (why then was the bird's-eye swooping view so common for so long?) or, in

Constable's case, the perfect cloud formation. The artist no longer needed to look at his subject and make a mark on his paper, look again and make another mark, and so on until his study was complete – all he had to do was follow the outlines of projected images and the essential work was done, and if a wealthy merchant had been his subject, then every detail of the portrait was absolutely in its place and the patron could not dispute its accuracy. 'No, Mr Arnolfini,' we can hear Jan van Eyck arguing, 'that is precisely how you look. You may think yourself a handsome dark Italian, but my camera obscura proves that you are as pale and ugly as an upturned Dover sole – and the camera cannot lie.'

Hockney goes further with the Arnolfini portrait; informed by the authorities of the National Gallery that no trace of preparatory drawing has been identified beneath the ornate candelabrum, he asserts that van Eyck 'could have hung' his portrait upside-down in the camera obscura instead of a sheet of paper, the bright white gesso priming of the panel having much the same effect, and painted directly the projected image of the candelabrum rigged to hang in the sun outside. Imagine the complications of this procedure; the candelabrum had to be suspended at precisely the right height outside on a windless sunny day, and the panel had to be fixed upside-down at precisely the right height and focal length in the darkness within the camera. Within the darkness van Eyck then had to organise his brushes and his paints, get his tones and colours absolutely right and somehow imagine and adjust the range of light and shadow of his painted candelabrum so that these were consonant with the light and shadow in the painted bedroom of this nuptial portrait, in which early morning light falls strongly through the windows (one visible, one implied) on the left wall. Hockney asserts proof of this idea with the instruction 'Notice how the chandelier is seen head on (not from below, as you would expect). This is the effect you would expect with a mirror-lens, which must be level with the objects you want to draw or paint.' Hockney is wrong; even to the most inexperienced eye the candelabrum is obviously seen from below, its perspective in general agreement with that of the room.

'Could have hung'. The book is littered with such ill-considered evasions – could have, may have, seem to have, surely it is no coincidence that, optics could account for, seems to suggest and could be explained by. As with van Eyck's candelabrum he constantly asserts that details are seen head on when they are not and, by urging us on with the intellectual sleight of the magician, he forces everything to fit the argument. If a detail is crystal clear it proves his point, if it is fuzzy at the edges, it proves his point; if preliminary drawings survive in quantity, or are utterly unknown, they prove his point – and his point seems to be that everything from the most meticulous verisimilitude to the most crass inaccuracy, elongation, disproportion or plain bad drawing, demonstrates that every artist from Jan van Eyck to Andy Warhol depended on lenses and projections for his realism or lack of it.

His interest in this nonsense began when, at the National Gallery's exhibition of portraits by Ingres three years ago, he failed to realise that the discrepancy between the care with which this master draughtsman of the nineteenth century drew heads in portrait drawings and the seeming carelessness in his treatment of the bodies, was then characteristic of much portrait drawing all over Europe. For Ingres, who tended to eliminate this discrepancy for his English clients and treat every detail of clothing with minute scruple, this was both a stylistic and a functional matter – the likenesses of the faces were important but the details of dress not necessarily so, and these could be dismissed with a fluent, but often quirky, shorthand. For more than half a century, from 1810 until the 1860s, the portrait drawings of Ingres are consistent in this discrepancy, but Hockney does not attribute this to the portrait painter who looks at his model and diligently makes delineating marks until the face is finished and then, with rapid strokes, dashes in the rest to give the head pictorial support, or, in a more annotating hand – in case a painted portrait might be commissioned from it – describes details that will recall for him a patterned or embroidered material.

Whether dashing, annotated or minutely finished, Hockney attributes every different characteristic to the use by Ingres of the camera lucida, a simple English invention of 1806 in which a prism is employed to project an image onto paper so that the draughtsman has no more to do than follow the outlines slavishly. It has many advantages over the camera obscura – ordinary light is sufficient, the image is the right way up and, without too much squinting, the draughtsman can see both the subject of his drawing and the projected image at the same time. No evidence, however, supports Hockney's assertion that Ingres used the camera lucida, and though a great deal of the old boy's personal and professional life was recorded by his possessions, no such instrument was found among them. 'Aha!' says Hockney, 'artists were secretive and kept such matters to themselves – that's why it has taken me, an artist, to discover what mere art historians could never know.' But it was not just the artist's secret in this case, for the hundreds of sitters who sat to Ingres kept the secret too; yet in 1855, a writer on Ingres as a then contemporary painter, told the world that with the help of a photograph by Felix Nadar, Ingres could compose the most admirable portrait without a sitter's presence; Nadar himself in 1857 published a caricature of Ingres chasing a camera that is running away on its tripod. How odd of Ingres to be so open about the conventional camera and yet so deceitful about the camera lucida – but then that, according to its inventor, William Wollaston, was designed to make drawing easy for those 'without an adequate knowledge of the art'.

The camera obscura too seems to have been a thing for amateurs. 'Nothing can be more amusing for great men, scholars and ingenious persons to behold,' wrote Giambattista della Porta in 1558. 'For the mathematician rather than the painter,' wrote Henry Wootton in 1620. Joshua Reynolds, who owned a portable camera obscura, discoursed against the contraption, the consequence of its use 'little and mean', the artist disdaining it a man of 'additional superiority', and George Adams, instrument maker to George III, who made and sold all sorts of refinements to the camera obscura – even a 'heliostate' for directing the sun's rays on a particular spot for several hours – wrote that 'the most able and successful artists . . . trust mostly to their eye and habit for success.'

There is no doubt that lenses, mirrors and optical deceits existed throughout the period covered by Hockney's book, but he has not proved one single example of an artist's using them, not even with Vermeer and Canaletto, the two cases most easily half proved. While there are many accounts of artists rare and famous at work among the ruins of Rome and in the Roman countryside, and many pictures and drawings of them, there is not one sight or mention of a camera obscura, and among all the portraits of artists by artists, not one is at work with a camera lucida. For every one of Hockney's proofs of their use of these technical aids by Caravaggio, Velázquez, Zurbaran, Fantin-Latour, Fragonard, Frans Hals and even Leonardo da Vinci with his Mona Lisa, there are far more reasonable and powerful explanations.

I must ask Hockney what part either camera played in the production of the *Martyrdom of St Sebastian* by the Pollaiuolo brothers and the portrait of *Madame Moitessier* by Ingres – popular pictures in the National Gallery. The Pollaiuolo is a typical example of the Florentine Renaissance struggle to apply linear, single-disappearing-point perspective to an extensive upright land-scape dominated by figures, at a time when aerial perspective (colour softening with distance) was just coming into play – no evidence of camera, mirror or lens. Ingres took twelve years to complete his portrait; the sitter aged from twenty-three to thirty-five, her daughter was put in and then scraped out, two earlier dresses, handsome and expensive, fell out of fashion and lie beneath the furnishing fabric of her final dress, her hairstyle changed from bouffant to severe and her jewellery and knick-knacks changed;

how many times did Ingres fix her behind his camera lucida and try again?

And my final question is, if the camera obscura was fundamental for drawing as the preparation for pictures, what has Hockney to say of preparatory drawings for sculpture? Did artists who were both painters and sculptors – Verrocchio, Leonardo, Michelangelo and Canova among them – really change their practice with their medium? Did Leonardo look at horses upside-down through a pin-hole for his *Battle of Anghiari*, but draw them freehand from the life for the Sforza and Trivulzio Monuments? No – of course not – any more than he asked an old man to pull a face and hold the expression while he drew it as a caricature, any more than he had a real dragon, tank or flying machine standing in the sun outside his studio.

This is a silly and meretricious book, a demonstration of naive obsession, of remote improbabilities presented as hard facts, of shifting ground for every argument, self-indulgently subjective, a farrago of feeble nonsense that should never have been published and, had it been sent to Thames and Hudson by Uncle Tom Cobleigh or Jack Sprat, would not have been.

David Hockney: *Painting on Paper*

ANNELY JUDA, W1

Evening Standard, 17 January 2003

The worst misfortune to befall the art dealer who specialises in the art of the past is to discover that he has been duped by a forger and has sold a fake to a valued client. The dealer loses face – is, indeed, made to look the gullible and greedy fool that in all probability he is – and his client feels that his trust has been betrayed. It is a not uncommon occurrence; it has happened often enough with such major figures as Van Gogh, Renoir and Degas, and from time to time there has been on the market a steady stream of watercolours thought to be by Sargent, oils by Sickert and drawings by Gaudier-Brzeska – the evidence for these last and a set of Omega Workshop chairs made by the sculptor Bill Woodrow, is to be found in Derek Jarman's journals.

Dealers in contemporary art, however, for the most part escape this particular embarrassment – though Picasso in his day was so constantly imitated that after World War II it was discreet always to consult him, no matter how distinguished the ownership of a painting or drawing, to prove that it was genuine. The menace in this field is, instead, the celebrated artist who has so fallen away in inspiration and execution, has become so habitual, repetitive, even regurgitive, that his work is no longer worthy of the collectors who have for half a century supported it. Year after year at the Royal Academy Summer Exhibition we see evidence of this phenomenon, this exhaustion of both intellect and skill, the one idea played out, the bottom of the barrel scraped, the imagery and handling automatic, and with some of these poor sods not even that – consider Kitaj, of whose once evident abilities there is now not the slightest token. Auerbach, Kossoff, Bellany, Caulfield, Hoyland, Hodgkin, Blake – I could continue this list of worn-out old boys with many much younger among the so-called sculptors of today, the installers and the mindless nincompoops who toy with video cameras, for mid-life exhaustion is a peculiarly British disease widespread and devastating in its strike. Like the ubiquitous Gormley and Kapoor, they do what they do because it is all that they can, and the only variation is in scale or number, never in idea.

I raise these melancholy matters because David Hockney is – as all the world by now must be aware – having another exhibition, long awaited, bated breath, and my heart bleeds for his dealer. David is the artist of whom everybody knows, the twin giant, with Alan Bennett, of Yorkshire culture, indeed, more than an artist, he is the Bradford polymath. David was the boy who put himself in the forefront of gossip in the Swinging Sixties when every member of the liberal intelligentsia in London had to have a pet homosexual under his wing. David was the young man who abandoned slap-dash post-COBRA influences for meticulous drawing and defied the dominant trend into abstract painting by portraying soft-porn bare-bummed boys in formulated swimming pools. David was the successful painter drawn into the staging business of the opera and the swagger business of the portrait – 'Posterity,' avers one well-known authority, 'may well acclaim him the greatest of modern portraitists.'

David is quite certainly the man who re-invented perspective and, not content with that, then re-invented Cubism; he is just as certainly the man who having made art with the junk polaroid photograph, then made it with the fax machine and that now forgotten contraption, the Quantel electronic paintbox. David is a grandee of such unassailable reputation that the publishers of his autobiographical ramblings felt able to present him, in the first year of this millennium, as the brilliant, scintillating, re-inventor of art history, for, having recontrived the camera obscura he thought he had the right to turn topsy-turvy the whole history of art. Not since Nazi art historians laid claim to the Renaissance has there been a more mendacious, misleading and meretricious book.

Some of us must argue that in his wild pursuit of every will-o'-the-wisp – the proper name of which is ignis fatuus and fatuous indeed most of the wills have been – David has neglected the areas of art in which he once gave proof of some small talent, skill and sensibility. Thirty years ago he drew wonderfully sensitive portraits in coloured crayons and touching evocations of Paris, Egypt and Morocco; with pen and line he lent immortality to his friends and lovers; and with his brush, he made acrylic, the most insensitive and least trustworthy of paints, breath life into still life. The brief Seventies were the decade in which it seemed that he could do no wrong, the years in which success justified every whimsical diversion. But in the Eighties it was no longer so and his progress has been downhill ever since, marked particularly by appalling greasy portraits of miscellaneous young men, dreadful daubs of sausage dogs David loved so much and a collection of *Some Very New Paintings* that could have been executed more than half a century ago by an infant Howard Hodgkin dribbling over a Picasso picture book. The only suggestion of survival as an eye and hand lay in many of the preparatory pastel sketches of 1998 for the vast and vile Grand Canyon landscapes in oil on canvas that were given a room to themselves in the RA Summer Exhibition of 1999.

His current consignment of new watercolours to the Annely Juda gallery must have appalled the Judas, Annely and David, when they first set eyes on them. I can imagine their silence as they masked their horror and searched desperately for words that would neither hurt with the truth nor cheat it with dissembling. It is easy for a critic to say bluntly what he sees (though very rarely done), but for the dealer who must act as the agent, proselytiser, promoter and prop of a much lauded painter famous from Berlin to Hollywood, a national celebrity and public pet, an icon of gaiety and hero of West Riding, such blurting is impossible. The Judas therefore did the only thing they could – put their shoulders to David's wheel, prepared a mighty handsome catalogue with almost a hundred illustrations, persuaded David himself to write a foreword and Marco Livingstone, an old hand notorious as a Hockney propagandist, to write an emotional and technically naive account of having his portrait painted in watercolour by the master. There then began the shrewd leaking of material to chosen sympathisers in the broadsheets – a portrait of Norman Rosenthal, panjandrum to the RA, in one, an interview by that great art expert Andrew Marr, the BBC's most indefatigable chatterbox, with a portrait of himself as part of the deal, in another, and so on.

Certain absurdities have been the consequence. David is now to be regarded as the inventor of watercolour, the inventor of the portrait in watercolour, the inventor of the double portrait in watercolour and, indeed, I am not at all sure that I am not expected to believe that he invented portraiture as well. Watercolour, managed easily enough by a million amateurs and by Edward Lear even while riding recalcitrant mules in Greece and India, is, it seems, the most impossibly unmanageable medium, to be tamed only by the genius of David; and portraiture too has to be conquered with multiple systems of perspective if 'wild foreshortening' is to be avoided. 'The lessons of Cubism,' we are portentously assured by Marco Livingstone, 'are much in evidence in these new works.'

And the results? The results are so crude, so clumsy and insensitive to both subject and medium that, as with the late work of Picasso, one is compelled to wonder how a painter whose work was once so beautiful, so intelligent, so skilled, so masterly, could have so unself-critically, sunk to this nadir. The portraits are little short of frightful, without focus and without composition; David's apologists may blether about the importance of body language and the intimate relationships of sitters, but in truth, in David's hands his victims are uniformly gauche and unrelated, their faces florid and flushed, all of them caricatured and uglified – and all the praise of his perspective skills is specious, for in every case he views his sitter as though he were a Kodak Brownie camera of 1937.

These portraits, their importance inflated by hanging five of them in the National Portrait Gallery, the Trustees of which were fools enough to commission a double portrait of the Glyndebourne Christies (the perfect pairing of painter and subject, murmured a spokesman for the NPG), are a gross impertinence – and the mystery of it is that David, once so engaging in his modesty, is now so downright vain that he cannot see how graceless, inept and maladroit they are. No one close to him will tell him. The one sitter to whom I have spoken about the sad business was so star-struck by David's having chosen him as to be both blind and incoherent.

The other astonishing aspect of the exhibition is a group of Norwegian and Icelandic landscapes made as a response to Tate Britain's exhibition, *American Sublime*. Lawks a mercy! To have seen such wonders and then, in homage, to have produced such dross. They are, beyond words, bad. Anyone uttering the traditional riposte that his six-year old daughter could do better, is for once telling a profound truth. We shall soon, I prophesy, be as troubled by fakes of late Hockney as we are of late Lowry, and when he's dead, who shall we trust to know the difference? Dr Livingstone, I presume.

The first words of the catalogue are a dedication by Annely and David Juda – 'Thank you, David, for this incredible exhibition!' How tactful. At last they found the perfect words; how suitable the emotion of the exclamation mark. I know exactly what they mean. After David's early achievements, incredible indeed.

David Hockney: *Painting on Paper*, Annely Juda, W1 2003
http://www.bbc.co.uk/london/entertainment/galleries/hockney_art.shtml

David Hockney Portraits

NATIONAL PORTRAIT GALLERY

Evening Standard, 13 October 2006

David Hockney, younger of the two grandest old men of British art still living, was once told that his double portraits conform to the traditional iconography of The Annunciation – one figure permanent, the other 'kind of visiting', one the Virgin Mary concentrating on a book, the other the Archangel Gabriel arriving with news that is not entirely welcome. I thought, not of this, but of something very like a week or two ago, when David and I encountered each other as, in Kensington High Street, we crossed a busy side road; for a moment we were frozen in unexpected recognition, and then, in imminent danger from uncaring traffic, with tender touches each old buffer steered the other to the kerb. This, I thought, was just like The Visitation, though which of us might be the Virgin and which Elizabeth her cousin, I did not pursue. For once in my life I wished that a photographer had caught us in the act, for the act, in gesture, stillness, colour and tentative relationship was the perfect enactment of a Hockney double portrait not yet painted – one that never will.

From 1955, when David, then eighteen, sold a portrait of his father at an exhibition of Yorkshire artists, he has been more continuously engaged with portraiture than any other genre of painting. For promotion of those who were to benefit from his occasional work for opera and theatre there was always the noisy business of a shrewdly exploited press; and now that late in life he has taken to painting landscapes with the affectations of the amateur, all the mechanisms of a boastful art market are employed to keep him in the forefront of public interest and amusement; but for himself and the pictures that he has always painted for himself — that is without the involvement of commissions and the judicious steerings of art dealers — it was enough, almost from the very beginning, to declare his homosexuality and paint with a decidedly homoerotic cast, the body of the naked male in attitudes formerly the preserve of furtive homosexual pornography. It was these paintings that brought him to the fore and provided the opening for formal portraiture, for this was the Sixties, the merry and generous decade when wealthy and influential non-homosexuals could declare his genius and give him dinner and patronage as a means of demonstrating their newly liberal attitudes to sex and class. I wondered at the time if David ever realised the extent to which he was, on the one hand, a powerful tool of social change and, on the other, a pet clown of the rich, regarded by them as a good investment. Years on I wonder still.

As a painter, the unformed adolescent Hockney emerged from the drab school of Euston Road — a group of dreary London painters whose muddy influence was well suited to the smog-blurred cities of the north; as a draughtsman, however, his portraits were far more distinct, his characteristic concentration on the head already evident, the body clearly defined as its pictorial support, but with a lighter touch that offered no competition for the spectator's concentrated eye. Two decades later and into the Seventies, this was still the case, but then distilled, the imbalance in the plain pen drawings perfectly contrived — the eye may wander the elegantly assured lines of shirt and jacket, hand and foot, astonished by the uncluttered clarity of forms so simply described, but always drawn back to the head where the definition, subtly heavier of hand, is more demanding.

With colour the drawings edged away from the occasional hint of caricature into high seriousness; they became more pictorial, the emphasis more even. The colour came from crayons so deftly applied that the effect is as soft and ethereal as the diaphanous touch of watercolour, the crayon point evident only when particular form demanded definition. There were fashionable draughtsmen in Paris a century ago, Helleu for example, who had something of David's skill in this technique, but only something; David lifted it to levels never reached before and I have no hesitation in suggesting now – as I did at the time – that his drawings of the earlier 1970s, not only of portraits, but of still lives and empty rooms, prove him to have been one of the very few great draughtsmen of the twentieth century.

Greatness was, alas, not to last even to the end of the decade. David is reported to have said to Salvador Dalí 'I believe in the primacy of drawing as the ground base for fine art' – certainly not his exact words, but the sentiment rings true. To the onlooker, however, drawing seems not to have been the ground base but the be-all and end-all of David's art, for when he buried it under paint it was utterly destroyed. Dare I declare that David has no feeling for paint whether oil or acrylic, that paint is for him the deadly substance of colour and no more, an opaque material that is, without life, without brushmark or impasto, yet in its flat intensity enabled him to make a bigger splash not only with the depiction of a swimming-pool and the bare buttocks of his boy friends, but with the large portraits that can dominate a hall or room in much the same way as an altarpiece dominates a church or chapel?

In these often huge paintings David retreated into accumulated formulae and the brash assertion of the roadside hoarding. With the current critical custom of transvaluation – that is the mention in the context of David's work such great names as Picasso, Van Gogh, Rembrandt, Caravaggio, Leonardo and Jan van Eyck, as does one scribbler in the exhibition catalogue (why not Piero della Francesca and Edward Hopper too?), they have become iconic (another jargon word in modern criticism) in the Greek or Russian Orthodox sense as in themselves sacred and to be honoured with great reverence. And honour them we do: they are beyond criticism: they were and are the great banners of figurative painting when all about us we saw and see minimalism, conceptualism, abstraction with edges hard and soft, subjectless expressionism, the installation, photography and video.

Mr and Mrs Clark and Percy may not yet be thaumaturgical, but post cards of it have long been among the most popular with visitors to the Tate even when the canvas has not been on view, and I dare say that it will be the first choice of editors picking illustrations for the plethora of Home Chat interviews with Hockney engendered by this exhibition (there was indeed a women's magazine with that title). Is it Percy the cat that leads everyone astray? I have never been seduced by the artless additive quality of the composition, the lilies here, the telephone there, to fill the empty flanks, its hard-edged detail and its silhouettes, its falsely benign light, the wallpaper balustrade and view beyond, and the scribbled paint in the walls in an attempt at painterly effect. It is a picture that can only be read haltingly and never as a whole, its various elements so disparate as to seem there only by impulse in slow motion.

As the Clarks parted company soon after the painting's completion, it is often interpreted as David's brilliant intuition that a sense of their alienation is so strong, but the separation of his sitters in the double portraits is a constant characteristic, never more abundantly clear than in the portrayal of his mutually devoted parents in 1977, uncannily still, both figures subservient and expressionless. This is a picture so rigid and awkward in construction that, in comparison, the domestic photographs of ageing nudists at home taken by Diane Arbus in the early Sixties, make widely separated sitters seem convivial and comfortable in ad hoc compositions of a kind to which David, who perhaps knew them as he knew the work of so many photographers, lent dull and almost primitive aesthetic discipline.

As the Seventies drew to a close there followed the pieced-together Polaroid portraits – tedious and trivialising, every one of them, in their empty ingenuity – and the mock Picassos, terrible defacements that traduce old friends. How could David retrieve for this very public occasion his dreadful dismemberment of *Peter Langan* in 1984, a man who had by then been his devoted friend for fifteen years and of whom he had earlier drawn uncaricatured truths with exquisite quality? Peter was, when he died, an irretrievably drunken slob, but David had known him far longer as a warm, generous and impulsive friend, as wild as an Irishman can be, as witty too and as casually sensual – but of all this there is nothing in the portrait, just a fragmented Dan Dare with a glass in his hand instead of cow pie. No doubt David thought it clever – and so it is, in the worst sense of that word, and shallow too.

In the Eighties, though once in a while the old genius flickered in the gloom, nothing interrupted the appalling decline in David's work – 'O Hockney, what a falling off was there'. His recent portrait drawings are a little better than those of the street artists of Montmartre, but no more significant, and for his recent paintings his sitters are so uniformly red in face that the prerequisite of sitting must for all have been an hour boiling in a sauna. His double and triple portraits of 2005, the latest works in the exhibition, are – if they are finished – the worst he has ever attempted, the stuff of student imitators, worse even than his recent landscapes. Let me again misquote Hamlet: 'O, what a noble eye is here o'erthrown.'

David Hockney, *Portraits*, National Portrait Gallery 2006
http://arts.guardian.co.uk/flash/page/0,,1867112,00.html

David Hockney RA: *A Bigger Picture*

ROYAL ACADEMY

Evening Standard, 19 January 2012

My predominant response to David Hockney's exhibition of Yorkshire landscapes at the Royal Academy is 'Why?' Why is there so much of it? Why is so much of it so big, so towering, so vast, so overblown and corpulent? Why is it so repetitive? Why is everything so unreally bright, so garish, discordant, raw and Romany? Why is the brushwork so careless, crude and coarse? For me this overwhelming accumulation of his recent work is the visual equivalent of being tied hand and foot and dumped under the loudspeakers of the Glastonbury Festival.

This exhibition is at the Royal Academy because it will bring in a multitude of punters and, with the outrageous admission price of £14, mightily increase the profits of the grand old whore of Piccadilly, masquerading as a charity. It is so big because Hockney, following the footsteps of Gormley, Kapoor and Gilbert and George, now works to fill the available space, and the 'Bigger' of the title suggests that he has not yet identified the Biggest – but if he continues to follow Kapoor, he will, he will. It is repetitive because that is Hockney's way – he takes a subject and wrings it to exhaustion, constantly repeating tricks of handling to lend shallow interest to his fields of canvas. As for his discordant range of colour, I fell to wondering if he is the Monet of our day, his vision so dimmed by cataracts that he must paint in vile greens and viler purples if he is to see anything take shape on his innumerable canvases. And the brushwork is crude because that is what so easily happens when a painter works beyond his, or the subject's, natural scale, or does not care if, when a landscape requires the jig-sawing of fifty canvases, the junctions are jerkily approximate.

As no one who knows anything of Yorkshire's wolds has ever seen them clad in the ghastly gaudiness of Hockney's vision, I must ask, if he is not purblind, from whom he borrows this jangling, jarring, grating palette? Has he, perhaps, a man of sudden enthusiasms who, on discovering the art and practice of water-colour only as late as 2002, immediately became the greatest watercolourist of all time, now just discovered the Fauve painters of Paris a century ago, Derain, Dufy, Vlaminck et al, and replaced them too, the wild man of the wolds, the savage of Scarborough, the beast of Bridlington? Fauvism was recently defined as 'a movement characterised by a violence of colours, often applied unmixed from tubes of paint in broad flat areas, by spontaneity and roughness of execution, and by a bold sense of surface design'; to make it the perfect fit for Hockney we need only add the occasional employment of heavy outlines and dependence on recurring detail.

It matters not at all if, in his dotage (he was born in 1937 on the day that Ethiopians devote to Pontius Pilate), his work is nourished by a new influence. His apologists are almost too anxious to declare his kinships with Bruegel and Turner, Van Gogh and Picasso, and his variations on a theme by Claude – dubbed by Hockney himself 'A bigger message after Claude Lorrain's Sermon on the Mount' – form a whole section of the exhibition, but of the Fauves there is no mention, nor of Walt Disney, whose Bambi would be comfortably at home in all these paintings.

If he denies the Fauves their influence, then perhaps we should look at their near contemporaries in England, at the work of Harold Gilman and Spencer Gore, and even to Gore's long-lived son Frederick who, as a Royal Academician, overlapped with Hockney. Those who delighted in the way that Freddy Gore, well into his nineties and the first years of this century, continued to hack out the landscape formula that Hockney now enlists and with the same bright vulgarity, will at once recognise the close parallel.

For all their up-to-the-minute modernity in Kapoorian scale and the smell of ill-considered paint still drying, these landscape vastnesses are disconcertingly old-fashioned. Technically much the same, technologically Hockney's work is very different from that of his more modest predecessors. The Fauves, the New English Art Clubbers and Freddy Gore brushed paint onto single canvases of unambitious size; so too does Hockney, but some are almost as large as Leonardo's *Last Supper*, and in most of his recent work the motif is spread over an assemblage of anything from two to fifty-two canvases abutting each other in a rectangle. This industrial scale apparently requires an industial approach, and technologies far loftier than the low technology of brush and paint come into play. Conventional drawing we should expect, and it is present; photography we should, perhaps, forgive, and it too plays its part in the production of a painting and, independently, it is included in the exhibition; but should we not dig in our heels and resist when Hockney pays homage to such mysteries as synchronised printing, digital video stills, the simultaneous operation of nine cameras, and the iPhone and iPad as instruments of drawing?

David has always adopted new technologies as they became available – the computer, the fax machine, the photocopier, the Polaroid and so on (and we all know how the Polaroid collages lost their colour and definition, and the faxes faded into oblivion) – but I feel compelled to ask if, for all this gadgetry, his paintings have improved. They have increased mightily in number, but in quality they have, no matter what the subject, as mightily deteriorated. There was a time in the 1970s when I thought him one of the best draughtsmen of the twentieth century, wonderfully skilful, observant, subtle, sympathetic, spare, every touch of pencil, pen or crayon essential to the evocation of the subject, whether it be a portrait or light flooding a sparse room; nothing has made me change that view, but Hockney has tried very hard. As a painter he has never had so sure a touch, has always seemed mannered, always a borrower affecting this approach and that (and in his heyday, very well) and, as though uncertain with the material of paint, has used it to colour between the lines rather than create with it the structure, form, volume, texture, atmosphere and space of whatever different reality lies beyond the picture plane. Now, in this new work, every blade of grass, every stalk of stubble, every hedgerow flower is reduced to a cypher and, when diminished by erratic perspective, to a blur.

In old age [Hockney is 74] he has acquired a clumsy bravura and he strokes, stabs and dabs the canvas with seeming confidence, but in truth much of this is the stuff of habitual gesture, of industry, repetitive, for he knows no other way of covering such an acreage of canvas. He is surrounded by sycophants, none of whom has the honesty to tell him what he needs to know – that he has fallen far from the saturated brilliance of his last brief fling with quality, the *Grand Canyon* drawings and paintings of 1998 or so, one of which acts as a benchmark in the scene-setting first room of the exhibition; no one has warned him that in dogged repetition what fire he once had has become a thing of ash and ember; and no one has dared suggest that though all the cocksure recent stuff dashed off for the exhibition works well as braggadocio, it is ultimately dull. Indeed, half these pictures are fit only for the railings of Green Park, across the way from the Royal Academy, and would never be accepted for the Summer Exhibition were they sent in under pseudonyms.

As for Hockney's rivalry with his master, Claude, this is sickening impertinence, contemptible. Hockney is not another Turner expressing, in high seriousness, his debt to the old master; Hockney is not another Picasso teasing Velázquez and Delacroix with not quite enough wit; here Hockney is a vulgar prankster, trivialising not only a painting that he is incapable of understanding and could never execute, but, in involving him in the various parodies, demeaning Picasso too.

David Hockney RA: *A Bigger Picture,* Royal Academy 2012
http://www.royalacademy.org.uk/exhibitions/hockney/about-the-
exhibition/#photos=gallery_%252
Fgallery.html%253FLgalleryHandleId%253D632

Howard Hodgkin

HAYWARD GALLERY

Evening Standard, 12 December 1996

To Howard Hodgkin, a 'major international artist' who has 'truly expanded the vocabulary of European painting', we are compelled to genuflect, or worse, to perform the low kow-tow, in part because we must acknowledge greatness with humility, and in part because the labels for the pictures in his current exhibition are only inches from the floor. The titles on these remote and inaccessible labels are vital to our understanding, for all Hodgkin's paintings are autobiographical and evoke 'memories of holidays . . . bodies, love affairs, sexual encounters . . . ' and without them may be mistaken for mere abstract touches of the laden brush; to discover whether it is *Down in the Valley* that we contemplate, or through a *Bedroom Window* that we peer, we must bend either the creaking knee or aching back, and one of the most engaging sights seen at the Hayward Gallery in recent years is the current spectacle of so many spectators faces down and bottoms up, as though performing some strange ritual native to Stanley Spencer's Cookham.

That HH, as he is known to many who have interviewed him, is perceived by many more as 'one of the leading British painters', is due to something approaching a conspiracy of critics (conspiracy is here a collective noun, one of several, creep and crawl among them), and their constant repetition of the mantra. This exhibition, for example, was immediately preceded by a filmed interview with Melvyn Bragg (an interviewer quite remarkable for the depth of his knowledge, inspired perception and intellectual rigour) in which HH wept with anguish at the neglect he suffers in this country, and by another interview, given a broadsheet's full front page, in which he complained 'how extraordinarily difficult it is to be an artist at all'. At the exhibition itself, the visitor is handed a lengthy essay by one Bruce Bernard (he who claims that HH has expanded the vocabulary), remarkable less for illumination than for sycophantic drivel, for he calls on support for his enthusiasm from Matisse and Vuillard, Van Gogh, Baudelaire, Stendhal and Degas, and from Lawrence Gowing he borrows the spluttered encomium 'splendidly shameless and assured, with a splendid clumsiness which is the ultimate skill and deftness of painting' – a paradox beyond absurdity.

None of this fits any conventional picture of neglect, nor does the almost unbroken series of one-man exhibitions since 1962, some supported by the Arts and British Councils. Representing Britain at the Venice Biennale scarcely suggests neglect, nor does winning the Turner Prize, nor does long Trusteeship of the Tate and National Galleries, nor does a Knighthood (he too has done his share of genuflecting), and few artists could help but envy the some five hundred entries in the bibliography of the current catalogue. To ensure that critics continue to prate the party line, on the press day of the Hayward exhibition, a drove of them was driven round the pictures by a harridan urging on them the customary words – presence, vehemence, volcanic energy, praising the sweeps and dabs of the broad brush, and, above all, the sumptuous, sensual and vibrant colour.

What an uncommitted sceptic finds at the Hayward Gallery, on walls painted a grey so drab that it takes the edge off Hodgkin's colour, dulling its transparency, is an exhibition carefully selected to eliminate the feeble early work, which is unquestionably derivative, and to reveal him only as a painter fully formed and consistent within his own conventions. Hodgkin, born in 1932, claims to have drawn and painted from the cradle, but not until the mid-Seventies did he manage to mature, only then to discard the gaucheries of youth and organise into uneasy coherence the various mannerisms of his handling and the crude devices of his composition. It is these pictures, of the last two decades, that we are allowed to see – of the adolescent fumblings that stayed with him into middle age, we learn nothing.

For twenty years he has painted more or less the same picture – an abstract notion of a stage set, with proscenium arch, vertical flats, a distant backdrop, and even the boards of the stage, on timber roughly the size of a tea-tray, sometimes physically framed, in which case the frame too is painted as integral with the composition, sometimes framed only with broad bands of paint. This very simple architectural business holds the smaller paintings together, but on a larger scale the compositions disintegrate in the welter of fussy touches with the brush; the worst of them resemble the painted tea-trays of Roger Fry's Omega Workshops – of which, no doubt, there were examples in his nursery, for Fry was a relative of sorts – and the best seem to spring from the imagination of old Ivon Hitchens, who was still very much alive when HH found his form. 'The essence of my theory,' said Hitchens to Herbert Read in 1951, 'is that colour is space, and space colour,' and he keyed his colour ever higher, with clarity and brilliance and bravura brushstrokes, until his death in 1979. The kinship between the work of the old genius in his late eighties and the plodding amateur in his early forties is unmistakable.

Hodgkin is far from being a great painter, but the role having been thrust on him, and so much money invested in it (only the tiniest tea-tray for £70,000), he must act the part until his dying day. He acts it rather well – with perhaps a little too much of Greta Garbo's influence, and his melancholy pose too close to that of Alice's Mock Turtle, his seeming modesty a useful camouflage for overweening *amour propre* – and most onlookers here are gulled by the affectation of genius misunderstood. Not so, however, in New York, whence the exhibition comes, for there, though HH insists that the reaction was 'amazing, absolutely astonishing . . . gratifying', the distinguished critic of *The Village Voice* observed that 'Hodgkin's peppy little pictures (the littler the better, mostly) jump into your lap like little dogs, and wear out their welcome almost as fast.'

The exhibition does HH no service, mercilessly exposing the repetitious handling of paint as he struggles to provide variations on the one meagre idea. Were it a proper retrospective, including his juvenilia, the crude competitions with Hockney and other near contemporaries in the early Sixties, the Pop-Non-Pop pictures, and the slow emergence of his characteristic tricks and mannerisms in the late Sixties, one might see some academic purpose in it – its purpose, however, is not to reveal the truth, but to further promote the man as lonely and exceptional genius. Authority, knowing how easily seduced we are by fat paint, bright colour and broad brushstrokes, would have us bow to these gaudy daubs as icons, awe-inspiring and thaumaturgical, but in this, as in all other propaganda, Authority cheats.

Howard Hodgkin, Hayward Gallery 1996

Down in The Valley **(1985–8)**
http://www.howard-hodgkin.com/
product.php?tab=2&searchtitle=down+in+the+valley&paintings=
1&categories=&dates=&imgid=2355

Bedroom Window **(1992–4)**
http://www.howard-hodgkin.com/
product.php?tab=2&searchtitle=bedroom+window&paintings=1
&categories=&dates=&imgid=2410

Howard Hodgkin

DULWICH PICTURE GALLERY

Evening Standard, 10 August 2001

Since late June thirteen paintings by Howard Hodgkin have been hanging in Dulwich Picture Gallery. They are not confined to a single room, there to be venerated in a cataleptic trance; they are instead scattered among the distinguished pictures in the permanent collection, rubbing shoulders with Poussin, Ricci and Guercino, keeping company with Claude, Rubens and Rembrandt, illuminating all – or so we are told – the juxtaposition leading to our greater understanding of the present and the past, Hodgkin and his wonderful precursors speaking the same language.

That is the official way of perceiving this chalk and cheese display. The sceptic might equally well suppose that the Gallery, remote in Dulwich (where there is nothing else to do) and likely to be overlooked by even the most passionately dutiful members of the art world, feels compelled to try almost any antic to draw in the punters, and the universal formula of the fashionable moment is to mix the old with the outrageous new – of this an extreme example is about to happen in Rotterdam where an important exhibition of paintings by Hieronymus Bosch is to be larded with the videos of Bill Viola and the waxworks of the Brothers Chapman. It seems that today's curators of old masters have lost confidence in their charges, believing that as they lack the bright hues of television and illustrate episodes from irrelevant old stories of which we now know neither the beginning nor the end, they have no hold on the interest of the wider public and must, by almost any means, be jollied into the present empty-headed and illiterate century. 'Look, look,' they say, 'in this seventeenth-century picture of a church interior a dog is emptying its bowels behind the font; and here, to demonstrate the continuity of old and new, Chris Ofili offers us a clod of elephant dung and Gilbert and George a huge photograph of human defecation.'

Galleries of old masters have no need to employ such deceits, no need to justify the old by conjoining it with the new as though the new is the superior, no need to prove the value of Rembrandt's flayed oxen by hanging them with Damien Hirst's halved cows and calves. Dulwich may, having received a vast Lottery grant to let Rick Mather build a hideous and shoddy restaurant and lavatory wing in its front garden, feel the need to increase its visitor numbers, but it does its permanent collection no service by peppering it with gaudy Hodgkins. It is, of course, just possible that Dulwich is being subtle, guileful and subversive, its intention quite the reverse of what at first it seems – that Dulwich is, in fact, demonstrating how fatuous and vacuous contemporary art can be by hanging a sloppy Hodgkin between a pair of Poussins that we all know to be monuments of scrupulously careful pictorial construction, the contrast made deliberately to reassure the visitor who perceives the work of Hodgkin as pretentious trash.

Trash? How could one use this word in the context of Howard Hodgkin, famous man, knight of the realm, winner of the Turner Prize, known to the close many as HH and to the distant more as GOD, the Grand Old Darling of the English art world, a painter and panjandrum so eminent that one must speak of him only in the hushed tones of awe? Well, quite easily. Try saying shallow of his pictures instead of ruminating on their depth, substitute slick for painterly bravura, try vulgar, crude and overwrought; think of wild swipes with a house-painter's brush, of paint dabbed and splotched and swabbed with turpentine, of paint thin and thick, of paint fluid and sticky, tacky, blobby and resistant, think less of the painter's vision and more of his retreat into repeated and repeated and repeated formula. These are paintings of such unmediated gestural habit that GOD could do them in the dark; they have no complexity of structure, no subtlety of tone – indeed they depend for their shock effect on the dissonant palette of the Indian sari in bright light, exciting in the bazaar of Benares, but shrill and acid here, the pitch sharp enough to set the teeth on edge. There is, too, something of the dirty dinner plate about these pictures, of gravy smears, exotic chutneys, mustard and tomato sauce, indeed *Chez Max*, a circular picture, resembles nothing so much as one tipped over the wastebin to discharge uneaten baked beans and mushy peas.

Hodgkin's pictures have titles that suggest some autobiographical experience evoked by memories of bedrooms, lovers, restaurants and melancholy holidays in uncharitable weather, but the stories are half-told with the revelation and the gossip halted in mid-phrase; one senses that HH is himself such an artificial self invention that he cannot, dare not, reveal an intimate truth and that every one of his abbreviated stories is a *roman à clef* to which he will never make the key available, Was *Chez Maxim* indeed a ruined dinner in a restaurant? Was *Afterwards* a tearful post-coital tristesse over some too rewarding boy? Was *Out of the Window* the way the condom went? It hardly matters; these teasing disclosures HH deliberately obscures to prevent our discerning an underlying narrative, but if his pictures are to be recognised as more than gaudy decorative objects, he knows that he must allow us our measured glimpse into his sensitive soul, for then, as aesthetes, we will detect that his images are of his feelings rather than events.

Feelings? What feelings should we see in *Out of the Window*, from which dense swathes of yellow, orange, bright green and magenta lap onto a decent antique frame as though seeking to escape its oval bounds? Is this another tearful tantrum? If so, why stop at the frame? Why not extend the sloshes of bright pigment across the drab intervening wall and onto the distinguished neigh-bouring canvases? That would add violence to rage. What are we to make of *Memories*, a frame turned face to the wall, levelled with a sheet of timber and painted as an unframed landscape that is a distant echo of Ivon Hitchens (who died in 1979), the honest painter whose influence converted GOD from a mindless muddler into the one-stringed fiddler that he is?

Over the past quarter of a century HH has painted more or less the same picture over and again; they have a certain hapless amateur charm on a very small scale (the therapy of the maiden aunt), but his larger variations on the inevitable theme dissolve into a flaccidity so weak that the spectator wonders at his letting them leave the studio. Both extremes are to be seen at Dulwich, where the hang is, to HH, so compellingly beautiful that he burst into tears when he saw the work complete – a bit like God sanctifying the seventh day. I vowed that I would not visit this exhibition, certain that GOD's work would be the mixture as before and that I should have nothing new to say of it, but it is August, the dry season for the art critic, and *force majeure* came into play. It is indeed the mixture as before, perhaps even feebler than five years ago, and I have no reason to revise my opinion of Hodgkin's extremely limited imagination and abilities – I need only express astonishment that the Grand Old Darling has grown so vain that he cannot see how much his daubs disrupt the serenity of the permanent collection.

Howard Hodgkin, Dulwich Picture Gallery 2001
http://www.howard-hodgkin.com/exhibitionsearch.php?exhibitions=16

Howard Hodgkin

TATE BRITAIN

Evening Standard, 16 June 2006

There is general agreement among the cognoscenti of the contemporary art world – that is those who through compliant journalists and even more submissive broadcasters form the opinions of the uninformed rest of us – that Howard Hodgkin is 'one of the most important artists at work in Britain today, celebrated by a wide public internationally . . . ' Internationally? Apart from my own amused dissent I know of only one respectable protesting voice that is international. The American critic Peter Schjeldahl, reviewing a Hodgkin retrospective exhibition for a New York readership in 1995, put British painting of the day firmly in its international context by damning Hodgkin (and Freud and Hockney) as 'on cosy terms with mediocrity'. 'Hodgkin's distinction,' he continued, 'is to be tremendously pretentious in a modest way . . . merely looking at his art misses the point – you've to imagine taking him home to bed or tea.' 'Phooey' is the climactic one word summary of his review – a review that is cunningly omitted from the sixteen-page bibliography of Hodgkin's current retrospective exhibition at Tate Britain.

Hodgkin is, as another writer opined in 1996 – this time a man almost spent in the exhausting throes of adoration – 'a painter who paints the unpaintable'. This is poetic hyperbole at full stretch, but manifestly not true, for every one of Hodgkin's paintings has a title so specific that it must conjure an image of sorts from what, to the uninformed eye, may appear to be a haphazard accumulation of paint in brushstrokes of heroic length, breadth and practised certainty, of paint in swirls and dots and splodges. These do not depict the subject; they are intended to evoke it, each stroke, swirl, dot and splodge a synecdochism for a person, place or event, dinner here, a holiday there, desire for a lover sated; where Rothko lets us see what we will in his still fields of colour, for they are intended to imply nothing, Hodgkin commands us to see what he wills in his energetic turbulence – and if we fail to obey, we are damned as fools by his apologists.

I have used the word splodge only because a thousand other critics have done so, tempted unconsciously by the rhyme with Hodge perhaps; for a painter who consistently employs high and often unmodulated colour, it is quite unsuitable, for to splodge means to plod splashily through mud, and very little about Hodgkin is either muddy or splashy; nevertheless, splodge came into art criticism in 1882 in a review of the Royal Academy Summer Exhibition where, no doubt, it did mean muddy. Criticism is not the proper word for most of what is written about Hodgkin. Put very simply, he is not much of a painter in any intellectual sense and no one could write of him in the language with which Hugo Chapman brought us close to the master in the current exhibition of Michelangelo's drawings at the British Museum, or in the terms with which Constable is elucidated in the catalogue of his six-foot landscapes now hanging in the miserable lightless rooms of the Tate's basement.

With Hodgkin, the scribbler must fall back on the ecstasy that was once the province of religious identification with the agonies of Christ. Consider the final sentence of the catalogue: after observing that 'the more he inhabits his body', the more 'Hodgkin-like' his paint-marks become, the writer ends with 'It is this body with which we, as spectators, identify when standing before the great, late pictures.'

Hodgkin is a painter who has always, since boyhood, wanted to be a painter, but until the mid-1970s, when he was well into his forties, he seems never to have had anything significant to communicate, nor to have commanded a sound means of painterly communication. His early work suggests decades of fumbling, of plucking a single idea from Matisse or Ivon Hitchens or even the younger David Hockney, without understanding the whole from which it came, of borrowed styles ill-mixed and in conflict, of no clear intention in any single picture or in any sequence. With the wisdom of hindsight and the certainty of peer approval, critics, curators and, particularly, novelists and literary exquisites, look back at these groping immaturities and weigh them down with interpretation and shared feeling – feeling, Constable's weasel word. The sane man, on the other hand, searches for, and occasionally finds, hints of the simple architectural framework, the bold sweeps of the brush and the bright splodges that are the essence of the later work, and observes too the prominent, hard-edged and decorative elements that Hodgkin eventually discards. Until well into the 1970s all these are crammed into congested compositions, tight and uncomfortable, their colour garish, their symbolism caricatural, obvious and shallow, and Hodgkin's handling of paint remains as tentative and uncertain as his construction of a composition – nothing of shape, colour or decorative embellishment seems essential, seems the only way in which this picture or that could have been resolved.

Even so, very slowly, the characteristics of the Hodgkin style were, perhaps unconsciously, being developed; by the end of the Seventies certain constants had emerged, the patterns of spots and splodges, the blurring over-paint, and the simple framing elements of heavy verticals and horizontals that suggest in miniature the massive proportions of Stonehenge. In some cases these last may be real picture frames onto which the painted surface is extended (something of a homage to Seurat and the Omega Workshops perhaps), converting the ensemble of panel and frame into a three-dimensional object or an abstract relief.

The Tate's exhibition omits all juvenilia; it begins with a handful of paintings from Hodgkin's late twenties and with another handful takes us into his mid-forties. Then, it seems, he had a near-death experience with amoebic hepatitis in 1975, and in 1978, having discovered that he was homosexual, he separated from his wife. Bruce Chatwin, travel writer, novelist and immaculately beautiful Peter Pan (but with scant knowledge of the visual arts), promptly identified these as years of crucial change: ' . . . a sharp and unexpected swerve; gone were the portraits of forlorn married couples in rooms, to be replaced by . . . a new mood . . . overwhelmed by dots, splotches, flashes and slabs of colour.' I suspect that Chatwin, having recently discovered his own homosexuality, supposed that every middle-aged man who discloses to himself and the world that he is queer, rejoices in the consequent relief and immediately dances a mad fandango in fresh fields and pastures new. I perceive no 'sharp and unexpected swerve'; I see only and at last the near resolution of recognisable mannerisms into something that can be recognised as a personal, if still incoherent, style. With the passage of another decade into the mid-Eighties the style gained the polish that comes with constant practice – less became more, so to speak, elimination proved wiser than addition, and small superior to large.

The American professor who wrote the forty-page essay in the catalogue (why was he asked, one wonders) dwells too much on Chatwin's view. Hodgkin's is not erotic art in any sense and is better interpreted in straightforward art historical terms – simple enough, and simpler still if we liken his working life to the long hard slog of the almost non-swimmer who, having failed to recognise the difference between the ends of the bath, has stepped into the deep and floundered his way to the shallow. With his feet at last on the bottom, from *c.*1985 to *c.*2000, Hodgkin has repeatedly dog-paddled from side to side in perfect safety.

In 2000 or so we sense the beginning of a change. In the Creation myth God transformed chaos into order, into day and night, earth and sea, but Hodgkin reversed the process; most of his newest paintings are significantly larger, the colour often brash and vulgar, the compositions as flexible and uncertain as they were when the formula first came into play some thirty years ago. The ugliest example of the deterioration is *Rhode Island* of 2000–02, the prettiest – in that it is a scrap of post-Fauve colour enormously enlarged and a century post factum – is the idiotically titled *Come into the Garden, Maude* of 2000–03. *Undertones of War*, of 2001–3, is painted with a loosely scribbled touch that, were it not distantly justified by American practice, one might mistake for the work of an Outsider artist; it raises only one point of interest – that Hodgkin has always been, when he takes to tone rather than colour, a much more subtle, less abrasive painter. I must argue that colour, a cheap attraction always putting weightier things at risk, has as often as not been his worst enemy. These three pictures, painted concurrently, suggest that Hodgkin has indeed now swerved – and lost his way.

The exhibited paintings are the victims of extraordinary errors of display. They hang in Tate Britain's ugliest and most ill-proportioned rooms (those with ceilings that were first designed as cooker hoods); of these the walls have been painted, successively, dappled charcoal grey (the dappling seemingly an attempt to give an all-over Hodgkin effect), then a sudden shift to a less dappled but ghastly acid green, followed by a hot and glowing cream that resonates between the pictures. From this we move to muddy orange and more brushstroke swirling, then creamy yellow and finally a vomit-inducing gold, the tone and sheen of which are a close match for rare Chinese porcelain in tea-dust glaze. Only a man of wholly aberrant sensibility could choose such bruising contrasts. The hang itself is pure Serota preciosity, acres of blank wall swamping the dinky little icons before which we are to genuflect; only the larger pictures can compete with so much background colour. I cannot recall a more insensitive presentation.

Hodgkin is always flattered in reproduction – but not when illustrations are guttered across two pages, as in the exhibition catalogue; in this there are no notes on the exhibits and only the scrupulous chronology redeems the price, £19.99. Thames and Hudson have just published, at £60, a catalogue raisonné, *Howard Hodgkin: The Complete Paintings*, more than 450 of them to the 65 of the exhibition, all illustrated, with detailed notes. From this the reader will learn much more than from the bare bones in the Tate.

Howard Hodgkin, Tate Britain 2006

http://www.howard-hodgkin.com/exhibitionsearch.php?exhibitions=75

Gary Hume

WHITECHAPEL GALLERY

Evening Standard, 17 December 1999

In the summer of 1991 Andrew Graham-Dixon, now a world-renowned historian of the Renaissance, but until then merely an art critic who showed some independence from, perhaps even some contempt for, the Contemporary Art Establishment, sold his soul to it and played curator to an exhibition at the Serpentine Gallery in which the formaldehyde fish of Damien Hirst jostled the hidden depths of spaces sculpted by Rachel Whiteread. One of the lesser artists there was Gary Hume, of whose life-size imitative painting of the dull doors of modern schools, restaurants and institutions – architects' ready-mades, so to speak – Graham-Dixon, not quite aboard the bandwagon of the Serota Tendency, felt compelled to write in high seriousness, ' . . . there is, it is plain, no . . . significance. The paintings repeat themselves . . . but cannot be said to get anywhere. Accumulating, pointlessly, they flaunt their own lack of direction . . . Hume's failures are deliberate.'

That, one might have supposed, was that; failures, pointless, going nowhere, sans direction and sans significance they may have seemed, not to some spiritually shrivelled Victor Meldrew scribbling in the *Evening Standard*, but to the one bright young critic of the day – but no matter, for Charles Saatchi had bought one of the door paintings in 1988, Hume's year of graduation from Goldsmith's College, and more the following year from a canny dealer – and when Saatchi jumps, the whole contemporary art world too must jump. By the time that Graham-Dixon mounted his exhibition at the Serpentine it was far too late, foolish indeed, to say that Hume was going nowhere, for he was already on his way to Paradise, the

Arts Council and influential dealers in London, New York and Germany assisting in his *Himmelfahrt*. The British Council too at once joined in, buying some of his paintings for its own collection and shunting others off to the São Paulo and Venice Biennales and other international exhibitions, even as far as Korea and Japan. A quick flip through Hume's curriculum vitae suggests that the Arts and British Councils have, between them, at not inconsiderable public expense, subsidised his inclusion in no fewer than twenty-five exhibitions between 1990 and 1999. With the Tate short-listing him for the Turner Prize in 1996 and a coterie of pushy dealers offering yet further assistance, it should surprise none of us that at an auction last week one of his drawings sold for not far short of £15,000, and that the price asked by his dealer for his largest paintings is now £45,000.

The first thing one sees on entering the Whitechapel Gallery, where Hume now has yet another exhibition, is a begging-box for small change to help keep access there free of charge. The Arts Council grant to the Gallery for the current financial year is £598,000 and the Hume show is indeed free – but think for a moment what such a show is worth to him in terms of increased prestige and prices; a line in his CV reading '1999/2000: Solo exhibition at the Whitechapel Gallery, subsidised by the Arts Council, in association with the *Observer*' (whatever that may mean) must add at least ten per cent to his current prices, for that is what notable exhibitions do – just as Saatchi knew when his *Sensational* possessions were exposed at the Royal Academy, just as he knew when he sent them over the Atlantic to be shown in Brooklyn; in the latter case Saatchi even thought it worthwhile to offer the museum there a subsidy of 150,000 dollars, though he asked for its return if a profit happened to be made.

No fewer than twenty-four of the thirty-four paintings in Hume's exhibition have been executed this year, thirteen of them as large as 10 x 8 feet, only six as small as three feet tall, the rest six or more feet – an acreage that indicates mechanical facility as much as industry and more than intellectual depth. If we suppose that Hume sells all this year's paintings for the sort of sums they are known to fetch (and with this laudatory exhibition his prices are bound to rise), the gross figure represents an annual income not far short of a million quid and both the painter and, particularly, his dealer are doing very well (a dealer's commission is often 50 per cent, very rarely less than 33.3 per cent). Has either of them, I wonder, offered the Whitechapel a ha'penny? And dare I ask if promoting the protégés of very rich and successful dealers is the proper business of the Arts and British Councils?

Here lies a dilemma. It is, of course, the proper business of the Whitechapel, the Serpentine, the Camden Arts Centre and so on to exhibit artists who may be thought important, successful, of international interest and so on, but we would think the Arts and British Councils in grave error if they gave public money to wealthy commercial promoters of drama and music, or paid the rent of the Albert Hall for Raymond Gubbay's seasons of opera and ballet. Surely there must be a point at which these Councils should call a halt to subsidising contemporary visual artists so settled in the public eye and leave it to their dealers to continue their promotion? Consider how wrong we say it is when the National Gallery exhibits pictures that dealers have for sale.

It must by now be clear that I have very little to say about Hume as a painter, though other critics have managed to masturbate their sensibilities over him at inordinate length – including, inevitably, Richard Cork, who shared with his few readers some kind of religious Revelationist experience, and one Gordon Burn who, writing at length for the *Observer* ('in association with', you will remember) had five full pages in the magazine to tell us that Hume's work 'doesn't chew up the furniture or piss on the carpet'. Well, no, indeed it doesn't, but I would much rather have my old dog Titian (who did both throughout his life and sorely tried me) back in my arms than any painting by Hume on any of my walls.

They are in household gloss paint on sheets of aluminium, gleaming like enamel, that on this scale would do very well as platform decorations on the District Line and, in swiftly becoming invisible, are perfect for that purpose. They offer nothing but a moment's glister and demand no contemplation; they are at most pictures for the idle glance, the question 'What's that?' answered with 'Who cares?' The colours, shrill and pastel, are those of cheap and nasty clothes for the beaches of Ibiza, though once in a while he toys with close tones that have a hint of subtlety. The compositions are rather more accidental than composed, the human subjects (in which category the fatuous angels must be included) glibly featureless or reduced to the pastry cook's cypher, 'Aren't I clever?' Hume's insistent question. Hume's empty wastes masquerade as ingenious simplicity, but in truth he is a witless painter haunted by the naive devices of the recent past, by the mechanics of the stencil and painting by numbers, by the heavy unmodulated lines of Patrick Caulfield and Michael Craig-Martin (the Goldsmith's genius), by the posters of the Thirties, by children's illustrated books and above all by Walt Disney in his heyday.

The simplest and most agreeable panels, though most disagreeable when the colours are drab and pallid, are wholly abstract hard-edged things that faintly echo Ellsworth Kelly but have nothing of his quality. The most complex are in a form of drawing on plain grounds of lurid pink and yellow that in the most densely scribbled examples suggest the influence of Feliks Topolski, but I doubt if Hume knows of that old master (at his best) and must suppose that he has hit upon the reckless idiom by accident; in those with larger figures – a series called *Water Paintings* – the scribbling clears a little to leave a multiple overlapping image of a naked woman, a technique much used for mild pornography in the Sixties in which the discerning prurient could discover nipple and rima if he stared long enough at an image pretending to be art.

I can understand Saatchi's early purchases of Hume's work for they fit perfectly with his hit or miss collecting and his preparedness to dump young artists when no one follows in his footsteps, but the indefatigable support offered by the Arts and British Councils is beyond comprehension. From the day of his graduation from Goldsmith's Hume has shown no intellectual grasp of what he has chosen to do, whether hard-edge abstract or feebly figurative, and after a decade of publicly funded approbation all that he can offer us are vapid images of no significance, half acres of aluminium lurking under repellent glossy surfaces, the damned things (yes, things) so empty that we should have no patience with them. Their emptiness, however, may well be their point, for Hume concluded a recent interview with Graham-Dixon (in which, playing wily critic once again, the great art historian evaded criticism with lubricious aplomb and did not recall the 'going nowhere' judgement of his youth), with ' . . . pictures start off empty. For me, that, basically, is the process at all times. You start off with nothing and you try not to ruin it.'

Anish Kapoor

HAYWARD GALLERY

Evening Standard, 14 May 1998

Anish Kapoor is a darling of the Serota Tendency and the Arts and British Councils. Born in Bombay in 1954, his training as an artist began in 1973 at the now forgotten Hornsey College and ended in Chelsea in 1978, but was for the most part self-inflicted. In 1990 he represented Britain at the Venice Biennale, in 1991 was given the Turner Prize, and is now so universally acknowledged and acclaimed as one of the brightest stars of contemporary British sculpture that no public gallery director dares ignore his powerful dealer. His proliferating work is thus to be found hither and yon across the supposedly civilised world, combining the manufacturing technology of modern western sculpture with the mystical impalpabilities of Indian philosophy.

This, for other sculptors, is an enviable combination, for it enables him to offer in his current exhibition at the Hayward Gallery, objects with the aesthetic virtue of a Ford Fiesta hub cap, yet demand from us the rapt contemplative response of a devout nun when a tooth of John the Baptist is pressed into her palm. In the presence of any work by Kapoor, the sceptic wishing to retain his sanity must remind himself of Roger Fry in his dotage, inanely teaching us how to respond to pots made by Mexican peasants – in front of these he expected us to maintain a mind of tense passivity, ever 'ready to vibrate in harmony' with them, 'a faculty which can be increased indefinitely by constant exercise'.

Kapoor's is the craft, rather than the art, of the curious object writ very large indeed – reduce his sculptures to the size of tennis balls and they take on the character of the tiresome glossy things with which the rich and foolish once decked their coffee tables, and in photographs many could easily be mistaken for Fornasetti baubles made for this very purpose. It is their sheer size that inflicts the first and dominant impression, for things of such weight and width inevitably assume significance even if utterly lacking in aesthetic substance, but remove them from the awe-inspiring circumstance of the art gallery, where the visitor is inevitably inclined to be as reverential as in a church at Mass, the agnostic here suspending his disbelief, and how then shall he perceive them? A sculpture by Henry Moore (no matter how many misgivings we may have about the man) remains a sculpture wherever it may be, but the sculptures of Kapoor would blend very well if despatched to Blackpool to keep company with amusements on the Front; they would be quite fitting as embellishments to the foyers of every vulgar hotel in Miami Beach and Disneyland; and those that are made of stone without pigment would be perfect as the mysterious objects beloved of fashionable contemporary gardeners, or standing among the granite chippings of the funerary mason.

This is not to suggest that Kapoor is a mischievous prankster entirely lacking the impulses and interests of a sculptor — only that these have not developed beyond the rudimentary stage of enquiring into the abstractions of form and void in the material's bulk, and reflection and absorption in the material's surface and colour. He is intrigued by concavity and convexity, but in treating these with gleaming metallic surfaces arrives at solutions no more subtle than a hall of distorting mirrors. Optical confusions are an obsession; we are tested to decide whether a void cut into a block is deep or shallow, or even cut at all — perhaps painted instead; we are tempted to peer into a vortex of polished stainless steel and see it as a force calling us to plunge to hidden depths; and we are drawn to look into great empty cups painted with such dense and unreflecting pigment that we lose all sense of their dimensions. This pigment is menacing stuff capable of destroying the material nature of anything to which it is applied: the most extensive work in the exhibition is an installation of large and intriguingly eroded limestone rocks soaked in the intense dark blue that Kapoor favours, blanking any natural glitter in the stone, flattening the contrasts of light and shadow, and denying their weight – they seem like nothing so much as the polystyrene rocks of Hades on which Orpheus sat howling for Eurydice last winter at the ENO.

If much of this suggests that Kapoor is trying, in small, to deal with matters of galactic space, black holes and their accompanying forces, or even of oblivion, we should perhaps recall the nature of the drawings that he exhibited at the Tate Gallery in 1990, then described as metaphors of the sexual act, of male and female characteristics in unity and opposition peculiarly and specifically genital. These were works of outright adolescent prurience, and they are not included in this exhibition, but one can recognise their spirit, albeit prinked and polished, in the vortices of his current work, recalling, as they do, Mona Hatoum's explorations of her orifices. The one overtly sexual image is the single great white breast, sans nipple, of *When I am Pregnant*, protruding from the wall at visitors' head height – but this is an idea taken from a Dutch sculptor's exhibition in Eindhoven nearly forty years ago; it is just possible, of course, that the untitled standing black slabs of 1997 are a reference to the meteorite of the Emperor Heliogabalus on the Palatine Hill, the worship of which involved mass masturbation by the Roman Senators. It is at such mysteries that Roger Fry seventy years ago would have had us 'vibrate in harmony' – Kapoor, however, has his own latter-day Fry in a Professor of Humanities named Homi Bhabha, to urge on us the virtue of such activity.

Kapoor is marvellous material for the writer of verbose nonsense. Extolled though he may be by the Establishment, he is matter of fact about himself – 'I've got nothing particular to say, I don't have any message,' and 'The method of manufacture is not the point. The question is whether or not an object is well and truly made' – but he believes that it is his duty to produce work that encourages others to interpret his intentions, discover meaning and explain, and he stimulates them to extraordinary flights of ekphrastic fancy in the exhibition's catalogue. He is splendidly rewarded by Professor Bhabha, for not since that old fraud Rabindranath Tagore relinquished his all too ready pen has any writer on the visual arts so bored us with impenetrable vagaries of thought made to seem significant by a deliberate smog of pomposity; it is enough to quote from his first paragraph – 'Kapoor's vast tolerance of empty space expands the space available into another ongoing disruption of time' – but this professorial gibberish is sustained for twenty-eight pages more, in which Kapoor is placed in the company of Giacometti, Caravaggio and the Apostle Thomas poking his finger into Christ's wounded side.

Professor Bhabha is a Trustee of the Institute of International Visual Arts, a prodigal body recently devised by the Arts Council to promote the art of ethnic minorities here (and majorities overseas), and at £522,000 in the last declared accounts, by far its most extravagantly funded visual arts client. Kapoor has every right to a major exhibition in the Hayward Gallery, no matter what his ethnic origin, for he works in Britain and his sculpture is no more vacuous, frivolous, pretentious and nonsensical than that of the other British sculptors of his generation more familiar from recent exhibitions there and in the Whitechapel and Serpentine Galleries, and it is, moreover, 'well and truly made', and skilfully sited to make the best of rippling reflections, particularly from the Hayward's beamed ceilings. That Professor Bhabha, however, a member of the Arts Council team, so to speak, should have been commissioned, and presumably paid, to write the inflated maunderings of his over-wrought and meaningless introduction, is preposterous. Such a text does no service to Kapoor, for it gives the impression that his work cannot be comprehended by a western writer – to which the response must be that if it needs the support of Bhabha's feeble pseudo-philosophical jabberwocky, it must indeed be meagre stuff.

Anish Kapoor

ROYAL ACADEMY

Evening Standard, 1 October 2009

The Anish Kapoor exhibition at the Royal Academy is a damp squib – literally so in that its two most sensational kinetic exhibits are given to failing their essential functions.

The first is a cannon that fires hefty plugs of blood red wax from one room to another in what used to be known as the South Rooms, the angle unsatisfactory, narrowing the visual field so that very few can witness the plug's reaching its target. The ritual is religious. An altar boy performs it with all the flurrying fervour of High Anglicanism, the extravagant gesture and the grace, whipping up anticipation with his fetching and feeding the plug into the cannon's breech, the ceremonial stacking of the empty cartridge case, his dextrous manipulation of valves and levers to control the heavy breathing in the system as the pressure builds, and then, finally, the firing. Were we shocked by the dramatic recoil of the cannon? No. Did the blood red plug fly into the far corner of the further room? No. Did it disintegrate in flight and spatter with the shrapnel of wax the walls, the floor, the ceiling of the nearer room? No. The red plug just peeped from the barrel like the corona of a half-stimulated penis from its foreskin and plopped onto the floor. Was there applause? No. The blushing altar boy wished himself anywhere but there as the audience first broke into helpless laughter and then scuttled off to catch the train.

The train is yet another example of Kapoor's making things to fill the available space – it runs east–west on a track through the northern galleries in which nothing else can be exhibited. I caught it in the last inch of a slow slither to a halt well short of its terminus.

Shades of the District Line, I thought, another signal failure at Barking. It is a solid block of the same red wax that the cannon fires, a windowless and doorless carriage, seemingly self-propelled, its shape and proportions dictated by the enfilade of arches that connect the galleries, and on these the wax shavings as it passes have congealed. Its role as juggernaut – Kapoor is Indian – is evident, and visitors are constantly reminded by the Academy's attendants not to throw themselves in its inexorable path. Visually it and its track reek of blood and sacrifice.

Both cannon and train have been exhibited before – in European galleries – for Kapoor can tinker with his jolly japes to fit with any circumstance. The one work that appears to be original and so far exclusive to the Academy is *Greyman Cries, Shaman Dies, Billowing Smoke, Beauty Evoked* – an accumulation of cement excreted by a computer-assisted piping machine that at best suggests the Sorcerer's Apprentice let loose in the kitchen of a pastry-cook, but at worst vividly reminds me of the floor of the public lavatory in Başkale, the highest town in eastern Turkey, after months of extreme water shortage. That these repellent absurdities are mounted on timber pallets no more than a few inches apart, crowding the floor in ankle-scraping proximity, a menace to the infirm and elderly, should be of interest to officials concerned with Health and Safety.

Most visitors will instantly (if unwillingly) have recognised the infant's interest in faeces. I am not in the least surprised by it, for Kapoor has always seemed to me less a sculptor in any grand sense than victim of arrest in the common infantile and pre-pubertal obsessions with body orifices and functions that here seem so evident. This exhibition is nothing but the indulgence of the nauseating fancies of perhaps the most vain, self-regarding, pompous, pretentious and wealthy celebrity artist of the day. I am surprised to find it sponsored by the Henry Moore Foundation, a charitable body that should find worthier subjects for its largesse, for Kapoor and his dealers, both of whom will profit mightily from exposure in the Royal Academy, could well have afforded to hire it from their own fat pockets. Who will pay the bill for clearing away all traces of the blood-red faecal mess? The Royal Academy levies an admission charge of £12 for a coprophilous joke worth neither tuppence nor the sane man's time.

Anish Kapoor, Hayward Gallery 1998

http://www.anishkapoor.com/305/Hayward-Gallery-1998.html

Anish Kapoor, Royal Academy 2009

http://www.anishkapoor.com/252/Royal-Academy-of-Arts-2009.html

or

http://www.guardian.co.uk/artanddesign/gallery/2009/sep/22/anish-kapoor-royal-academy?INTCMP=ILCNETTXT3487

Exhibition poster

http://www.royalacademy.org.uk/exhibitions/anish-kapoor/

Ron Kitaj

Evening Standard, 16 November 2001

If it is the nature of art institutions to run out of steam, as indeed it is – witness the Royal Academy, the New English Art Club and the Institute of Contemporary Arts – it is the nature of painters too, most fortunate the genius who dies when young. Others just plod on with the mixture as before, sans inspiration and invention, some become celebrated personalities of whom the public is as fond as of a panda or an elephant, and some descend and descend before an audience amazed that a painter once so good can become so irredeemably bad. In 1985 it was possible to recall that Ron Kitaj was once 'the greatest living draughtsman' but lament that in the underlying drawing of his paintings he had begun to lose his grasp of figures and the space containing them, the manifest flaws masked by urgent short cuts and ill-considered bravura that convince only those who look for performance without depth and meaning. There was still hope, I suggested, without being particularly hopeful.

By 1994, at the Tate's major Kitaj retrospective exhibition, hope had to be abandoned. A number of critics, some of them not known for plain speaking, damned him for his slipshod, slapstick carelessness, for having been so promising but offering promise no more, offering not even sustained achievement but decline, deterioration and enfeeblement. Here was a man who had once been more than promising, a man capable of considerable profundity, of images that stopped the spectator in his tracks stock still, sensing levels of meaning deep within the drawing and the paint, sensing sensibility, anguish and experience inherited, generations old. Here was a man who could once have matched Degas, descended to the level of the scribbler.

If it was anything, the critical outcry was one of miserable disappointment at having been cheated of confident expectations. It was not 'a systematic attempt to cut the painter down to size', as an essay in the catalogue of Kitaj's current exhibition at the National Gallery has it. Critics do not enter into conspiratorial agreements with each other – they are far more likely to lick the arses of such panjandrums as Kitaj than take a common line against them. A painter with his hubris under control would have recognised that the critics had seen something in his work that he had not; instead, he expected them, blind and unquestioning, to nourish his vanity, railing at them not only for their shrewd criticism but for their perceived attitudes to what he called the Jewish Question (a matter more of his Jewishness, aggressive, whining and self-pitying, that he thrust in the way of his art), and to his wife Sandra, whose death he attributed to the cruelty of our criticism. This last I could not accept, for I had known Sandra for some years before she married Kitaj in 1983 and, once he had begun to slide into decline, had told her that she was becoming rather the better painter, more sympathetic, more sincere.

This current exhibition, seven years on, of his response to paintings in the National Gallery, inspired by painters as diverse as Giorgione and Cézanne, reveals his recent work to be a betrayal of all the skills he once commanded as draughtsman and painter. The National Gallery must be embarrassed to display paintings so perfunctory, shoddy, slapdash and downright bad, so profoundly witless. We learn nothing of old masters from these deplorably shallow interpretations, but we have our noses rubbed in Kitaj's vanity, a vanity that blinds his judgement utterly. 'It is impossible not to be struck by the visual weight and intellectual power of Kitaj's work,' writes his devout apologist within the National Gallery. What codswallop; on the contrary, it is impossible not to be struck by its childishness, its screaming tantrum quality.

Leon Kossoff

ANNELY JUDA, W1

Evening Standard, 9 June 2000

Of Leon Kossoff as a student, one of his contemporaries at St Martin's School of Art in the early Fifties wrote that he was 'a blasted distraction in the life painting room, rattling the hardboard on his easel with the fearsome vigour of his attack, always sighing and groaning, always walking back and forth, a trodden path of yellow ochre, black and the various siennas squelching on the woodblock floor; the same oily gunge hung from his easel as though it were a guano deposit'. The memoir continued with the tale of a nude model posing for a group of students that included Auerbach, Joe Tilson and Sheila Fell as well as Kossoff, so spattered about the breasts with the latter's paint that she felt compelled to rebuke him with 'Kossoff, not only do you paint the floor and the ceiling, but you paint the bloody model as well.' Half a century on, nothing has changed; among many articles in a carefully contrived wave of publicity for his latest exhibition, one distinguished critic writes of Kossoff's studio as 'a manifestation of primal chaos', and another as a room 'hit by a pigment-and-charcoal-bearing typhoon. The walls are thickly spattered with paint; a dense archaeological layer of it covers all horizontal surfaces.'

One of the oddities of critical comment on Kossoff is the evasiveness of so much of it. He is widely acclaimed as a grand old man of British figurative painting, one of the half dozen or so who have clung, through the thick and thin of abstract and conceptual art, to the ancestral traditions of the recognisable subject, and yet to talk of form and volume or sensuality and eroticism, is not only irrelevant but tends to expose the paintings as wholly lacking these characteristics. The critic, anxious above all not to be critical, not to suggest that Kossoff suffers an irrepressible compulsion to turn his nudes and townscapes into inert bogs of feculent pigment, not to imply that the ooze and sludge and slop bewilder him, not to intimate, even ever so cautiously, that perhaps as a figure painter Kossoff is hopelessly inept and that in his surrender to the mere material of paint all else is desperately lost, turns from the melancholy challenge of these raked and raddled surfaces, and writes of other things.

Thus it is that we are told of 'the scale of the artist's vision', but not how it compares, nude for nude, with Michelangelo's, of his 'agonised, simple but dignified world', a phrase much better said of Rembrandt with whose handling of paint Kossoff's is too often blindly likened, for Rembrandt knew precisely what he was doing with every brave bold stroke, while Kossoff leaves us in a state of dismayed disbelief that any man claiming to be a painter should so utterly fail to transcend the material nature of his paint. Thus we are told that Kossoff's 'are heroic pictures because they demonstrate that humanity is not exclusive' – but what one earth does that mean? What too the assertion that Kossoff's art is 'part of the quest for a universal language capable of expressing the frailty and vulnerability of the individual's predicament' – as a translation from the French of an article on Goya, this one might understand, but as a comment on Kossoff not at all. Thus Lawrence Gowing, that hack weeper whipping his emotions into play for yet another dealer's shekels, could write 'the random yet rapturous traces have some of the character of what Constable called his dew . . . we are aware that we have been taught . . . the language of the heart.'

All this emotional and ekphrastic clap-trap is not, alas, an end to the nonsense written about Kossoff. Still avoiding the issue of criticism – Kossoff is, after all, a man whose work has been sent to the Venice Biennale and who has to his credit a major retrospective at the Tate, and is thus, in a sense, above censorious comment – timorous critics tell us, in tones of purest Betjeman, of the tea, biscuits and home-baked cake dispensed to them by the painter's wife in the suburban wilds of Willesden, of the shrubs in his front garden and the roses round his door. By a railway cutting at the bottom of his garden, through which diesel trains run from Kensal Rise to Brondesbury, Gowing even felt impelled to write of both 'the emotional world of Post-Impressionist Provence' and of the cool and lustrous light of the Suffolk Stour, conjuring kinship with Van Gogh and Constable, again. By invoking Monet, Cézanne, Giacometti, Soutine and Titian, all painters whose names and reputations are virtually unquestioned and unquestionable, other critics have implied that Kossoff must share the same esteem, and in this fervid climate of adulation it has become possible for one of them to raise the stakes and begin his eulogy with the words 'The great figurative painter . . . '

Kossoff is nothing of the kind. All his talk of drawing a subject or a sitter over and over again and for year after year before he even begins to think of dipping brush in paint, may suggest the integrity of Michelangelo and Leonardo, Rembrandt and Raphael, but one glance at any Kossoff drawing and we see the crass ineptitude of the frantic scribbler. His are not the drawings of analysis and under-standing; nor are they the drawings of a man concerned with space and form; nor are they the plotting and preparations of a composition; nor are they the impetuous and delighted trapping of transitory effects or movements that are momentary and fleeting. Kossoff's are drawings entirely without subtlety of mind or hand, sensibility or comprehension – they are the rough stuff and ritual habit of the lunatic. All Kossoff's talk of taking years to paint a picture, of painting it, of scraping it down to the board and chucking pounds of pigment in the bin, of painting it again and scraping it again, until out of the mire that is the consequence of this 'constant activity' (his mantra) something emerges from the squelch and squitter that appeals to him, should convince no one that he is a genius. His assertion that a finished painting emerges from constant activity is the justification of the head-banger; his coy plaint that he never quite knows what he does nor how he does it, is less a claim to divine inspiration than a frank admission that he is in control of nothing and wholly in the hands of hopeless chance as he piles on the paint, puddles, muddles and confuses it until he has the option of scraping it off and throwing it away or roughly drawing outlines on it to persuade us that within the congealing mass he has discerned the ectoplasmic image of a subject. It is an activity as intellectual as seeing faces in the fire, figures in the clouds, or fancies in a Rorschach blot.

Anyone who looks back over the half century of Kossoff's work will see little change or development since 1960. A few earlier paintings survive, haunted by his teacher, Bomberg, and by Auerbach, his friend, but by 1960 his familiar facture was well established, the paint thick, the handling wild, the drawing crude, seeming to have a struggling promise in something of the way that young Cézanne's first paintings had – but the promise died away and in their frequent repetition the paintings became caricatures of themselves and have remained so ever since. In his current exhibition we have seen everything before, nothing is new and no painting shares with the spectator a fresh engrossing insight; the crowds at King's Cross Station are of ugly puppets tangle-stringed, gawky, twisted and grotesque, the nudes posing in his studio are stunted and misshapen, the portraits gnarled travesties of face and soul. Like Lowry in Manchester, Kossoff in London has become a local painter; like Lowry, his is work of constant repetition; like Lowry in his dotage, what quality and energy Kossoff's work had long ago, has slid into decline.

To some extent one can understand how Kossoff reached his undeserved and perhaps untried-for eminence; the support of Helen Lessore, an often remarkably perceptive art dealer, gave him in the late Fifties a mighty professional push – enough to draw him to the attention of the Contemporary Art Society, the Tate Gallery and, eventually, the Arts Council, and to establish him as one of a loose group with Auerbach, Kitaj and Freud. Kitaj's use in 1976 of the term 'The School of London' to consolidate (quite speciously) this informal coterie, ensured that Kossoff could no more thereafter be detached from the coat tails of the more celebrated painters than bobtail from rag and tag or Wilfred from Pip and Squeak. Ten years ago the distinguished New York critic, Hilton Kramer, dubbed them the Cold Porridge School of Painting; since then Kossoff has added sloppy ice cream and the wrinkled skin of old milk puddings.

Of one thing in Kossoff's favour we must, however, be convinced — that he is an honest painter, not a scheming old fraud like Lowry, who knew precisely what he did; Kossoff is driven, manic and possessed, his painting necessary activity as essential to the well-being of his temper as the urgently repeated acts of those suffering obsessional-compulsive neuroses. We should look on it as therapy, not art.

Leon Kossoff, Annely Juda, W1 2000
http://www.annelyjudafineart.co.uk/artists/kossoff/kossoff.htm
or
http://www.theartsdesk.com/visual-arts/leon-kossoff-
new-works-annely-juda-fine-art

Leon Kossoff and Drawing

NATIONAL GALLERY

Evening Standard, 23 March 2007

It was once, many years ago, my misfortune to encounter a small boy who delighted in employing his faeces as a medium with which to ink his finger, as it were, and draw. I have since learned from friends in the business of understanding the mysteries of the human mind, that this is by no means a rare phenomenon, but both a primal urge to make an image and a primitive response to a tactile material so easily available. This field of enquiry is of only marginal interest to the art historian and should be left to those who follow in the wake of Donald Winnicott, Melanie Klein and other late Freudians, including Anna of that ilk, but in the course of working as a critic I am occasionally reminded of faeces and the infant's finger by the work of contemporary artists — none more so, indeed, than of Leon Kossoff, master painter of the London School.

A painting by Kossoff is encrusted with paint that seems more crudely trowelled onto the canvas than daubed there with the brush, the surface texture faecal, the colours faecally subdued in tone, the subject so blurred and indistinct that he has been compelled to reinforce its outline with a finger-brush dipped in faecal matter of a darker strain. Without this clumsy over-drawing Kossoff's paintings would be fields of muddy matter, nothing more; it is therefore not entirely surprising that his apologists now proclaim him to be a master draughtsman, but to the sane man who in the past twelve months has had the opportunity to see, close-to, drawings by Michelangelo, Leonardo, Holbein, Leighton and Guercino, it must seem that to Kossoff's work, the definition *drawing* has been misapplied.

There is currently much debate about drawing, a sense of regret that it has fallen away as the habitual practice of the artist as a means of recording the thing seen, whether suddenly and momentarily or as the subject of long concentration, fallen away as the means of analysing form and structure, or of clarifying composition and motif from a torrent of ideas. The sketchbook used to be the vade-mecum of every artist, the instrument of immediate response to both the outer and the inner eye; and drawing used to be the fundamental armature of painting, its underlying hidden strength, its scaffolding, its corrective to elements misbegotten on its surface. Drawing, I must argue, is also so deeply instinctive in the eye of the informed beholder that it conditions his response to every work of art he contemplates, as the great Leonardo himself was eager to acknowledge, 'for we know very well that though a man may not be a painter, he may have a true conception . . . '

Much of the current debate is led by appointees to influential positions who preach that almost every action of the mind and hand results in drawing, that any mark or movement is a drawing. At a recent symposium on Lord Leighton's drawings, a professor at a London art school argued that the biggest drawing in the world is the road map of the United States (surely those of Russia and China must be larger?) and that, offered the choice of a preparatory red chalk study by Raphael of a naked man or a primal smudge of soot from a cave occupied by Neanderthals, he would take the smudge. With such politically correct tuition, what hope have the students of today of understanding drawing in any sense that was its purpose in all the centuries between Botticelli and Burne-Jones, Masaccio and Mucha? Again and again I hear it argued that drawing is a means of self-expression – and indeed it is, but it should also be much more than that, and charcoal, the oldest, but now the most contemporary medium in that it responds so crudely to the act of drawing, in its mess and sputter and even in the noise it makes when hard forced across the paper, masks ineptitude with seeming vigour and lends every stroke a spurious intensity.

When asked what drawing is, these worthies prattle of its universality and primal nature and tell us that it pre-dates language and writing as a means of record and communication. It is, they say, a tool of conceptualism and, seeing no distinction in definition between the clean lines of a wiring diagram and the drawing over drawing of the master draughtsman clarifying images in his mind's eye, they aver that these have equal value. They do not; one is an instrument of scrupulous technical instruction for which a thousand men could be equally responsible, and the other an irresolute aesthetic idea in the process of resolution unique to one man only, every stage of which is in itself an object of aesthetic worth to which other abstractions are connected – beauty, insight, emotion and empathy among them, all qualities evident in the great masterpieces of painting in the National Gallery.

Ah yes, the National Gallery. Kossoff is apparently so great a painter that there he has free rein to prowl at any time he chooses. And there he draws large but raggedly feeble copies of great paintings; and there he now exhibits these. Why? It is beyond the sane man's understanding of the purpose of the National Gallery that it should foster Kossoff or any other contemporary artist – surely the place for his bathetic offerings is any of the several Tates, or has the Gallery become yet another outstation of the Serota Tendency? Freud, Auerbach and the even more execrable Peter Blake are among those who have preceded Kossoff in Trafalgar Square with work based on paintings there, yet not one picture, print or drawing by any of them has been of the slightest consequence or quality, providing only overwhelming evidence of arrogance and vanity.

Are the Gallery's grandees in thrall to the nonsensical notion that there is some sort of continuity between the great masters of the past and these Lilliputian noodles of the present? It is all very well for a commercial dealer in the art market to promote Kossoff as a significant and respected artist, a Blake of the quotidian today, a peculiarly London visionary whom fellow Londoners must therefore clutch to their bosoms with unreserved affection, to claim that Kossoff has a 'deep relationship with the Old Masters (in general) and with pictures in the National Gallery in particular', and thus gull the gullible rich, but for the Gallery itself to join in the deception is deplorable. Do the Trustees not realise that an exhibition in these hallowed walls implies to those who through ignorance can know no better and therefore trust the Trustees' judgement, that this exhibition must seem to put Kossoff on a par with Velázquez, inflating not only his reputation but his prices too. The beneficiaries of this exhibition are not the misled public, but the Bond Street Boys who trade in Kossoff's work.

To the cold eye of the scrupulous critic, Kossoff is a wretchedly incompetent painter for whom one cannot even claim show without substance. To many blind observers he is Bomberg's natural successor, but in no aspect of his work or eye is he the older painter's heir. He is wholly lacking in Bomberg's assurance; he takes no risks with lurid colour or vertiginous perspective, with thunderous shadow or bright sun; with the loaded brush his heavy hand is clumsily tentative, the paint torpid, jaundiced, feculent; what evidence there is of drawing in his paintings (we are back to the finger-brush) suggests either that he is a child or that he affects the naivety of a child. Every one of his mature pictures has been a thing entirely of the few deliberate tricks and mannerisms into which he had retreated by his early thirties; now eighty, these have remained the hallmarks of his painting for fully half a century. Few painters have changed so little for so long.

Much the same is true of his drawing. 'I draw,' he said in 1979, 'mostly with charcoal or compressed charcoal. Looking back, it seems that I have been endlessly engaged in the self-imposed activity of trying to teach myself to draw from life. I think of painting as a form of drawing' – endlessly from life, endlessly too from paintings by old masters, for the practice apparently began when he was a student between 1949 and 1956. In abandoning what little he had in those early years borrowed of Bomberg's certainty, he was left with nothing but the scribble over scribble with which he developed a private world of stunted ugliness. This he imposed on paintings by Velázquez, Goya, Poussin, Rembrandt and other painters for whom he professed his admiration. It is the admiration of the uncomprehending dunce, the parasitical dependence of the *pediculus humanus* on its host, of which there is no more grotesque example than his reworking of the beautiful act of mystical piety that is Velázquez's *Christ after the Flagellation contemplated by the Christian Soul.*

The National Gallery has, of course, issued a catalogue laden with the empty awe and fulsome admiration of curators who have acquired the trick of mindless veneration commended by Roger Fry. Its authors write of Kossoff's energy and dynamism, of his heightened emotional states and, conversely, of the slow emergence of things fundamental, of his discovering some elusive truth that has for long stubbornly refused to reveal itself, of excavating buried secrets, of psychologically inhabiting a painting, of experiencing a picture on a deeper level than the solely visual, and they and Kossoff pun on his insistence on the description of his studies as 'drawings from', not drawings of, implying that he has drawn from them some previously invisible essential just as the slaughterer draws entrails from a carcass – and just as heartless, just as messy too, the sceptic adds.

When, however, made excitedly expectant by all this, the sane man attempts to discern what really is there on the paper, he finds, matching the infantile feculence of the canvases, only such ludicrous incompetence and downright ugliness as prove, not that Kossoff is a fraud, but that his apologists cozen us with ekphrastic flimflam. Kossoff, poor pathetic soul, is as much a victim of this as the rest of us; I suppose him to be an innocent, a genuine naive, a simpleton, a perfect and imperfect fool, an Outsider driven, not by art, but by obsession and compulsion, for half a century of self-delusion trapped in the ante-chamber of idiocy, a possible case for treatment by psychiatrists.

Leon Kossoff and Drawing, National Gallery 2007
http://www.culture24.org.uk/art/painting%20%26%20
drawing/art45147

Richard Long

HAYWARD GALLERY

Evening Standard, 18 July 1991

Those who expect sculpture to be hacked from stone, moulded in clay, or cast in bronze to stand in public places, may have difficulty in coming to terms with the notion that Richard Long, who neither hacks nor moulds nor casts, and works as much in the wild wilderness as anywhere, deserves to share the description 'Sculptor' with Michelangelo and Rodin, or even the deplorable Glyn Williams. We live, however, in an age when artists so often claim that it is the idea that matters and not the execution, and that the bounds of convention and the bonds of tradition must be broken so as to extend one art into another, that we should at least attempt to appreciate Long's work with the same high seriousness as that of the great sculptors of the past, and not simply dismiss it as yet another wearying aberration of the wayward present, to compete with the *Dirty Word* photographs of Gilbert and George and the wedges of accident-prone animal fat that were fundamental to Joseph Beuys.

Long has been much praised by critics and curators. Born in 1945, he was in his early twenties when he was given the first of the now much repeated exhibitions in Düsseldorf (where Beuys was a noisy and notorious teacher), New York, Paris, Milan and many other European centres of contemporary art. In 1976 he represented Britain at the Venice Biennale, and in 1989 he was awarded the Turner Prize by the Tate Gallery's puffed-up Patrons of New Art. He is now the subject of a major exhibition at the Hayward Gallery.

The Hayward, from the outside, is the ugliest gallery in England, yet Long has transformed its interior into a place of peace, repose and considerable beauty. The walls of the first room and the room beyond the ramp are decorated with rectangles and circles of mud smeared and dragged by Long's hands to give a sense of action-splash and rhythmic squiggle, the sputters of superfluous material flung away like sparks from a Catherine wheel to extend and soften the simple forms and leave a residue of waste fallen to the floor below; on the floors are disposed the careful rectangles and circles of white flints and broken stone in red, white and grey, the spiky erect forms of some seen, at first, at eye level, a worm's eye view that gives them something of the effect that can be had when climbing to a peak, a tor, or hilltop ruin. The alliance between the sculpture and the space is so convincingly theatrical that the visitor is immediately removed from the bustle of Waterloo Bridge, drawn in and up the ramp, and put into a contemplative mood.

There, however, lies the problem, for one wonders whether the mood is evoked by Long's neat arrangements of the natural materials that tumbled from the tipper-trucks, or by the things natural and man-made that they in turn evoke. At their most successful the circular floor sculptures suggest Stonehenge, Avebury and Grey Wethers, and I suspect that the spectator's response is, at a remove, to these haunted places that are man's mysterious early interventions in the landscape, at least as strongly as to the symbols laid out by Long. As it is no longer possible to see Stonehenge as Constable and Turner saw it, unfenced, menacing the fork in the westward road, a ring of stones placed by man yet having the grand scale of nature, it is perhaps – in small – possible to retrieve some-thing of the effect from Long's sculptures, to let them work as catalysts. At their least successful they do nothing of the kind, but merely resemble bleak garden embellishments no more interesting than the sad offerings of the Chelsea Flower Show.

Long makes his pieces for particular exhibitions in particular places, and (though they may easily be reconstructed in a loose sense) they are transitory – but permanence seems of no interest to him, and he is just as likely to make a sculpture of twigs, driftwood, pebbles or turf on the Alaskan shore, the Andean plateau, the Cairngorms or a country garden at the mercy of a lawnmower; these, neatly described as 'knots in the handkerchief of memory', must take their chance with Nature.

He also makes literary 'knots' akin to those of any scribbler on the move who wishes to keep hold on some small experience, and these he uses in printed form to record his marathon treks from the Atlantic to the Mediterranean across Spain, from Aldeburgh to Aberystwyth, and over many more hostile lands. This orienteering, or sticking to a straight line come what may (which I know, from trying it, to be impossible) is recorded in notes that sometimes have rhythm or structure – 100 Tors in 100 Hours, or Twelve Summits in Twelve Hours, or seven coloured things seen in the correct order of the rainbow – and sometimes are random, as with Deserted garden/still water/sheep on her back/slanting rain/squashed greengage/lost foxhound/drowned pony in a leat (though these I have to admit are my own notes on a day's walk on Dartmoor, as evocative for me as any by Long); such observations range from deliberate contrivance (and they are sometimes as shaped as the mouse's tale in Alice in Wonderland) to the bare bones of the travel writer.

Long has never before seemed to me to be anything more than a provincial disciple of Joseph Beuys, his range of ideas narrower and their manifestations repetitive, his work with mud regressive and infantile, and more a matter for the Freudian analyst than the art historian. His work with stone has always seemed the industry of compulsion or obsession, and I can think of few things more amiably dotty than trampling a path over grass or sand and calling it a work of sculpture – but then Beuys swept and garnished a whole forest and called that sculpture too. Beuys maintained that even thought and speech were forms of sculpture, that concepts that stimulate emotion are at least as valid as sculpture as any solid artefact by Rodin, and that art is no more than the supreme riddle to which man himself is the solution. Such notions, propounded by the one artist who can be said to dominate post-war art in the West, justify all that Long has done – though we in turn are justified in rejecting them if we so choose.

In the Hayward Gallery many of Long's orderly treatments of disorderly materials have an effect that elsewhere has escaped them. The materials, tones and textures of this unlovely building are so much in sympathy with Long's inventions that they seem part of them; but if Long's work is transitory, the Hayward is not, yet something must be done about it and the present thinking is that it should be destroyed. I wonder instead if Long should be asked to treat the exterior of the building as a place of wilderness and work his magic on it, for, with his stones and mud he has converted the interior into an astonishing decorative unity of architecture and applied art; as sculpture it may seem whimsical, but as interior decoration it is superb.

Richard Long, Hayward Gallery 1991

***A line the length of a straight walk from the bottom
to the top of Silbury Hill*** **(1990)**
http://www.richardlong.org/Exhibitions/2011exhibitions/
silburywalk.html

Ron Mueck

Evening Standard, 4 April 2003

Dead Dad is deeply disconcerting. Three feet long, the hands as broad as the narrow thighs, the penis oddly pink against their grey, and oddly tumescent too, the lifelike little waxwork seems much less a work of art than the consequence of a bizarre and aberrant accident in those sequestered rooms of the funeral parlour where the dead are drained of blood and body-waste and then cosmeticked into presentability for loving mourners. *Dead Dad* was the sensation of *Sensation*, the exhibition through which, in the autumn of 1997, the Royal Academy saved its financial bacon by borrowing the then upstart collection of Charles Saatchi, and lending it, in turn, all the authority of that august historic body. This exchange was seen by many of us as a Faustian bargain in soul-selling, for by it the stature of the once esteemed Academy seemed as much diminished as *Dead Dad*.

It was an exhibition of works by artists who attacked the taboos of sex and nudity, wounds and mutilation, squalor and religion, paedo-philia and murder, with the subtlety of the blunderbuss, but death, the last taboo, obfuscated by a thousand euphemisms – at rest, peace or repose, departed, taken and gathered to the bosom of the Lord, even, though dead and buried, enjoying eternal life – was the target chosen by Ron Mueck, a sometime puppet-maker for Australian television, and *Dead Dad* is his father's funerary monument.

It is not a waxwork – at least, not in the sense of being a work in wax, though devotees of Madame Tussaud's (if any there be) must be forgiven for seeing something of the Chamber of Horrors about it. It began life (or death) as a clay model from which a cast was made, the materials fibreglass, silicone and acrylic, the lifelike pigmentation diligently added in the process. In the basic elements of this procedure Mueck is as much a sculptor as Rodin – first the tiny model constructed in pinches of clay attached to an armature (a simple outline skeleton that prevents the soft clay from collapsing – unnecessary in a recumbent figure), then perhaps a larger model in more clay to clarify the detail, and then the finished sculpture to full scale, destroyed when the cast is made. If not technically a waxwork, it is at first aesthetically indistinguishable from one, for access to which Tweedledee and Tweedledum might say, as they did of themselves, 'If you think we're waxworks, you ought to pay, you know. Waxworks weren't made to be looked at for nothing. Nohow!' And at *Sensation* we had indeed paid to look at *Dead Dad*, and when the new Saatchi Gallery opens on the South Bank, we shall pay again.

For the moment, however, we may, in the National Gallery, look at Mueck's latest works for nothing – again not waxworks, but with the same disturbing something of their character. For the last three years Mueck has been Associate Artist there, his task or purpose to be both himself, that is an artist pursuing the normal course of his development and, in whatever sense occurs (subliminal or deliberate), an artist reflecting or responding to the paradoxical privilege of being able to work in a studio at close quarters with a wide range of ancestral European paintings. If we substitute the term Associate Sculptor for Associate Artist, the paradox becomes even more pointed, for we ask of Mueck that he should respond in three dimensions to inspiration derived from the two of a flat surface and an image that is an illusion.

In this we reverse the not uncommon course of the painter's derivation from the sculptor – and how many of us can readily point to sculptors' derivations from painters, apart from Anthony Caro's foolish student exercise conceits when he preceded Mueck in the National Gallery? Consider Donatello, Bernini, Canova, Rodin, Moore – when did they succumb to a painter's influence?

The authors of the National Gallery's catalogue of Mueck's four works in three years illustrate as precedents Holbein's *Dead Christ* and Jan van Eyck's *Adam and Eve* – but as these are in Basel and Ghent, not Trafalgar Square, Mueck might just as well have worked from picture books as a studio in the Gallery. The pictures there that they adduce as evidence of influence, by Murillo, Campin, Costa, Tiepolo and others, are evidence of nothing – but then it is the common device of critics with an axe to grind to drop the names and images of old masters into the argument when they need to consolidate the status of a contemporary artist to whose wheel they have put their shoulders. Give Mueck his due, he is reported to have been disappointed that in his three-year stint of duty so few explicit links with the Gallery's possessions had developed – 'Never mind,' the authors say, 'We'll find them and they shall be thrust upon you.'

Links abound, however, with at least half a dozen contemporary artists of widely varying kinds – with Lucian Freud's starkly naked women and gross Leigh Bowery, with Robert Gober, whose lifelike bits and pieces of the human body appear to grow real hair, with Duane Hansen, a maker of lifelike and life-size human figures stilled in day-to-day activities, with Jeff Koons, whose naked sexual conjugations verge on pornography, and with Bill Viola, whose videos have been much concerned (at inordinate and intellectually numbing length) with matters of birth and death. Mueck's contribution to this figurative field has been to vary the size of the human figure from the midgetry of *Dead Dad* to the gigantism of the *Boy* that was one of the vacuous entertainments of New Labour's Greenwich Dome, and to focus on nakedness with an obsessive interest in detail – not a follicle or pore, not a varicose vein or pubic hair omitted, the corona of the penis examined with the curiosity of the pubescent boy and the labia of the vagina with the slug-hunting care of a sous-chef preparing an organic lettuce for a salad in the Ritz. I use the word nakedness rather than nudity, for nudity has nobility about it; nudity elevates the human being to an abstraction, an ideal, and has been, since western sculptors first achieved – in ancient Greece – the ability to conjure with it ideas of heroism, sacrifice, virtue and gravity, the device through which we have discarded the mere likeness of nakedness for the communication of concepts, visions and beliefs.

Mueck, when he is not playing the waxwork fool or the Disney fool of cute Pinocchio and cuter Bambi (the most irksome of the sub-genres of his work, providing the strongest arguments against his being considered a sculptor), contributes images at least of high seriousness to his chosen field, but they are so extraordinarily literal as to descend into tedious verisimilitude for its own sake – 'Look, look,' the two curators say with relish, 'here are flesh, blood, hair, substance and texture with breathtaking accuracy.' 'Well, well,' I say, 'it takes breathtaking accuracy to fart the tune of Annie Laurie through a keyhole, but no one could claim that that is music.' And I have no doubt that anyone who painted with such breathtaking accuracy would be sent away with a flea in his ear by the Serota Tendency.

Mueck's exhibition themes – pregnancy, birth, a swaddled baby and a fool in a ship deserted by all wiser fools – do not, for conviction, require pale flesh and pubic hair, moles, warts and acne. With such details, his is the art of hospital drama, of television midwives crying 'Push, push,' and 'It's a boy!' and in the very detail he diminishes our empathy and diverts us from the fundamental enquiry that we would like to believe is his pursuit. The distracting accuracy of an ugly, crumpled, half-boiled baby glistening with natal slime, is a crude sentimental appeal to the maternal instinct, the pulled-back foreskin and the stretched vagina are perverse, our contemplation of the veined and swollen belly a prurient intrusion at Mueck's insistent invitation. Whatever Mueck seeks to communicate with these obsessive details could be better achieved without them, the illusion of real flesh replaced with patinated bronze, emotion distanced, the intellectual response elevated, elemental and abstract. Imagine, for one moment, Rodin's *Burghers of Calais* in Mueck's idiom, or Donatello's *Habakkuk*, or Michelangelo's *David*.

Astonishing accuracy — the stuff of sex toys in the Soho shop — smothers art, and surface is no substitute for depth. Disconcerting shifts in scale are merely diversionary tricks — and the larger the scale, the less convincing is the finish, the smaller, the nearer we approach the Dinky Toy and miniature railway engine, and the criteria associated with them and the model-maker. Colour, though once one of the currencies of sculpture, particularly in ancient Greece, the medieval north, the German baroque, is now a mere distraction, a thing to be inspected and judged for accuracy, and Pygmalion's may well be the old myth by which to justify meticulous realism in sculpture, but we are all agnostics now. Try, as the curators do, to champion and vindicate Mueck's work in terms of Renaissance painting, the traditions of Spain and Northern Europe, the lost inessentials of the distant past, the *Little Dancer* of Degas with her real tutu, and anything else that they can adduce in support of the waxwork genre, Mueck's figures remain resolutely unlike the living human beings that they are intended to resemble — like, but unlike. Rodin confronted the same human bodies, the same emphatic genitals, male and female, and some of the same themes, but communicated his emotions, understanding and ideals without a single real hair, a single immediately subcutaneous vein, a single disconcerting hint of skin texture or colour. Mueck's apologists argue that his art is not that of the waxworker, but pleading that clay, fibreglass, silicone and acrylic make him the true heir of Donatello is, like these materials, an ingenious deceit.

It has taken no more than the magic seven years for the art establishment to construct the television technician into a great sculptor with *Dead Dad* an icon of the age — a seven-league stride if ever there was one. Buried in Mueck's nature there may well be the instincts of a true sculptor, and Saatchi had the eye to see them — the initial small clay models are a strong indication of their presence, as is the tug of hidden meaning in three of the exhibits at the National Gallery – but they are almost imperceptible under the baggage of his past. Given time, given isolation from critics, curators and hyperbole, appointed Associated Artist to the Cast Court of the V&A, and he may fulfill the promise now just discernible beneath the gloss and glister.

Ron Mueck, National Gallery 2003

Mother and Child (2001)
http://www.ncbi.nlm.nih.gov/pmc/articles/PMC1125681/
figure/FN0x9a75688.0x9cf8958/

Chris Ofili

SERPENTINE GALLERY

Evening Standard, 8 October 1998

I am sick of shit masquerading as art. Readers must forgive the vulgar word, Old English though it is, and from an even older German root, for it is now the common parlance of Britpack artists and the gleeful critics for whom they can do no wrong, and to employ Latin, baby babble or a drawing-room euphemism would be ridiculous. Gilbert and George broke the taboo on dirty words in art more than twenty years ago, and now any of them will do as the title, the subject and even the material of what we see in galleries subsidised by the Arts Council. The emerging turd, the ejaculating penis, the urinating vagina – think of the body, male and female, emptying its wastes or engaged in a sexual function, and think of the associated dirty words used by schoolboys and the rugger scrum to prove what men they are, and you have the art of the immediate present day encapsulated in the words scrawled upon a wall or decorously printed on a label, supported as much by laddish women with the cucumber standing as a phallus, the fried egg breast, the semen spurt emulating Jackson Pollock and even the wonders of the medical camera recording on video the vagina after intercourse.

Painting with Shit on it, Spaceshit, Seven Bitches Tossing their Pussies before the Divine Dung, Popcorn Tits, Captain Shit and the Legend of the Black Stars, The Adoration of Captain Shit . . . These are the labels now in the Serpentine Gallery, the titles of paintings by Chris Ofili, the young painter tipped by betting men to win the Turner Prize this year. The shit in question is that of elephants, the turds brought from the London Zoo, dried, steeped in resin, embellished with glitter and the bright plastic heads of map pins and other trinket tawdry, resembling nothing so much as chocolate truffle mixture prepared for a children's party by some idiot apprentice to a pastrycook. As each turd falls a considerable height when extruded by the pachyderm, it has a broad flat surface as a base ideal for application to the canvas and, in matched pairs, for acting as feet on which to stand the canvases as they lean against the walls, for Ofili prefers not to hang his pictures. They have a passing resemblance to decorative screens in which Ofili the multi-culturalist blends traditional elements of both African and European decoration, delicate fabrics from dix-huitième Lyon, Victorian Paisley and the horror of the slattern's cotton frock combined with the bead and basket work of the native African. We should not, however, see Ofili as a slave to political correctitude in this, for he is as willing to poke fun at himself as at the Virgin Mary, offering us a self-portrait head in which an elephant turd embellished with lengths of dread-lock cut from his, grins at us with real teeth; had this been made by any artist of white origin, he would have been shackled and whipped before the Race Relations Board and then crucified by the yes men of the Arts Council.

If we ignore the elephant dung and their challenging titles, Ofili's pictures are no more remarkable than those thousands now commercially produced in southern Africa, their painters self-consciously striving to be primitive and to convince the buyers that they speak from the black man's heart – spurious rubbish, most of it. Ofili is not African; he is black, his name is African and his parents are Nigerian, but he was born in Manchester in 1968 and is to be counted, with his education at the Chelsea School of Art and the Royal College, as well and truly English. Even so, while he was still a student, a visit to Zimbabwe in 1992 – a country where local art has become as much a bogus cottage industry for the benefit of tourism as the Aboriginal rubbish churned out in Australia – encouraged him to discover his own identity and literally put Africa itself into his art by incorporating elephant dung. That he could have discovered an inborn cultural heritage among the marvels of Benin and the sculpture of the Yoruba is obvious, but as Nigeria is some 2,500 miles from Zimbabwe, looking for his roots in east Africa makes as little sense as a Mancunian educated in Patagonia claiming to have discovered his spiritual roots in Rostov-on–Don and plastering his canvases with caviar; 'discovering himself' amidst the bastard rubbish of the art market in Harari says very little for Ofili's aesthetic sensibilities.

We must, however, make what we can of Ofili as he is and not as he might have been – and that, alas, is very little. The exhibition of his work in the Serpentine Gallery is pompously catalogued as though we are confronted by a sophisticated and eclectic genius of wit, irony and humour, the paintings exquisite, spirited, assertive, radiant, significant and remarkable (I borrow the language of the author). He and they are none of these. Every London shop with a decent fabric department puts on a braver show of colour and pattern, outdone by Ofili only in surface texture, for he works with layers of acrylic and oil paint, collaged paper details, glitter and map pins preserved in the aspic of resin that runs, dribbles and lies glutinously deep on it all, translucent yet muffling and obscuring, the mixture repellent to the fingertip and deceitful to the eye. Ofili himself is immature, laddish, adolescent, challenging us with deliberate offence on an inoffensive scale. Saatchi owns *The Holy Virgin Mary*, a picture timorously excluded from this exhibition though the whole London art world knows it well enough and exclusion brings it to our notice far more forcibly than inclusion; this mother of Christ is African – a political correctitude that we must accept – but is set against the gold ground mandorla of ancient Christian tradition, at second glance seen to be embellished with small obscenities, mostly female buttocks naked and parted to reveal the mysteries between when observed from below as well as from behind, cut from pornographic magazines. The point of this challenge, other than deliberate adolescent affront, escapes the sane man. Hints of timid pornography appear elsewhere but are at first unnoticeable, for as with the paintings of Professor Lari Pittman recently at the Institute of Contemporary Arts (another painter of the impastose dot and spot, with whom Ofili has something in common in decorative confusion and obsessive finish), it is only when the spectator learns the painter's visual tricks and mannerisms that he can see beyond them easily – but then, of course, he may discern more phalluses and vaginas than Ofili intended. But why should we bother? – if any of us wants pornography of this feeble kind then most local newsagents have it in plenty on their upper shelves, and for far less than the £15,000 that the chrysophilous Chris Ofili now charges.

If anything is to be said for these pictures it is only that all the damned dots and spots are mind-numbing triumphs of idiot industry, and their concentrated tedium is in no way relieved by the random application of pachydermal turds. These lumps of elephant shit are, the writer of the catalogue earnestly informs us, 'objects of desire . . . irresistible jewels (and) sites of energy'. How can curators, critics and directors write such rubbish and uphold it with straight faces? How can the Arts Council subsidise such thinking? How can even the Serota Tendency, notorious for its driving fascism in current art politics, compel its members to laud such shit and commend it for the Turner Prize? I am sick of shit in art: has no one in authority the courage to resist it and the infantilism that promotes it?

Chris Ofili

TATE BRITAIN

Evening Standard, 28 January 2010

The catalogue of Chris Ofili's retrospective exhibition at Tate Britain is introduced by Nick Serota with the sentence: 'Great art often emerges when cultures cross boundaries.' So there we have it – with the one word 'Great' we have the official assessment of Ofili's position in contemporary art, and with the other weasel words are encouraged to bracket him with Picasso, Kirchner, Heckel, Epstein and all the other European artists who, in the early years of the twentieth century, expressed enthusiastic interest in the primitive fetish art of central Africa and Oceania. But with these Ofili is a false comparison, a hundred years too late, and lacking all their skills.

Though Mancunian by birth, education, circumstance and opportunity, deference to his Nigerian ancestry has, it seems, compelled him to adopt the conventions of African rather than western art. Yet Ofili's early work did not cross boundaries – it established them. With his notorious exploitation of clods of elephant dung as their support, or incorporated as simulated breasts and nipples, or simply applied to make *Painting with Shit on it*, his canvases compelled attention. With myopic decorative techniques that reflected nothing of any European tradition but were founded on the souvenirs-for-tourists art that used to flourish in Zimbabwe (where he was on a British Council scholarship in 1992), like basket and bead work they proclaimed an African origin that was shrewdly assumed but utterly bogus. His five years at Chelsea Art School and the Royal College of Art were wasted and irrelevant.

Nevertheless, his rarity as a black male in the white male milieux of King's Road, Kensington Gore and Cork Street makes him the perfect candidate for positive discrimination from the Arts and British Councils and all arms and outstations of the Tate.

In one way and another the state invested generously in young Ofili and it cannot now withdraw its support – that would be the admission of error. It even, in 2000, when he was only thirty-two, made him a Trustee of the Tate which led to many other trustee-ships and appointments through which to dispense patronage; and while in that enviable position the Tate bought from him his *The Upper Room* for a punishing and greedy £705,000 – the vice of chrysophilia now twinned with coprophilia. A monstrous imper-tinence, *The Upper Room*, a deliberate reference to the Christian iconography of The Last Supper, were it not so profoundly trivial, might well be interpreted by the sane, civilised and reasonable man as blasphemous; had Ofili mocked in Islam as a feast of monkeys so serious an event as the institution of the Eucharist, our con-demnation would have been forthright and immediate, but as lukewarm liberal Christians, thoroughly unconvinced and with no respect for those with conviction, we refused to recognise the insult and praised the gaudy bling as art. And bling it is – bright trumpery, the dozen shrill colours of the twelve apostles blasted with bright light, each canvas a thing of tinsel tawdry, the trademark Brummagem, fit only for the embellishment of bathrooms in the mansions of footballers' wives.

Ofili was never anything but a decorator of cheap and shallow sensibility (if sensibility at all), the minuteness of his industry obsessive, the sexual humour puerile, soft and sniggering, until, four years ago, he began to paint on canvas without the tinsel touch and elephant dung. In these new paintings, however, there is further proof of his inadequacy, for they are first-year student stuff on overblown scale, best summarised as a wretched fusion of Edmund Dulac, Walt Disney and Art Deco – what can have been in his Christmas stocking in 2006? In these, first having floundered where Picasso marched triumphantly a century ago with *Demoiselles d'Avignon* (no shit), Ofili flounders again. Such ephemera may be new to him but they are stale in the history of art. They extend nothing, consolidate nothing and lead nowhere. They make a sorry show.

Chris Ofili, Tate Britain 2010
http://www.guardian.co.uk/artanddesign/gallery/2010/jan/25/
chris-ofili-tate-britain-art

Grayson Perry

THE BRITISH MUSEUM

Evening Standard, 6 October 2011

As Grayson Perry, one of the most prominent figures in the world of contemporary art, is a potter, it has never been necessary for me to say of him more than an odd word on such an occasion as his winning the Turner Prize. Pottery is only pottery, the craftsman stuff of the kitchen and the cabinet of curiosities, and never to be mistaken for a work of art, never to be put on a level with Raphael and Titian. One might well preserve pickled herrings in a Perry pot, drown a Duke of Clarence or even pee in it – none of which things can be done with Michelangelo's *David* or Rembrandt's *Samson and Delilah*; indeed, the very uselessness of a narrative painted on canvas in a frame, or a block of marble carved into the image of a naked hobbledehoy, is the simplest of all distinctions between art and craft.

As a craftsman Perry is by no means exquisite. The vehicle of the imagery with which he prettifies his pots is not the fine porcelain of Sèvres and Meissen expertly shaped on the potter's wheel – that low technology defeats him. His is the common clay of the school art room with which the first attempts to construct pots are made with long ropes of clay formed between the hands and then coiled upon themselves in exactly the same way as for primitive rope baskets. Born in 1960, that is how he began as a potter in the mid-1980s, at an evening class near his Camden squat; and as it is how he still makes his pots it is reasonable to assume that he has no craftsman's interest in refining his skills.

The gaudy pots are, in themselves, of little importance, their forms and glazes utterly conventional; they are, as it were, only the paper and canvas on which he inscribes, crudely, the episodes of sexual variety and deviance, of frank obscenity, child abuse, violence, murder and masturbation with which he subverts his commonplaces of the mantelpiece, table-lamp and umbrella stand. At first glance they could well have come from a John Lewis emporium, but the curious, looking closely, will find them embellished with graffiti that often have much in common with the pornographic comic strips now found on the bookstalls of Madrid and Tokyo, and once infamous here on the walls of public lavatories. Such irreverent subversion of a craft that, plain and decorated, is as old as the civilisation of man, makes Perry the perfect example of a Post-modernist.

Tate Britain's jury, when awarding him the Turner Prize in 2003, ignored the obscenity and praised 'his use of the traditions of ceramics and drawing in his uncompromising engagement with personal and social concerns'. Perry himself described his work as that of a guerilla – it appears to be a beautiful (his word) work of art, but instead confronts us with a polemic or an ideology. Not so; much of his imagery is autobiographical, exposing a troubled childhood, vaguely implying that parents are perhaps worse than paedophiles for children. As a consequence he developed a female alter ego, Claire, who is now, in adult life, his public persona and has become not only much the subject of his work, but the work itself, with the sedulous promotion of being Claire a constantly performed performance that more or less obliterates his un-memorable pottery.

Unlike Gormley's *Angel of the North* and Hockney's *Mr and Mrs Clark and Percy*, no single example of a Perry pot stands for all and, with no *pars pro toto*, in recollection, all blend into a glistering blur. In the quarter of a century that he has been making them they have remained essentially the same – perhaps bigger and more provocative in imagery and narrative, but so much undeveloped that they demonstrate stultifying intellectual and aesthetic limitations. Meanwhile Claire has gone from strength to strength and it is for her tasteless and preposterous dresses worn on every possible public occasion, that Perry is now notorious. I have no doubt that many find the grotesque and posturing pantomime a barrier to any appreciation of Perry as a potter; we are confronted not only by Widow Twanky and Alice in Wonderland, but by an adult child for whom his teddy-bear, dubbed Alan Measles, is God, guru and St Winston Churchill, and an unwholesome infantile constant in his recent imagery; an adolescent too, this transvestite man of fifty, this husband, father and international high flyer, signs his pots with an anchor and a capital W that are to be read as Wanker. Wanker indeed, in the word's wider sense, yet the establishment is fool enough to take him seriously; I'd wager that had he not been so brazen and cunning as to let Claire take the lead, the art world would never have noticed him.

This Claire, this High Priestess of the Alan Measles Cult, this Hell's Angela in lavender and yellow motorcycling kit, this sour-faced old bat glowering from a daisy-decorated helmet, has been given the freedom of the British Museum to mount an exhibition of artefacts in which he perceives some affinity with his own work. These are largely unsophisticated primitive things by anonymous craftsmen, imbued with elements of faith, fetish and native tradition, often whimsical and charming, occasionally menacing. These we must see as though on a pilgrimage through a world of Perry's imagining but, too much diluted by his pots and his vast, vile, vulgar tapestry, they are reduced to the status of goods in a curiosity shop that has something of Harrods and the Hirst Sale at Sotheby's about it.

I quite see why the Director of the British Museum accepted Perry's proposal for this wretched little show. Boyishly provocative, aesthetically levelling, too clever by half and ultimately shallow, the reasoning was that with Perry's name, face and persona attached to it, thousands of loyal Perry fans will become fans too of the British Museum. How naive – exhibitions of Hirst and Freud made no new friends for the Wallace Collection, and they were not held in such derision. Perry is not a man of scholarship, nor of credibility, and neither informs this puerile, silly and self-aggrandising show. Everything is subordinate to Perry's work – the largest exhibit is his, the exhibition's feeble climax is his, and his pots will rise substantially in price now that they have been exhibited in the BM. If the Director was too unworldly, the Trustees should have recognised the commercial implications of Perry's impertinent proposal. Dealers in his pots are certainly rubbing their hands with glee, while the rest of us must pay £10 to see these pointless juxtapositions of Perry's current stock in trade with BM property. Was he paid a fee for his curatorial services and for writing the embarrassing nonsense of the catalogue? 'Do not,' he writes in it, 'look too hard for meaning here.' Do not look at all.

Grayson Perry, The British Museum 2011
http://www.guardian.co.uk/artanddesign/gallery/2011/sep/18/
grayson-perry-tomb-of-the-unknown-craftsman-in-pictures?intcmp=239

Yinka Shonibare

NATIONAL GALLERY

Evening Standard, 19 August 2007

To what extent, I wonder, should the National Gallery be used for political propaganda, social engineering and as an out-station of the Tates? That it is in Trafalgar Square and not in Bloomsbury, an adjunct of the British Museum, is entirely due to the arguments of its founding fathers in 1824 that it should be sited 'on the gangway of society', for only with ready access could it 'civilise and humanise the public at large'. They were convinced that free admittance, unhindered by the conventions of dress and manner, would, by osmosis as it were, gentle the ruffian, educate the ignorant and inspire the unawakened aesthete in us all, and thus, without a penny to be paid, the gallery's doors must always be open 'to all ranks and degrees of men . . . to the indolent as well as the busy, to the idle as well as the industrious'. Historically, then, the institution itself was designed to be, not just a plaything for the educated, middle classes (the aristocracy had galleries in plenty of its own), but an instrument through which the working classes might be elevated, intellectually if not in economic terms.

Aesthetic-cum-intellectual elevation by both osmosis and through the academic disciplines of art history, are processes of education and experience that lead to greater understanding of man's inherited primitive impulse to illustrate, embody and develop ideas. The art of the ancient Greeks and Romans was influenced by the way they saw themselves, but with the spread of empire, art itself became the influence; we have seen much the same in the twentieth century with the arts of Communism and Fascism, and for the best part of two millennia we have seen this same propaganda element of art in the service of Christianity too. The objective of the National Gallery at its founding, however, was not the employment of art as propaganda – that was then, as now, the business of the contemporary artist – but the isolation of paintings from whatever their purpose had been (though the writer of a catalogue entry might remind us of it) so that we might concentrate on their aesthetic content, on the underlying drawing that is their armature, on composition, light and colour, the sense of sculptural weight and volume, and on the very business of the painter, the strokes of his brush, the weight of his paint, and the sense of self that he communicates.

When *The Raising of Lazarus*, by Sebastiano del Piombo, became NG1, the very first painting in the National Gallery's inventory, it ceased for ever to a rich man's boastful chattel or a cathedral's venerated altarpiece (it had been both) and became simply the possession of the nation, its status irrevocably changed. In a sense it was neutered; no longer a demonstration of Medici pride and power, nor a vehicle of Christian example, as a picture in a public gallery it had become the subject of aesthetic argument and art historical debate. Two thousand more have followed it to Trafalgar Square, and there they hang to be enjoyed, repeatedly, as we enjoy re-reading a poem and hearing yet again an opera. This, I am convinced, is the prime purpose of the National Gallery. That it should occasionally enquire into the making and meaning of paintings is properly and comfortably within its sphere of responsibility; so too it should inform us of the life and methods of a painter or a group of painters united by a time or place or working within a particular genre – and, indeed, every other highway, byway and dead end pursued by art historians – but that it should invite contemporary artists to demonstrate their wares within its walls is a grave nand continuing error.

The Gallery used to invite eminent artists to choose paintings from the permanent collection and re-arrange them in the Sunley Room – an illuminating frivolity once made serious by Bridget

Riley's selection and her exquisitely intelligent exegesis. Now that it asks artists to be influenced by paintings on its walls and to respond with shallow copies, pastiches and misinterpretations we have had to endure dreadful stuff from Auerbach, Kossoff, Freud and Peter Blake, and the currently favoured artist, Yinka Shonibare, has dipped below even their dismal standards with one installation in the splendid Barry Rooms and another, its explanation, in Room One. *Scratch the Surface*, as it is called, is a belated contribution to the bicentenary debate over slavery – a subject that by now, more than half way through the year, has been exhausted in every possible vehicle for its discussion, including other major galleries and museums in London.

Shonibare's laggardly contribution in the Barry Rooms – yet another of his fanciful costume pieces – is a jibe against what he perceives to be the upper crust sport of shooting, and in Room One hang the portraits by Zoffany and Reynolds from which he developed this feeble idea, together with a video in which, faltering and incoherent, he offers a bumbling explanation unworthy of a schoolboy. The Zoffany was painted in the early 1760s and the Reynolds in 1782, a period when shooting was far from the exclusive sport of aristocrats and a skill on which poorer men depended for the rooks and seagulls in their pots and ovens; shooting as Shonibare understands it was a phenomenon of the later nineteenth century long after the abolition of the Slave Trade, and his premise is thus wrong. The National Gallery nevertheless justifies it as 'a classic example of Shonibare's subversion of conventional readings of cultural identity', but the Gallery's duty is surely not to subvert, not to diminish and distort two of its own great paintings, and not to damn the considerable artists who painted them without a thought of the rights and wrongs of slavery and how their sitters benefited from it. Had Zoffany and Reynolds themselves been the subverters of formal conventional portraiture with snide comments on the sources of their sitters' fortunes, that would indeed have been remarkable and worthy of special exhibition, but that centuries later an artist from another cultural tradition (Shonibare, of Nigerian origin, defines himself as a cultural hybrid) should be given space and subsidy for such subversion, founded on error, in the Gallery itself, seems wry in the extreme. The proper place, if there is one, for political nonsense of this sort is in the Tates, but in Trafalgar Square it is claimed as 'part of the National Gallery's ongoing commitment to the support and display of contemporary works'.

Why is there such a commitment? Who decided to make it and on what grounds? A director past or present? The trustees, obliging the whims of political masters? Turn it on its head and we have Tate Modern promising an equally ridiculous commitment to Raphael and Rembrandt. I see some point in asking Damien Hirst to select his choice of pictures and explain it – even Tracey Emin hers – but I see no point in making the National Gallery an exhibiting out-station for wealthy artists already favoured by the Tates, the Arts and British Councils and any other institution that has cut itself off from the historic past in the cavalier, even dishonest, way that the Arts Council has, abjuring its once accepted duty.

Elsewhere in the National Gallery the despairing visitor may encounter its latest travelling exhibition, a condescending little offering called *Work, Rest and Play*. For the past six months one of the two paintings by Avercamp in the permanent collection has been in Bristol and Newcastle, so too its only figure painting by Courbet, its most intriguing canvases by Manet and Monet, the one Moroni that everybody wants to see, *The Tailor*, and ten other paintings of which the subject is work, rest or recreation. To these have been added borrowings from five other London museums, a Lowry from Salford, a Gauguin from Newcastle and other random trifles. Haphazardly they hang and haphazardly they are catalogued, as though by a lazy teenager on a course of work experience, to whom the coherence of display and the purpose of exegesis are as yet matters of no importance.

Paintings belonging to the National Gallery should always be there for everyone to see and not away in Perranzabuloe or Little Piddlehinton; they are in the Gallery's catalogue and every visitor has every right to see every picture listed there when he makes the journey to Trafalgar Square from Dundee or from Dunedin; this is the Gallery's responsibility, national, international and worldwide. Let me put it this way: had any of us in the south gone to Newcastle to see the Gauguin, only to find that it was on its way to London, we'd not have been best pleased. Paintings should leave the galleries known to possess them only for the most serious of reasons – a major retrospective, for example. *Work, Rest and Play* is not a serious reason – in twenty-seven paintings and four photographs of daunting banality it offers only arbitrary illustration of three unrelated subjects each of which, considered seriously, could have provided the theme of a much larger exhibition – imagine a survey of the painter's observation and changing attitude to work as a subject from, say, Konrad Witz's *Miraculous Draught of Fishes* of 1444 to Stanley Spencer's *Shipbuilders* of 1941, to rest from Giotto's dreaming Joachim to Tchelitchev's idly masturbating peasant, and play from Bruegel's *Children's Games* to Paula Rego's sinister variations on the theme of Girl and Dog. Compared with these we have a trite little offering wholly unworthy of a national gallery.

The only conclusion to be drawn from *Scratch the Surface* and *Work, Rest and Play* is that increasing provincialism is à la mode at the National Gallery, that with kow-towing compliance it accedes to fashionable political demands for intellectually undemanding accessibility, and that it is dumbing-down in precisely the same way that is so evident at the BBC. Why is the Gallery now so fearful of reaching beyond a low level, arrogantly presumed, of intellectual and aesthetic response, the very things that its business is to stimulate at a high level? Why is it so intent on the literal explanations of subjects and utterly ignores the ways in which paintings are painted? Newcastle's *Breton Shepherdess* is far less interesting for its subject than for the way it is composed, its colour, its tonal contrasts, and Gauguin's varied handling of paint – it is an intriguingly transitional picture in which Gauguin is not wholly at ease with either past or future – but none of this is mentioned in the catalogue.

The National Gallery should be heightening our perceptions of paintings as paintings, not reducing them to illustrations. The National Gallery once set standards of connoisseurship, scholarship and presentation; it has now abandoned them. The National Gallery was once elite, but the retiring director would rather run a mile than take pleasure in that word; elite, however, is precisely what it should be, superior, illustrious, pre-eminent.

Mark Wallinger

Mark Wallinger is an artist who, until recently, has been largely ignored by commentators on the contemporary art scene in Britain. Even Matthew Collings, who must now have some claim to be the Vasari of today, has had all but nothing to say of him and other writers either omit him or employ the none too subtle compromise of introducing his name as a second string when discussing someone else's work. This has always seemed, since he first came onto the London scene in 1986, a well-deserved position, for in whatever he has done in painting, sculpture, video and what-not, he has clung to coat-tails already flying, if not already landed and moved on. As a dull painter of horses he has not been a twentieth-century Stubbs (though some have called him so) and in other subjects his canvases have seemed poor mimicries of the inn sign, Michael Craig-Martin, Scottish social realism, the alphabet pictures that have been in currency for a full generation on both sides of the Atlantic, and any other vogue that has caught his eye. As a photographer he has done nothing not already done a million times in the sports pages of daily newspapers; his idea of figurative sculpture has been not to hack at stone or make a clay model on an armature, but to cut short these labours by taking a full body-cast of a standing boy; and his videos, remarkable for their tedium, are outdone in this particular by those of Gillian Wearing.

He has had three audiences. Of these the first was the small body of cognoscenti (for want of a more appropriate word) who have fostered his career, his dealer, his dealer's customers, Saatchi, various agencies of the Arts Council, the jurors of the Turner Prize in 1995 (one of whom, the then Director of the Ikon Gallery in Birmingham, had promoted him at an exhibition a few months earlier) and one devoted critic who told us that in all his work Wallinger adopted the strategy of parabasis. For the life of me I cannot see the relevance of this assertion, but then I know of parabasis only as a digression by the chorus in the drama of the ancient Greeks, addressed directly to the audience and not connected with the action; to me, Wallinger's work is above all things straightforward to the point of tedious banality and his audience is invariably addressed directly, not as an aside, by the subject, be it horse, sets of racing colours, the Queen, a homeless beggar, the sculpture or the video and it is, whatever the medium, utterly lacking in depth, complexity, subtlety or parabasis, but parabasis is a wonderful word with which to make the hoi polloi feel small.

His second audience was the countless number on the tops of buses as they swept past the formerly empty plinth in Trafalgar Square, then occupied by the stark white resin cast of the standing boy who played Christ, stripped and whipped, tugging at our sympathies for six months a year or so ago. *Ecce Homo*, said Mark Wallinger, behold the man. The man? No, this was a boy, as much pretending the role of Christ as any altar-boy in an Easter Passion Play in the days when such things were performed in churches up and down the land, the days before we became a secular society. In this, much praised for its piety by many who should have known better, Wallinger was no nearer the spirit and predicament of Christ the man than his resin cast was sculpture.

Wallinger's third audience was the international mob that saw his work in Venice at the Biennale this past summer and raved about it, as the fashion-conscious invariably do at that absurd beano (here to be pronounced in the Italian manner, bay-ano, as did Henry James). The British Council, the agency that fixes this and other such prestigious businesses, thought him 'very different' –

from what, one wonders? – 'quizzical . . . and worth a punt'. Even the eximious Waldemar Janusczak, once the presiding genius of that part of Channel 4 that fosters the Turner Prize, thought the choice of Wallinger a mistake, but most critics were compliant, assessed the show as wonderful and ensured with all their flatulence that Wallinger ceased to be perceived as somehow a peculiarly British painter and secured an international reputation.

His recent work is now on view at the Whitechapel Gallery. It is, alas, much more a series of morbid entertainments than anything to do with art. We enter the Gallery to find it deep in fashionable gloom, with to right and left a television monitor on which we see a man in an electric chair, presumably Wallinger himself since he is so often the core character in his work, singing an incoherent dirge as though he has five humbugs in his mouth – it is, in fact Ariel's 'Full fathom five thy father lies . . . ' from *The Tempest*. We then, through two more doors, enter the execution chamber as though through the ceiling, and look down on the empty electric chair; to either side are huge photographs of clenched fists with LOVE and HATE tattooed on the fingers.

So far, so what? So much for so little? This was a theme better and more sinisterly explored by Warhol, a so-called work of art that is no match in horror for the real-life, real-death executions that are witnessed by so many in the USA and seen on television by the rest of us, an idea that is no match in imagination for the cage pieces made by Damien Hirst ten years ago, particularly his *Acquired Inability to Escape*, which insists on and achieves an equally powerful act of imaginative identification from the spectator. Wallinger leaves us cold with his installation and if it is a comment on the death penalty, it is ineffectual, its visual edge blunted, as in so much of his video work, by the clutter of indecipherable sound.

Next we come upon what seems to be an eye focusing and blurring on a cinema screen; it is meant to suggest our slipping in and out of consciousness on an operating table while a voice – the kind of common voice that suggests unenlightenment unpenetrated so often employed for announcements on the BBC – recites by single letter after single letter, the opening words of St John's Gospel – I,N,T,H,E,B,E,G,I,N,N,I,N,G,W,A,S,T,H,E,W,O,R,D. Some of us are unfortunate enough to have heard Wallinger's abuse of the Gospel before, not at a Christmas Mass, when even to the sceptic it must seem the most mystical sentence ever written in English (and, oddly enough, wholly consonant with Islamic belief), but from the lips of Wallinger himself, recited backwards, reduced to gibberish, as he, pretending to be blind, ascends and descends the escalators of the Angel Underground station to occasional bursts of Handel's *Zadok the Priest*, the Coronation anthem. Why take Shakespeare's verse and a quotation from the Bible as beautiful as this, muffle it, deconstruct it, destroy it and then call the infantile wreckage art? Wallinger's *Angel* and this *On an Operating Table* are works so repetitive, tedious, pretentious and sedulously silly that no one sane or without investment in his reputation could ever take him to be either an artist or an intellectual.

Things are little better in the upper gallery. *Whistlejacket*, the National Gallery's sublime horse-portrait by Stubbs, wonderfully sculptural, one of the greatest paintings of the eighteenth century (if not the whole history of art), is reduced to the semblance of an X-ray photograph and given the horn of a unicorn. More deconstruction. Why? A tardis-cum-telephone box is presented in stainless steel, glistening, reflecting and very, very heavy. Why? A video of railway lines viewed from the front of a train is made to seem portentous with the title *When Parallel Lines Meet at Infinity*. Why? And in *Threshold to the Kingdom*, travellers to the City Airport emerge into the arrivals area in slow motion to the accompaniment of Allegri's *Miserere*. Why? And why should Wallinger present this nonsense as though it were so moving and profound that we must stand entranced by it for more than eleven minutes?

The exhibition is presented with something of the panache to which we were accustomed at the Whitechapel Gallery before it fell into menopausal desuetude some years ago, but skilful window-dressing cannot conceal how dire and superficial Wallinger's inflated trifles are. None of his utterly negligible conceits, his silly semi-blasphemies – though amusing enough, no doubt, over pints of beer with his mates in Camberwell – is worth such large-scale installation. Wallinger is yet another example of the artist who has little skill and less education, accorded for the half-baked ideas of an idiot, signifying nothing, seer-like status by the art establishment.

Coda

When Marcel Duchamp, the unwitting author of most of our misfortunes, turned a urinal bowl on its back in 1917, he almost brought the history of art to a halt; certainly he maimed, crippled and arrested it for the rest of the twentieth century and it has not recovered yet. With this act he asked if it is possible to create a work of art from an object that is not only not art but wholly associated with an alien purpose, asked if it is possible to be a creative artist without creating a work of art, and waited for the answers to be provided by the spectators, who were confounded when the critics answered for them that through the force of Duchamp's imagination this plumbing accessory had indeed been transmuted into art. Years later, Duchamp said, 'I threw the bottle rack and the urinal in their faces, and now they admire them for their aesthetic beauty' – but this denunciation the critics chose to ignore, just as they ignored him when he said of his *Large Glass* (an unsatisfactory work with which he was in some sense occupied for forty years), 'I have offered no explanation myself . . . what is intended is of no interest; what is interesting is the effect the work has on the spectator . . . it is nothing to do with me; I have nothing to say . . . it is up to the public' – an apologia that fits almost every artist cherished by the several hegemonies of contemporary art.

I have always defended, supported even, Duchamp's excursions into unknown territory, but like Botticelli and Beuys, he needed no followers and his influence has harmed his reputation. It is the futility of his imitators that I deplore, and now that we are within spitting-distance of the urinal's centenary, we are at the end of the third generation of imitators of imitations, now worn very thin. To those for whom Duchamp is as remote as Michelangelo and

Rembrandt, and perhaps even forgotten or unknown, his current imitators are still entertaining in their stale Post-Duchampianisms, theirs a harmless, pointless, dead-end, whimsical form of art to balance the amusements of art forms that are incomprehensible and bizarre, freakish, scatological and nauseating. Recognising art as entertainment might indeed be the basic definition of contemporary as opposed to modern art, which, if we give it the date bracket *c.*1870–*c.*1950, extends from Impressionism to Surrealism, and was still, even in such extreme movements as Cubism and Constructivism, within the traditions of ancestral European art, if predominantly in their lines of intellectual enquiry rather than subject and seductive surface treatment. Contemporary art has largely abandoned intellectual enquiry; it is subject to no formal discipline, nor has it a formal language; it is not concerned with aesthetic or empathic consequences for the viewer and, having no rules, has become unjudgeable self-indulgence by largely self-declared but wretchedly ignorant and ill-educated practitioners. Art in most manifestations supported by the public purse is now neither the learned profession of the High Renaissance and the Age of Reason, nor the skill-based trade of the earlier twentieth century – it has become the business of the circus freak managed by the circus barker.

Brian Sewell, London 2012

Index

Besides the listing below of all the artists mentioned in this book, the publishers have included a number of related themes and subjects which might also interest the reader. These are listed in bold type.